BOOKS BY JAMES MERRILL

Poetry

Fiction

Essays

A Memoir

A Different Person

James Merrill

A Different Person

A MEMOIR

HarperSanFrancisco
A Division of HarperCollins*Publishers*

A hardcover edition of this book was published in 1993 by Alfred A. Knopf, Inc. It is hereby reprinted by arrangement with Alfred A. Knopf, Inc.

FIRST HARPERCOLLINS PAPERBACK EDITION PUBLISHED IN 1994

Library of Congress Cataloging-in-Publication Data
Merrill, James Ingram
   A different person : a memoir / James Merrill.
   p. cm.
   ISBN 0–06–251079–7 (pbk.: alk. paper)
   1. Merrill, James Ingram—Biography.
   2. Poets, American—20th century—Biography. I. Title.
[PS3525.E6645Z464 1994]
811'.54—dc20
[B]   94-7687
                                                   CIP

---

94 95 96 97 98 RRD(H) 10 9 8 7 6 5 4 3 2 1

This edition is printed on acid-free paper that meets the American National Standards Institute Z39.48 Standard.

For J. D. McClatchy

Contents

*Photographs of some of the people spoken of
in the text will be found following page* 116.

A Different Person

I   *Decision to go abroad.*
My dearest friend and my latest love.
A Proustian party.
A night in Vermont.

MEANING TO STAY as long as possible, I sailed
for Europe. It was March 1950. New York and most of the
people I knew had begun to close in. Or to put it differently,
I felt that I alone in this or that circle of friends could see no
way into the next phase. Indeed, few of my friends would
have noticed if the next phase had never begun; they would
have gone on meeting for gossipy lunches or drinking together
at the San Remo on MacDougal Street, protected from en-
counters they perhaps desired with other customers by the
glittering moat, inches deep, of their allusive chatter. I loved
this unliterary company; it allowed me to feel more serious
than I was. Other friends, by getting jobs or entering graduate
schools, left me feeling distinctly less so. On the bright side,
I had taught for a year at Bard College, two hours by car from
MacDougal Street. My first book of poems had been accepted
by the first publisher I sent it to. And I had recently met the
love of my life (or so I thought), who promised to join me in
Europe in the early summer, by which time we should both
have disentangled ourselves from our past and present worlds.
Was I ever coming back? Yes, yes, one of these days. But of
course I would be a different person then.

    It took a fair amount of perversity to want to distance myself from my friends, for with them only—never in solitude or with my family—did I feel at ease. After a day that typically included lunch uptown at my mother's bedside, followed by an hour or two of "work" in order to deserve the evening's fun, I plunged giddily into their midst, drinking and laughing and "being myself" until my face ached and it was time to return, alone, to my apartment in the East Thirties. Following me out of the subway, my shadow wavered past a shop I'd never found open, its dark window dingily lettered in gold: LUST'S BAKERY. I slept late. By noon the evening's goblin pleasures left no trace, beyond a dim cranial throbbing, upon the ornate stanza under way about loneliness and pain. So there was a side to the story that my friends didn't know. And just as well, I told myself; the way they saw me—the way I had invited them to see me— was already straitjacket enough. How glad I would be to get away from them.

I was glad also to be putting an ocean between me and my parents. My mother was ill that year with a gastric ulcer, and I knew why. Four years earlier, she and I had each done things the other could not forgive. Since then, despite the rare hour when the old unconditional intimacy shone forth, each had felt a once adored and all-comforting presence slipping gradually, helplessly away. For good? Who could be sure? Our dear ones' behavior is seldom hard to justify; whether it can be tolerated is the issue. With hurt aplenty on either side and no quick or painless remedy forthcoming, it had begun to seem like mere human kindness on my part to speed up the process and distance myself from her. Keeping out of range of my father, on the other hand, might well have defeated me had he not himself, twelve years earlier, taken the first step by leaving my mother and persuading her to divorce him. (It "looked better" that way; and given this latest and most stubborn of his infidelities, what else could she do?) In time a series of heart attacks left him progressively more self-absorbed, less in control. Even so, he was talking of joining me in Italy

4

for the month of May. Not exactly what I'd had in mind, but my father had more irons in his fire than my mother did— two older children, *their* children, business interests, the third wife—and this spell of unprecedented closeness abroad would do for both of us for a long time to come.

As it happened, my father had taken a much earlier step to ensure his children's independence, by creating an unbreakable trust in each of our names. Thus at five years old I was rich, and would hold my own purse-strings when I came of age, whether I liked it or not. I wasn't sure I did like it. The best-intentioned people, knowing whose son I was and powerless against their own snobbery, could set me writhing under attentions I had done nothing to merit. So I looked forward to distancing myself from all that as well, in places where the family name cut no ice, the Firm had no branch office, and I might if need be, like the Duke of Mantua in *Rigoletto*, pass myself off as a poor student.

Friends, family, money . . . wasn't there something else? From the mirror stares inquiringly a slim person neither tall nor short, in a made-to-order suit of sandy covert cloth and a bow-tie. My bespectacled face is so young and unstretched that only by concentration do the lips close over two glinting chipmunk teeth. My hair, dark with fair highlights, is close-cropped. I have brown eyes, an unexceptionable nose, a good jaw. My brow wrinkles when I am sad or worried, as now. Not that what I see dismays me. Until recently I've been an overweight, untidy adolescent; now my image in the glass is the best I can hope for. Something, however, tells me that time will do little to improve it. The outward bloom of youth upon my features will fade long before the budlike spirit behind them opens—if ever it does. It is inside that I need to change. To this end I hope very diffidently to get away from the kind of poetry I've been writing.

That same March, not long before sailing, I accepted an invitation to read with Richard Wilbur at Amherst College, our alma mater. Poetry readings, in those days before Dylan Thomas and the Beats, had yet to become the rage. Still, the room was filled with faces, and I was proud enough of a few recent poems to fancy they could hold their own in such company. But the mere act of reading them aloud—something I was doing for virtually the first time—quickly disabused me. Despite all I had learned about "tone" from my teachers (many of them right there, nodding encouragement), despite the presence on campus, twice yearly, of Mr Frost and *his* campaign for the sound of sense, my poems remained verbal artifacts, metered and rhymed to be sure, shaped and polished and begemmed, but set on the page with never a thought of their being uttered by a living voice. As I read, part of me listened to how I sounded, nasal, educated, world-weary as only those without experience of the world can be, and thought how much I would like this sound to change; or failing that, what a relief it would be to live among Frenchmen or Italians, who wouldn't automatically "place" me each time I opened my mouth. At the reception everyone was very kind. Dick Wilbur—his own performance a master class in resonance and poise—asked for a copy of the poem I had closed with. But I returned to New York depressed, with a vision of my inner self as a lone teardrop glittering deep in tissues of shyness and plain incuriosity.

According to Rilke, a young poet can't have enough solitude. I pondered the dictum ruefully. Being alone was not my long suit. Aside from activities that might loosely figure as aesthetic—going to the opera or a museum, reading, writing a term paper or a poem—I was not in the habit of doing things by myself. I was eleven when my parents separated, old enough to be allowed some liberty. Instead I have the impression of proliferating guardians: no longer nurses and maids, perhaps, but schoolmasters, camp counselors, army sergeants. Grown up at last, I was free to board a train to a strange city, but to do so without a companion, or without the promise of meeting an old friend on my arrival, would by then have seemed a great oddity, doomed to failure. Like those children who, undetected until it is too late, lose the use of one eye by favoring the other, I functioned blankly, imperfectly, without a confirming viewpoint. The unexamined life wasn't worth living? Even so; only in my case the phrase meant a life not examined by someone else. This is where a lover came in. For could I truly have contemplated stripping and plunging into the unknown without Claude's life-preserving arms about me?

We had caught sight of each other in January at a party for the publication of Frederick Buechner's first novel. Freddy had been my dearest friend since boarding school. But for him I might have left adolescence behind without ever knowing the perfect admiration, the boundless trust one can, at fifteen, both feel and inspire. Each worried about the other, took to heart his triumphs and setbacks, loved his mother and his jokes. Freddy and I shared—had indeed mutually cultivated—a quasi-ideological passion for the "literary." The novel in question, finished two summers earlier in a house we rented on the coast of Maine, was called *A Long Day's Dying*, and its ecstatic reception would make him the wonder of that winter of 1950. More New York nonsense to be shrugged off? If so, it would take some doing—wasn't that Leonard Bernstein sitting at the young author's feet? It was then that I met Claude's eyes and remembered him as one of the little group who, four years earlier, saw Kimon Friar off to Greece. Because Kimon was my first lover and Freddy my best friend, I could pretend—by triangulation, as it were—that Claude was perfectly at home in my life, and I greeted him with a warmth that must have taken him aback. He had been brought to the party by Carl Van Vechten. That connoisseur of celebrities was already making plans to photograph Freddy in profile against the backcloth of unironed satin that was his trademark.

Claude Fredericks had a round, fair-skinned face, by turns

7

elfin and exalted, under thinning brown-gold hair. He was a printer, living in Vermont with another man. Thanks to Van Vechten, who was Gertrude Stein's literary executor, they were about to undertake the first edition of an early novella, too scandalous for its day and too forthright ever to fit easily into the Stein canon. He was spending the midwinter months in a hotel on Union Square; his partner had gone farther south. It seemed that the Vermont house had no furnace. By choice? I wondered, as much of the friend's absence as of the furnace's. Yes, said Claude, presumably meaning the latter—he believed in living according to classic patterns. I gave him my telephone number, and he invited me to an Elisabeth Schumann recital a few days later. We both had full engagement books—he because he was so rarely in New York, I out of my dread of solitude—but stole what hours we could together, meeting at midnight on a street corner near where one of us was dining, or walking back and forth between his hotel and my apartment until the sun rose. I wanted to show him off to everyone I knew, as if his discreet person and unfrivolous conversation would explain how little I'd be seeing of them for the rest of my life. Claude, two years my senior, took care that his friends and I didn't meet. By the third week we were both intensely committed, though we had yet to become lovers, and the plan of joining up in the south of France (as soon as the Stein book was finished and my father's visit over with) took shape. And then? Why, anywhere we pleased. A summer in the mountains, a winter by the sea. We could go to Persia, we could go to Portugal—

"Portugal!" echoed Claude, and the name from then on encoded every delirious possibility of love.

So it was all at once the easiest and most exhilarating thing in the world—this embarking upon a *vita nuova*, as we each trusted it would be. Claude had raised a few questions I found hard to answer. What, for instance, was *Wayne* still doing on the scene? If I no longer loved him or he me, why hadn't I

8

taken back his key to my apartment? Who were all these silly *girls* who greeted me with shrieks and kisses? What did my drinking champagne from a slipper kicked off by one of them mean? This wasn't Claude's world. He had grown up in a small town in Missouri, where nobody had heard of Euripides or Joyce. At fourteen, wearing, despite his mother's upbraidings, a kirtle out of Theocritus and a scowl out of Thoreau, he had raised "Greek vegetables"—beans and turnips and cucumbers—in their front yard. (The people I cared for most didn't, by and large, have fathers. Claude's had faded from view, keeping only minimally in touch after the divorce. Freddy's had killed himself. The trauma seemed in every case to have quickened the child's imagination.) With a dowser's blind instinct, Claude had found and devoured the *Symposium*, the sonnets of Shakespeare and Michelangelo, also a shelf of illustrated medical texts in a neighbor's house, and seen his path shining before him like the rising sun's over a rough sea. To a degree I'd have found inconceivable without his example, he had made—remade—a fussed-over only child into a proud, uncompromising young man. Not that I myself was innocent; I'd read every word in print about Oscar Wilde and knew by avid, pounding heart the juiciest of Havelock Ellis's case histories. But I was immature. My nature, like the slipper dripping champagne, sparkled messily, next to Claude's. I asked nothing better than that it, too, be remade according to his guidelines.

My second-best friend from boarding school, Tony Harwood, had arranged to sail with me. Tony lived abroad but had spent the past ten months in New York. Back when this was an uncommon thing to do, he rented and made livable an enormous loft in Chelsea. His next step was more conventional: he joined the dozens already fluttering mothlike round a young man named Bill Cannastra, whose incandescence I found cheap, perfunctory as neon. Why Tony felt ready, at winter's end, to put

9

Bill and New York behind him I can well imagine but not recall. The unimaginable thing was to leave without a party. After all, a chapter was ending for both of us. How better to signal closure than by some large emblematic gathering to glide knowingly through, like Proust at the end of his book?

Upon Tony's candlelit space over a hundred people in evening or fancy dress converged for pastries and champagne. (It was on this evening, I'm afraid, that I drank from a Miss Morrison's slipper and Claude's patience with my social instincts snapped.) There was a rented piano on which somebody played the kind of music one is meant to sit down and listen to. A soprano sang settings of T. S. Eliot's "Preludes." Tony's guests included quite a few patrons and practitioners of the arts. As I had agreed to pay for the champagne, I was allowed to invite whom I pleased, so Freddy and his mother were there; *my* mother as well, risen from her sickbed—and Claude, whom I now with studied casualness introduced to her. When I wondered the next day what she'd thought of him, she said mildly that she hadn't been impressed. It only strengthened my resolve.

Freddy, aware of my feelings for Claude, came over to greet him. My dearest friend was tall and well made. His large sea-green eyes shone from a face striking for its air of serenity—inviolable, masklike, benign—which somehow dignified whatever issued from it, whether a dirty joke or, as now, a bouquet of charming smalltalk. Claude looked puzzled—he had other ideas of discourse, even at a party—and presently moved away. It was one more sign of how different my life was going to be, with him. Freddy's Princeton of suntanned girls, gin drinks, and laughter in the primrose glow of late spring afternoons—setting and figures lifted straight out of F. Scott Fitzgerald—already promised little where I was concerned. With equal force I felt both the enchantment and my insusceptibility to it. Our sexual selves, so long untried except in wish, were bearing us off in contrary directions. Now, after putting our mothers into the same uptown taxi, we stood at Tony's, as we made a point of doing at the height of any good party we'd ever attended, in make-believe gazing back upon it from the far side of decades to come. We shook our heads sadly and tenderly over that dear droll distant hour whose participants knew no better than to have the time of their lives. "I still worry about you, old friend," said Freddy softly, almost to himself. He meant that he worried about *us*. Although nothing would change our loyalty to each other, and although he'd just finished promising to visit me in Europe without fail before the year was out, Freddy and I would meet less often from now on and have less to tell when we did. The candles had burned low in Tony's loft; even the younger guests were beginning to leave. We filled our glasses with champagne, and Freddy gave his favorite toast: "*La vie, la vie*—we'd be dead without it!"

Before sailing I went to Vermont with Claude. The handsome white Federal house stood on a hillside far from the main road and any neighbor. Claude had bought it during the war, along with a hundred acres of field and woodland, for next to nothing. Indoors it was very cold; the pipes had been drained since Christmas. Once both downstairs hearths were blazing and my teeth had stopped chattering, I was shown through a number of minimally furnished rooms: here a round table with four chairs, there a lamp. A mattress made up into a neat bed. A wall of books. These, consistent with Claude's decision after a year at Harvard that he would do better to educate himself, were of a breathtaking high-mindedness: Greek philosophers and Latin poets in scholarly editions, Aquinas and Dante, Gibbon and Donne, scores of the Bach Passions and the Beethoven quartets. Twentieth-century authors were strictly limited to "classics" like Frazer and Freud, Pound and Eliot, Joyce and Mann. I couldn't imagine any work of mine ever being admitted to this august senate. It was here, in the library-pressroom, that Claude and his friend, whose life together was now ending, set and printed the exquisite editions they published. The old press, painted dark red and worked by the rotation of one shieldlike wheel at its flank, stood five feet high, a presence challenging and inscrutable as any samurai in full armor. Late in the tour I was glad to see a fully modern bathroom and kitchen. Supper was under way; we would presently eat cross-legged by the fire.

"Who are your friends here?" I asked.

Claude hesitated, laughed, named a literary couple forty miles away. Oh yes, and the farmer's wife (down the hill, across the road) dropped in for tea every couple of weeks. I kept looking at him expectantly. "Friends from New York like to visit in the summer," he finished, looking shy and proud. Outside the glittering panes, night and cold stretched for miles. Was it here that I would live, in this disciplined isolation, if and when we ever came back from Europe?

The fire we slept by died during the night. All too soon day broke through uncurtained windows, a day so cold it sent us howling and dancing into our clothes. I thought of my New York bedroom with its carpeted floor and heavy curtains, which kept out every ray of light, while the steam heat rustled like a housekeeper through the pipes. I thought of my sitting room's dark tobacco-brown walls and black, flowered carpet, where even at noon you needed lamplight. I had a piano and the Mozart sonatas, along with every piece I'd ever learned as a child. And yet it didn't do, at any age, to put one's faith in arrangements. Wouldn't I live a wiser, freer life without twice my weight in scratchy opera recordings, and shelves overloaded with books very few of which were enduring classics? Alas, I had never thrown anything out. In its three small rooms this first apartment held all the accumulated "signifiers" of my twenty-four years—or am I misusing a fashionable term? These were the obvious things to strip myself of, or to turn the key on for an indefinite period, if I was to become a different per-

12

son. To that worthy end the cold bare light of Claude's house, and the fun and fluency of breakfasting with him by a new fire, felt like a suit of magical properties laid out for me by elves. Let yesterday's tatters be consigned to the flames.

※

A different typeface for that person I became? He will break in at chapter's end with glimpses beyond my time frame. Who needs the full story of any life? Biologists are learning how to reconstruct the complete organism from a cluster of cells; the part implies the whole. Here, too, is a likely spot for the reveries suitable to a pillow book, for gossip, for shoptalk.

I began writing poetry in my second year at Lawrenceville, soon after meeting Freddy. He had shown the way by publishing in the school literary magazine eighteen lines (they gave it a whole page) in a delectable pre-WWI mode. Cathedral imagery prevailed; "my soul" was the protagonist, "pale" and "dim" the most telling epithets. It was like a sibylline, aesthetic maiden aunt of those red-blooded lyrics by Housman or Rupert Brooke—the masters at St Bernards had to blow their noses after reading them aloud—and I hailed it at fourteen as the real thing. I set about modeling my writing—not just poems, my very handwriting—on Freddy's. Oddly, those period pieces took little work to imitate. The school magazine soon devoted a page to my "Sonnet" apostrophizing a "maid of Nippon," ivory-pale and passionless on her painted screen. Now that Freddy and I were both in print, we had our mothers buy for us at DePinna's identical overcoats whose contrasting lapels, formed by the lining of artificial, cocoa-brown fleece, suggested, to none but ourselves, something Oscar Wilde had been photographed in. We wore them all through college.

Our teachers meanwhile were busily exposing us to the whole of English poetry from Wyatt to Browning. On our own we pored over the Pre-Raphaelites, Baudelaire, and Verlaine, even the ground-breaking new names in Louis Untermeyer's anthology. Our schoolboy stories and poems gave off a dewy, fresh-faced unhealthiness, a Yellow Book fever from which Freddy recovered more quickly than I did—though to tell the truth, neither of us evolved very much during those years at Lawrenceville. A precocious adolescent makes do with whatever odd conglomerate of wave-worn diction the world washes up at his feet. Language at this stage uses him; years must pass before the tables turn, if they ever do. Our early efforts nevertheless filled us with wonder. Freddy's poems, just by our being friends, and young, quivered with a live magic barely attached to any historical context. I read them the way a spider in Hagia Sophia, oblivious to the great dome, might have scrutinized her neighbor's web.

> My long sealed memory recalls
> The perfect shadows we once made on walls.

Lines such as these, which he wrote at eighteen, embodied for me everything—chaste, cryptic, melodious, infinitely sad—a poet could ever dream of achieving. But Freddy had other strings to his bow, wit and semicomic human presences, like a certain Madame Fogg, who loved her suitor "none the less / When he proposed to her as less the nun / And more the lass"; images, too, that when I got round to him, seemed almost to prefigure Wallace Stevens—"Superfluous as angels in a dogwood tree." I wrote Freddy from Amherst to drop everything and read "Notes Toward a Supreme Fiction," saying that it reminded me of him. A tactless move, I fear. Freddy, who at Fitzgerald's Princeton had been gravitating towards prose, now more and more consigned his own poems to a bottom drawer, refused to read a single tercet by that insurance-mongering

14

humbug I claimed to admire, and with no further visible ado became a novelist.

In my second semester at Amherst one of my teachers arranged a tête-à-tête with Robert Frost, suggesting that I bring along two or three short poems. Sure enough we were presently left alone, I and the famous old man bent over my stanzas. When he looked up it was to say kind things; there were turns of phrase he liked, and touches of "seeing" he found original, whereas I knew secretly how much they owed, that year, to Rilke and Yeats. So no doubt did Mr Frost; only, gentler with students than with their teachers, he hadn't wanted to dampen me by saying so. What he didn't know was how much these juvenilia owed to my gifted schoolmate. I felt obscurely to blame for Freddy's defection from poetry, and lonely in the vast chamber full of voices. But relief was at hand.

I I *Tony puts one over on the French.*
Visit to Kimon in Greece.
Illness and recovery.

H ERE I WAS, off to Europe. My weeks in Paris during a winter break at Bard hardly counted. This time, long unbroken months—years if need be—lay ahead. Claude did not come to the sailing; it would be intolerable, he wrote, to say goodbye in a cabin full of my chattering friends. When I saw the space in question, big as a closet, with double-decker bunks and no porthole, I wondered if I shouldn't have stayed in Vermont with him. (*"Amants, heureux amants, voulez-vous voyager?"* asks La Fontaine in a passage I can recite to this day but have never sufficiently acted upon.) Tony, who had made the arrangements himself at the French Line's office on Fifth Avenue, was already at the purser's desk, two decks up, complaining. Wasted breath: the cabin was ours for the next nine days. So much for my old friend's savoir faire.

Tony had lately spent a season or two in London and Paris, and let it be felt that he knew the ropes. Even at fourteen he had been dazzlingly urbane. Tall and olive-skinned, with the features of, if not a Greek god, perhaps a Sicilian one; all willowy visibility in foxglove-colored tweeds and scarves that trailed the ground; in hushed accents holding forth upon French porcelain, English furniture, and the genealogies of "old New York," he was from the start the most insufferable boy in school, or would have been had he not so roguishly

16

endorsed the consensus. To be insufferable was the role of a lifetime, and he played it with style and nerve. His snobbery exasperated, his frankness disarmed. Tony's was also the biggest "tool" among us—a mixed blessing but one imprinted willy-nilly upon his fans and his detractors alike. The other boys never baited or tortured him as they did me, who, small and bespectacled, lived in provocative terror of them. From Lawrenceville he had gone on to Harvard. Tea-pouring women took him up; he attended meetings of the Vedanta Society. Soon he was referring to Those Who Know and calling what he wrote Poyetry. Behind his back I mocked his literary efforts; to my face he patronized my own. Our friendship, while allowing for flashes of uncommon intimacy, remained faintly unreal, tinged with irony and sapped by worldly claims. Once in Paris, for instance, Tony would be moving on. Friends were expecting him in Madrid.

We had ordered a small Citroën, to use alternately. Tony would drive it to Spain, I would take it over for the summer. The car needed only to be picked up; its co-owner, however, bored by the driving lessons he'd begun taking in New York, had neglected to get a license. I secured my own international permit without fuss, but at the same Parisian window Tony's blandishments were met with firm headshakes. Easter weekend was upon us. A driver's test before next week? Unthinkable. At length pure luck saved the day. A harried official at some remote, complacently francophone desk, mistaking an expired learner's permit for the real thing, issued the vital papers. Tony was off. So was I. As I hardly knew how to spend an hour by myself, and a whole month yawned before the rendezvous with my father, I had arranged to visit Kimon Friar in Greece.

My subsequent years in that country and the mix of memory and invention in a novel I wrote about those long-ago weeks make evoking them today problematic. Despite the rapturous letters Kimon had written me during his two previous stays there, I'd formed few expectations. Unlike Paris, where the most banal sidewalk set me quivering because Debussy or Wilde or Cocteau might have set foot on it, Greece and all its splendors would have to work long and hard, like Greek immigrants in the slums of New York, to earn their keep in my blocked imagination. My plane arrived at twilight; Kimon was waiting; the Athens we entered was dark, cheaply lighted, full of language. Having taken some ancient Greek at college, I could transliterate the billboards and street signs. But the great, the single luxury now freely available in this society shattered not only by the German and Italian occupations but by the civil war that in 1950 still smoldered in craggy provinces was talk, and this I could not share. Everybody else, from teenage surrealist to white-haired bootblack, was engaged in dialogue, in fluent speech and vehement gesture. New ideas glowed with the lighting of a fresh cigarette. It hardly mattered that these "ideas," far from originating with the speaker, were often little more than conventional responses picked up in a café or from an editorial. A conventional response so deftly internalized as to set eyes flashing and smoke pouring from lips wasn't to be scorned; indeed, it answered to the kind of poem I hoped to write.

Kimon took me to a large popular restaurant in Omonia Square. I sampled politely a number of specialties I had no taste for. He was, I could tell, equally touched that I had come to see him and saddened by the sight of me. Our story was fresh in both our minds. Early in 1945, when I returned to Amherst as a veteran of nineteen, Kimon was teaching world literature to the would-be army officers still on campus. This slight, graceful man, whose waxen brow and bespectacled austerity radiated self-knowledge—at once the ideal of his Greek ancestors and the fruit of his psychoanalysis—resembled no one I knew. Then in his early thirties, Kimon fraternized easily with the as yet small group of civilian undergraduates; some of us began to meet at "his" table in the college dining hall. Soon he was

18

regularly criticizing my poems and I was attending his weekly workshop and lectures at the YMHA in New York, for he had a career quite apart from his duties at college. As a lecturer he performed eloquently. His topics included Euripides and Djuna Barnes, the myth of the Medusa and the symphonies of Beethoven. After the lecture we would stop by the Gotham Book Mart and stock up on poets I'd never heard of. Then? Why not tea with Anaïs Nin, a drink with W. H. Auden, a late party at Maya Deren's? Anything was possible. In a matter of months my existing sense of how to write, who to take seriously, what to feel, and where to go from there had undergone lightning revisions. Not all of it stuck, but when the smoke cleared, the schoolboy imitator of Elinor Wylie had turned into this new person who read Hart Crane and Robert Lowell with an air of total comprehension and whose own poems—designed, after Stevens' dictum, to "resist the intelligence / Almost successfully"—now began appearing in magazines. By then, too, Kimon and I were lovers. The double goal of numberless adolescent daydreams was being realized.

And yet this first love, so largely the intoxication of *being* loved by such a man, failed to surmount the three obstacles in its path: my own callowness, my mother's horrified opposition, and a year away from each other. On his return from that year, in 1947—I was twenty-one then, able to do as I pleased—I nonetheless told Kimon that I couldn't cope; the break left both of us numb, confused, guilty. He went back to Greece the following spring. Our reunion this evening in Athens bore only the sorriest resemblance to the one we'd imagined together before Kimon's original sailing, when I, a snow-sculpture of constancy, had vowed to follow him as soon as I finished college.

Back in our hotel room after dinner, I was still too callow and, yes, too unthinkingly lustful not to take him in my arms. He might have been wiser to rebuff me without a word; instead he explained wryly that his Greek lover had left Athens only hours before my arrival, after a passionate couple of days designed to drain Kimon of every last erotic impulse by the time he met my plane. Had he so dreaded the sight of me? The thought left me morose but flattered. In return for his confidence I could now talk openly to him about Claude, whom he remembered with pleasure, having commissioned him to print a little anthology by the YMHA poetry class. (Claude's having set lines of mine by hand thrilled me like a kiss.) On this new, different footing with Kimon, I might even take in something of the world he now called home.

The next morning—it was early April, warm and blindingly bright—we walked downtown for my sojourn permit. The Tourist Police office, littered with ashtrays and tiny white coffee cups drained to the black siltlike dregs, was lined with dossiers old and dog-eared enough to have been carved in time-browned ivory by a Chinese master. We then went to call upon a friend of Kimon's, the not-yet-famous painter Yannis Tsarouchis, in a vast and squalid bedroom-studio only a step or two from Athens' smartest hotel. It stank of more than cats; a couple of barnacled amphorae served his models as chamber pots. Tsarouchis was youngish, slightly built, blotched and balding. He greeted me in a casual, amusing French I wasn't equal to. At Kimon's insistence he showed a number of small oils, freely and vividly brushed, of swarthy young men in and out of uniform, gazing without emotion at one another from unmade beds or barracks bunks, their bodies virtual cartoons of slim-hipped, lantern-jawed sexiness. The paintings cost little enough; why didn't I buy one? whispered Kimon when our host went to make coffee. What, and hang it in the back of my closet? I blushed, scandalized. Besides, who was the artist? Merely a living Greek, not Monet or Vuillard . . .

Time for lunch. After changing a traveler's check—twenty dollars stuffs your every pocket with ragged thousand-drachma notes—we enter one of the little vine-roofed taverns oblivious to their imminent replacement, here at the heart of town, by tall glass banks and world-class jewelers. The clientele includes, or so it seems, many of Tsarouchis's models—sailors, policemen, evzones. The latter, allowed in those innocent days to wear off-duty their short, petticoated foustanellas, sit with legs spread like resting dancers by Degas. When a phonograph strikes up the bleat and twang of a popular song, one or two of the sailors rise as if hesitantly setting out for a far place. A little cement floor serves their purpose. The dance, grave and slow and in no sense a performance, is never quite so introverted as to exclude the abrupt leap and glad slap of palm on shoeleather and tends to leave the dancer with both his empty glass and his self-esteem replenished. Even the brown marble faces out of Tsarouchis come to life when Kimon addresses them, shares a joke or asks a riddle, then with a conjuror's flourish presents me as an "American poet who is visiting your country." Does he speak Greek? Not yet? Too bad . . . But knowing the alphabet, I am able to amaze them by writing their names in Greek letters. The scrap of paper is then reverently pocketed, like a poet's worksheet by a Texas librarian.

The museums were still closed for reorganization in the aftermath of the war. We visited the Acropolis by moonlight and (through a curator Kimon knew) paid our respects to the great bronze Poseidon in his dressing-room. But Kimon was eager to take me to his island. Another day, and we had sailed for Poros. Approaching the harbor, our white steamboat passed the headland where I would spend the next two weeks. For over a year now Kimon had been the guest of a Mrs Diamantopoulos—or Mina, as I was told I must call her. She and I knew more about each other than most people do on the verge of a first meeting.

We were met on the quai, however, by Mitso, Mina's gardener and Kimon's lover. He loaded us and my baggage into a little rowboat over which a fringed canvas awning had been stretched, then, facing us, rowed across the kilometer of pale silken water to Mina's dock. Kimon and he chatted in Greek translated at intervals for my benefit. "He says you have a sincere expression," I was told at one point. So did Mitso. Unshaven, with curly blondish hair and a vulnerable smile, he resembled the models of Tsarouchis not at all. He and his wife and baby lived in one of the cottages on Mina's property. Because of the voracious local gossips, his trysts with Kimon called for the greatest discretion, usually a night in Athens on one pretext or another. Mitso's wife could then rest easy: the abstemious Professor would keep her young husband from the fleshpots.

Mina came down to the landing to greet us. She was in her early sixties, with dramatic Byzantine eyes, silvering hair in a bun, and a manner of perfected naturalness. Just as Kimon and I, to the degree that poetry filled our lives, shared a dozen interests and assumptions, so Mina and I, when we met, recognized the upbringing that marked us as deeply as any tribal scarification. Years before Kimon grew up in the linguistic no-man's-land of a Chicago slum, Mina had learned from her tutor in St Petersburg, where her father was ambassador to the Czar, the same manners, the same French and German courtesies, that my beloved Mademoiselle would try (with less success) to teach me in her day. Comfort and privilege, ours from birth, had left us with a lightness of tone that worked like a charm in the right company but could swiftly frustrate whoever wanted, as Kimon often did, to get to the bottom of things. His was the tragic view of life; the affirmation added inches to his slight frame. Mina's view and mine, however we might rail at the given moment, counted on its being seemlier to shrug and smile.

Above the door into the Medusa, as Kimon had named the cottage where I would be staying with him, hung an ominous assemblage, a large grinning head made of hardware and jetsam. Thus Kimon, bent over work under her petrifying eye, could see himself as a latter-day Perseus, saved by the mirror-shield of Art. Amused by his own snobbery, he added that Ghika, the maker of the gorgon mask, was not only a renowned artist but a prince. At once my personal snobbery set about ranking him beneath Tsarouchis, as if the misfortune of being well born would automatically prevent him from doing serious work. Kimon took me inside. I already knew, from letters and photographs, the two rooms, beds and windows, table and tiled floor. Here, too, I felt at home. Within hours my place, along with the baby's and the dog's, had been secured. I would play the young foreign guest in the ongoing *piccolo teatro* of Mina's domain.

The main house had been designed by Mina's late husband. Tall windows in the dark, paneled library framed views of the bay and the sunny lemon groves on the mainland opposite. This room I also knew from letters as the scene of anguished talks throughout the previous winter, when Mina and Kimon, drawing upon all the experience, irony, and compassion at their command, wrestled with her demon: she'd fallen in love with him. That drama lay safely in the past, Kimon assured me as we sailed towards Poros; they were at last the dear good friends life meant them to be. Sitting down to supper with these grownups in the afterglow of their recent ordeal, I kept glancing uneasily at them, like a child who has just discovered what his parents *did* in order for him to be born. By the meal's end, however, I had grown passive, suggestible, at peace. I'd landed in a benign revision of my own family romance: a father who read Yeats, a mother without prejudice—parents whose primary interests were cultural and whose mutual attraction, bewildering to a youngster, had burned off like fog in morning sunlight.

Beneath the gorgon's ghastly smile I wrote my letters to Claude, reassuring him of my love and conveying Kimon's hope that we would return together for a long stay in Greece before the year was out. The small patio in front of the cottage was never quiet for long. Mitso's wife came with a question from

Mina—did we want chicken for dinner? The baby was brought to be watched. The dog needed patting. Mina's grandson—a beautiful child of six, crowned with water lilies—ran up to ask the population of New York. Alone for an hour, Kimon turned gratefully to a mountain of books and manuscript on his desk. He was translating the modern Greek poets—and how many of them there were!—into English.

One evening Kimon and I went by ourselves on foot to a tavern on the port; he needed periodically to assert his independence from Mina's household. The food and wine here were terrible—it seemed to be the price one paid for eating where the sailors did—and I wasn't myself the next day or the next. Another afternoon we boated across to the mainland for a festival among the lemon groves: roasting meat, musicians, retsina. Arms draped over each other's shoulders, dipping and gliding in unison, Kimon and Mitso—or was I feverish?—danced the witty "butchers' dance" together. We returned after dark, and I spent the next day between toilet and bed, with boiled rice and tea for nourishment. A doctor came from the village; a white emulsion was prescribed. It helped but not for long. Was it too late for ordinary cures? Weak as a flower, I continued to waste away.

We canceled an excursion to Epidauros. I sat out the mild afternoons in a reclining chair under pines. Mina took to joining me for a half hour at a time. Did I see that mountain across the water? She and her brother climbed all the way to the top of it when they were twelve and fourteen. Yes, and their guide was a notorious bandit, feared throughout the region, but a man of honor too, as bandits were in 1900. He asked no more than the Christmas gold piece they had agreed upon before setting out. How angry her father had been, and how secretly proud, when— Here, with a worried glance at me, Mina rises. What can she get me? Do I need anything? I might have thought, or she might, to have the local doctor's prescrip-

24

tion refilled. But such are the risks we run when seeking far from home the loving care we can no longer accept from our parents. Mina's concern for my comfort is that of a hostess, not a mother, and I haven't yet learned how to look after myself. Her serene, candid presence charms me nonetheless. Listening to her talk about Kimon, in my eyes a middle-aged victim of his own habits and attitudes, I begin as never before to see the young man he still is, all fiery daring, resilience, ideals. She loves him as he (or anyone) needs to be loved, for "himself" and not, as I had done, for his greater experience, his faith in me, which I treated so cavalierly. In Mina's company I feel my own youth forgiven, along with my unmasculine tastes. "Here," she says one day. "I've had this ever since I was a child. Would you like it?"—handing me a tiny Russian needle-case of green and blue enamel.

A caïque full of young people connected with the British Council arrives from Athens on my second weekend, anchoring in the cove below Mina's house. The twilight rings with merriment. But they also have the Anglo-Saxon's healthy concern for his bowels—or in this case mine—and the extremists among them want to see me hospitalized. On Sunday evening, with the owners' cabin surrendered to Kimon and his glassy-eyed American poet, we sail for Athens. Half dreaming, I pluck from the shelf above my creaking bunk a memoir by an English traveler. The weather-stained book opens to his account of being received by Mina, before the war, in the house I've just left. My fortnight there recedes (as I blow out the lamp) to the dimensions of a paragraph.

At the hospital I had a room to myself. The nurses were nuns—Orthodox? Catholic? Nobody spoke English. I was given white pills and a painful injection every six hours. By the second day my diarrhea stopped. But I had been so strictly trained in childhood to perform "number two" each day or face the consequences (enemas, laxatives) that I dragged myself each morning to the toilet across the hall, where Herculean labors produced a few blood-smeared votive pellets. When the doctor arrived and asked his one question (*"Avez-vous fait quelque chose ce matin?"*) I was able to answer with a feeble but proud *"Oui."* Whereupon he ordered—like Scarpia's gruesome *"Insistiamo!"*—further pills and injections. After a week I gave up, confessed to failure, and was discharged from the hospital, cured.

Kimon and I flew to Rhodes for some last days together. No Colossos bestrode the entrance to the harbor, but in grassy yards behind the municipal buildings lay monumental heads and arms, fragments of Mussolini's dream. Kimon gleefully set about posing me with the broken statuary; his photographs looked like stills from an unsuccessful screen test for a Cocteau film. We spent an hour in the town's one nightclub. Too refined for Greek music, the band played tangos, to which the beau monde of Rhodes performed a mechanical two-step without variation, like so many wind-up mice. At the British Council on my last evening in Athens we saw Louis MacNeice, of all people, act the bumpkin suitor in *The Playboy of the Western World*. After that, just as on those evenings in New York after Kimon's lectures, anything was possible. As we drank our cognacs at the Café Byzantion in Kolonaki Square, all the figures who would mean most to me fifteen years hence strolled past our table—or might have been made to do so by only the slightest warping of my time frame: Maria in her perpetual black with movie-star dark glasses, en route to a polyglot dinner party; Tonáki (our darling Alexandrian Tony, not to be confused with my high-handed classmate) on leave from his navy clerk's office in Patras; Strato at nine or ten, the age when Greek males are at their cleverest, his joyous green eyes missing nothing. Save for a screen of undistinguished architecture, I might have seen, gazing vaguely into the purple dusk, the house halfway up the slopes of Lycabettos, where David Jackson and I

26

would spend so much of our long life together. But who in his right mind wants to know what lies ahead?

My friendship with Kimon, however smoothed over by these reunions, kept deteriorating. David, for instance, thought him stupefyingly pompous. The day came when we agreed not to see each other or communicate for a while, and twenty-five years passed. Out of sight wasn't, however, out of mind.

Kimon believed that myth was indispensable to poetry. In times like ours, when religion played no vital imaginative role and the political myths were turning to radioactive ash in the hands of the superpowers, the poet had no choice but to live by some personal mythology of his own construction. One day, when the time was ripe, Kimon planned to write a long poem based on Yeats's system: spiritualism, the phases of the moon, the gyres of history. A long poem was the test of any poet's powers. He cited Dante, Milton, Rilke, Pound. What would their shorter works amount to without the great achievements that crowned them? The notion struck me at twenty—at forty, too, for that matter—as a dangerous form of megalomania, and I wasn't buying any of it. But at fifty? Longer than Dante, dottier than Pound, and full of spirits more talkative than Yeats himself might have wished, the Sandover project held me captive. It was Kimon's dream, only I was realizing it in his stead. In his copy of the poem I wrote: "Dear Kimon, who'd have thought? You would!"

Then there were Kimon's translations. They began as a grateful gesture towards his heritage—after which he would be free to resume his "real" work, the projected epic, the novel, the theoretical essays—and ended by consuming the rest of his life. Once the first "definitive" anthology had appeared, full of big names like Cavafy and Sikelianos, Seferis and Elytis, he couldn't resist undertaking the thirty-thousand-line Odyssey of Kazantzakis. That alone took seven or eight years. Looking up dazed from the task, he saw a new generation of poets. They clamored like dogs round a stag at bay. How could they dream of international renown without being read in English, and who could they trust to bring this about if not Kimon? Critical articles, further anthologies, medals and honors from a government keenly aware of the steps leading to those two Nobel prizes—and suddenly it was close to a half-century later. Across from me sat, depressed and short of breath, the cricket-like husk of the man who had given so much to so many and taken so little for himself. If in retrospect his life gave off a paradoxical aura of self-absorption, one had to remember that, whether by accident or design, he had never found the right person to share it with.

Peter Hooten liked Kimon from the first. In 1989 we went to see him in a suburb of Athens where Kimon had moved to escape the bad air downtown. He was recovering too slowly from open-heart surgery, perhaps because his growing dependence upon sedatives left him restless at night and disoriented by day. More than once, he told us, during the past five years, since meeting my new love and seeing what we meant to each other, Peter and I had come to him in a dream, and our happy, wordless presence comforted him. Over lunch we urged him not to live alone, at least for the time being. Surely, said Peter, a student would be honored to occupy the spare bedroom, shop and cook for him, while helping with Kimon's current project, a selection of Kazantzakis' letters. But this had been tried two or three times already. And . . . ? Kimon gestured grimly at his depleted shelves. The books didn't just vanish without help. H. had come to stay with him a couple of summers ago, all friendliness, wanting to bury the hatchet. But when he left he took with him the dozens of intimate letters he had written to Kimon twenty years earlier, before his own success—for which indeed he had Kimon partly to thank—made their undestroyed existence, even at the bottom of a trunk in Kimon's storeroom, a potential threat.

"I'm surprised I still have that," said Kimon, meaning his Tsarouchis oil sketch of the tanned young sailor, cock a fat mauve daub in its inky thicket, glowering from bedsheets at a chocolate-suited buddy. Was it, I wondered, a painting we'd seen that distant morning? "When did I take you to Yanni's studio?" asked Kimon, shaking his head in amazement.

During the 1960s in Athens, when I was forever participating in life studies bold enough to have been dashed off by the master himself, I came to regret my decision not to buy one that day in his studio. Tsarouchis had in the meantime grown famous and changed his style. Now that he was dead, his prices, at least for such early work as this, unmarred by what its creator liked to call the bloom of decadence, were skyrocketing. "Oh, wow," said Peter, under the spell of Kimon's little canvas. "Cavafy lives! Let me take you and JM in front of it. Here we go, the flash is set—heads together now. There!"

I I I
With my father in Italy.
Dr Simeons operates.
Robin.
Acquiring a camera.

T HE Roman café is filling up. I am alone for the first time in many months, but without anxiety: my father docks in Naples tomorrow noon, and I shall meet him there. It is dark, yet not dark. Façades and fountains are lit as on the stage. Before long I shall find a restaurant and order not, thank goodness, Greek food but some perfect, undreamed-of *specialità*. Two smartly dressed Roman matrons meanwhile settle themselves at the next table. I have studied Italian at college, have read Dante in Dante's own tongue, and am now about to hear it *in bocca romana*. As the women flip silently through a newspaper, I glimpse my first headline. Thrilling, but does it count as Italian? RECITANO BAUDELAIRE VESTITI DA COWBOYS. A second headline, announcing the death of the actress Maria Montez in her bathtub, holds my neighbors' attention. The elder speaks in a richly derisive voice: "*Almeno è morta pulita.*"

The following morning I'm getting dressed, when a sudden awfulness afflicts me. Dropping my pants, I peer through my legs into the hotel-room mirror—yes, there *something* is, but what? A small pedantic voice advises me to look up "haemorrhoid" in my portable (two heavy volumes) *Oxford English Dictionary*. Thus the riddle is solved by a Greek word, in memory of daily heroics in a Greek hospital. The pain, however, stays.

I find my father at the Excelsior Hotel, where a suite has been booked to rest in before we catch the afternoon boat to Capri. He kisses me affectionately. It is always a pleasure to set eyes upon him: silver-haired, his round face lightly tanned, a small, compact figure in smart clothes. I am his youngest child; he has a daughter and son by his first wife. I've come to think of him as less paternal than grandfatherly. He was after all over forty at my birth, and two or three heart attacks have added a decade to his age. Conversation is happily just now out of the question, what with the two American factotums who met his ship, the come-and-go of waiters with sandwiches and tea, and the excited claims of his traveling companions. On a previous crossing my father enrolled his Negro valet in the passenger list as a banker from Cairo and enjoyed with this undemanding sophisticate a quiet table for two in the first-class dining saloon. This time my sister has talked him into bringing along not only a trained nurse—Miss MacHattie, who properly coaxed could pinch-hit as valet—but Neddy, my brother-in-law's brother and the spiffy grasshopper to his ant. He and I will be sharing a room for the next month. Why Neddy of all people? The reason ought to have been clear: my father dreaded solitude as much as I did.

He also dreaded the company of his third wife, for love of whom he'd left my mother, and her absence from the scene added measurably to the charm of Naples and its bay. That was merely a smoking volcano in the distance, not Kinta with her whims and irascible vapors. After the flurry of docking at Capri and settling ourselves—where was Miss MacHattie's brown suitcase? had Mr Merrill's caviar been consigned to the hotel's refrigerator?—high above the port in luxury that surpassed even his own arrangements in Southampton or Palm Beach, we could positively feel his blood pressure going down, day by brilliant, carefree day.

Capri. This ingenious toy amazed us by the number of its working parts. Starting from the miniature square with its mix of local and international beauty, any narrow walk led past baker and goldsmith, tinker and tailor. We gawked over fish and vegetable stalls like bumpkins in the Louvre. Here was produce grown on the island, here were monsters "which only the fisher looks grave at," hauled from waters we strolled above. Hoping to please Kinta on his return, my father had abstracted from her shoe closet one of the few pairs she spoke well of. After breakfast we sought out the shoemaker in his wee shop and asked if he could copy them. The man responded, hand to heart. Honored, overcome, he vouched in advance for the Signora's perfect satisfaction. How many pairs—one? two? *Twenty pairs?* His expression, as he revised his view of us from respectable spreaders of the wealth to cartoon Americans, never changed. *Benissimo.* The shoes, at a few dollars a pair, would be finished in eight days.

Leaving the shop, we ran into Miss MacHattie, who had ordered some ready-next-day velvet slacks around the corner. Nevertheless she looked grumpy. Last night's noodles and veal in wine sauce hadn't gone down well, and she had no use for the Eyetalians. She was a plain forty-year-old with curls blonde as tin and a good figure; from the first, men crooned like doves and pinched her as she passed. She didn't see how she could stand a whole month of it. My father out of long experience with discontented women shook his head compassionately. "I know just how you feel," he said. "How soon would you like to go home?"

Two evenings later—she was catching the early morning boat—we made a little party of it. Miss MacHattie wore her new slacks, and Neddy telephoned for "Mr Merrill's caviar" to be brought up from the kitchen along with toast, lemons, hard-boiled eggs, and a couple of bottles of champagne. No one could remember who sent the caviar to my father when he sailed, but we blessed the giver. The tin must have held a full kilo, glistening black and fresh and priceless, for our four selves to consume. We spread it lavishly on toast, washed it down with champagne, spread more, spread even a portion for the hovering waiter, who hoped it was tasty. At orgy's end we had him return the tin, two-thirds empty, to cold storage with Mr Merrill's name on it. We saw it next on the weekly bill, where it equaled the cost of our rooms. Charged for his own caviar? my father protested. No, sir, this was the *hotel's* caviar; nothing was known of his private supply. But . . . ! (Ah!) *Un momento* . . . Whereupon a tuxedoed gentleman from the great mirrored and chandeliered dining room returned with the quite intact two-ounce glass jar given him for safekeeping on our arrival. No matter; Miss MacHattie'd had her send-off. She was promptly replaced by an Italian nurse, Miss Beltrami, who knew how to flirt and added a festive, Continental note to her duties.

Donkeys bore Miss Beltrami and me to Tiberius's villa. A boatman in the Blue Grotto serenaded our gently rocking party. Neddy was already licking his lips at the prospect of a night in Rome with the Cockney divorcée he'd met in a piano bar. My father and I went by carriage to see the faience church floor at Anacapri. On our return, the driver, disapproving of our silence, pointed out a statue in a roadside niche: "*La Vergine*. The Virgin." "The only one on the island," said my father, and I laughed at his joke. A half hour alone with him could be all uphill. *His* talk flowed, the pauses companionable, the delivery frank: a business deal, an old mistress, family stories and boyhood exploits. He had played "semi-pro baseball" (whatever that was) and piloted a plane. Feeling his love and good will as we leafed, side by side, through these albums of his life, I despaired of showing him the least snapshot in return.

Young people often strike their elders as sleepwalking, drugged by youth, heads full of music no one over thirty

33

can hear. Is that how my father saw me? Or did he guess that I was all this while quivering with awareness—of sun and sea, of the lustrous phlegm coughed into his white handkerchief, of the hairs in our coachman's ears and the chip in the Virgin's smile? A thousand details reached me, but like a primitive painter ignorant of perspective, I had no way to order them; the mosquito was the same size as the horse or the purple blossom of the artichoke. Worst of all, this awareness, which ought to have been my lifeline to the world, at present divided me from it, every detail a pane of glass. No doubt the seedling psyche needed time in the greenhouse. Yet I felt stifled, unable to express a thought, my thoughts being primarily erotic. How could I? Hadn't my mother said more than once, looking me straight in the eye, "If your father ever knew about your life it would be the death of him."

Would it? My father despised secrecy. Demystification had been the key to his own great success: no more mumbo-jumbo from Harvard men in paneled rooms; let the stock market's workings henceforth be intelligible even to the small investor. I was visibly sharing in the profits of such openness. As our carriage ride ended, my father began a story I listened to with mixed feelings—gratitude for the broken silence, apprehension for the import of any given tale. "When I was about ten years old," he said, "some older boys who lived on our block ganged up on me after supper and started to push me around. I was faster than them; I made it home without getting hurt and complained to my father. He told me, 'Get back out there right now and stand up to them, son. Make them respect you. Sure, you'll get a thrashing. But you'll get an even worse one from me if you don't do what I say.' "

"So you went out?" I faintly asked, recalling that my grandfather wore "a silver plate in his skull" after having been mugged on the streets of Jacksonville. Had that old man with his terrifying white mustaches wanted my father to taste the same medicine?

34

"I went out," said my father. He turned to face me squarely—here came the homily—then broke into his widest, most charming grin. "And I had better sense than ever to do a damn-fool thing like that again."

The ointments and sitzbaths Miss Beltrami suggested for my complaint did little good. As our next stop was Rome, she arranged for the famous English doctor who attended Orson Welles and Ingrid Bergman to see me. My father put on the scowl of a thwarted little boy—he collected doctors—and demanded an appointment of his own. Came the day to settle accounts. We found the shoemaker bent over the nineteenth pair of Kinta's identical spectator pumps; he delivered all twenty to the hotel that evening. A new suitcase was purchased to carry them. "Have you ever known anyone as thoughtful as your father?" Neddy chortled. "It'll be a red-letter day when he gets back to Southampton!" "Don't count on it," sighed my father.

Dr Albert Simeons had a kindly face, sallowed by decades in India. There he'd run a leper colony, working to stamp out both the disease and the prejudice against its victims. His novel about this experience was soon to be published. A later book, *Man's Presumptuous Brain*, still turns up in popular-science or holistic bookstores. This work claims, as did its author when he examined me, that every physical symptom is to some degree psychological. Even my piles? Absolutely, said the doctor, warming to his theme. He unscrewed his pen to sketch first a normal, then a spastic colon, all the while describing the mental tensions likely to turn one into the other. Really difficult cases he treated in conjunction with a psychiatrist. He asked so many questions about my health and habits and self-image that, simply to keep the ball rolling, I complained of being fat. Dr Simeons appraised with new interest my slender person (what I'd meant to say was that I had no *muscles*, that I was essentially soft flesh and bone—an endomorph, had I known the

35

word) and told me to come back to Rome whenever I had a free month; a newly developed course of injections would change all that. As for my immediate problem, the quickest solution was surgery.

True to his theory, no sooner had Dr Simeons finished the short operation than up to my hospital room he trotted with a couple of psychological tests. The Rorschach cards looked like watercolors by Max Ernst, and I associated freely and fluently. But lest he dismiss me as a pushover, I balked at identifying as such an obvious phallic shape; nor in the Szondi test which followed (where the patient is asked to evaluate a rogues' gallery of mad crones and elderly murderers), would I explain, for all the doctor's urging, why I distrusted the one effete young man who looked like me. My local anesthetic was wearing off. Dr Simeons left to order a shot of morphine. Presently a girl mopping the corridor paused and, seeing me in pain, ran to my bedside with tears in her eyes. "Ah, *quanto mi dispiace!*" she breathed, beautiful as a goddess, clasping my hand before darting back to work. I returned to our hotel the next morning, well enough to take my father to a matinee. I had never heard *Zazà*—and when if ever had *he* gone to the opera?—but we both felt at home with the tuneful score and the plot's conventional characters. Husband and mistress, wife and child, how one knew them! It could have been another Szondi test.

A boy of fourteen now joined us for a weekend from his Swiss boarding school: Robin Magowan, my half-sister's son (hence Neddy's nephew as well as mine) and my father's oldest grandchild. Robin was only ten years my junior. I knew in my bones how the pressures of upbringing (tennis lessons, languages, the dress codes of Southampton) had told upon him. Naturally left-handed, he'd been "encouraged" to conform to a dextral world, a shift that marred his diction—so faintly, however, that

36

it sounded like a throwback to his father's Scotch ancestry. "I was so excited," he told us on arriving at the hotel. "I couldna eat breakfast on the train." Like my father and me, Robin was traveling equipped with the names of those tailors and restaurants without visiting which, in his parents' view, no Roman holiday was thinkable. At his shy suggestion we booked a table for that evening at Alfredo's, where the *fettuccine* were stirred by the proprietor with a fork and spoon of solid gold. Neddy had a date with his doxy from Capri, Miss Beltrami was put at liberty; the three of us sat among the music and lights, beaming in our newfound— But now what? Halfway through a story, my father, bent over, scarlet, is coughing up his dental bridge into the celebrated noodles. (It occurs to me that he's had one drink too many, yet this cannot be. Liquor makes us charming, witty, accessible, not—) In no time we are back at the hotel, and Miss Beltrami, dressed for her ruined evening, is receiving instructions from Dr Simeons. It isn't a heart attack, he says, putting away stethoscope and hypodermic kit, just a close shave; a couple of days in bed, some further precautions . . .

So Robin ate his first Roman dinner off a table on wheels in my room (and Neddy's) at the Grand Hotel. The couch had been made up into a bed, but he wasn't sleepy. He was frightened—was Grandpa going to die? I just happened to have with me some chapters of a novel I'd begun in New York, in whose prophetic opening scene the hero's invalid father, attended by a needle-brandishing nurse, weathers a crisis similar to the one subsiding next door. Meaning, perhaps, to reassure my nephew that this sort of thing occurred regularly, I put my pages into his hands. I must have known already that he was susceptible to words. Tonight, however, it would dawn upon him that actual people, people he knew, could be written about, and not merely in the local paper's society column but in *real books*, stories contrived for the hard-to-please grown-up reader he himself was turning into under my eyes. An old man's brush with death, a boy's glimpse into the secret workshop . . . When at last Neddy stumbled in, lipstick on his jowl, the young initiate was sleeping as fast as he could.

I wasn't to learn for many months what Dr Simeons said to my father at their consultation. Now that he was again on his feet, and Robin back in school, we undertook the full-time job of seeing Rome. A limousine appeared every morning at our hotel. Its high-spirited young driver, Marcello (who spoke ten words of English and twenty of French), whisked us to museums and churches, to lunch at Tivoli, to the Vatican. Marcello, like everything else, had been pulled from a hat by those two Americans who danced attendance on our first day in Naples. Their calling was to foresee, make feasible, make positively festive for clients such as my father, every aspect of the Italian Experience. Through their uncanny connections they could smuggle a della Robbia relief back to Tulsa as casually as they could book a private dining room. An audience with the Pope? Nothing simpler. Here my father came into his own. First calling the concierge to make sure that the Pope had no monopoly on white raiment, he appeared in snowy, double-breasted swank. A gold bill-clip shaped like a dollar sign held his blue silk tie conspicuously in place. "Hey, Charlie, great!" cried Neddy. "His Holiness'll kiss *your* hand when he sees that." Miss Beltrami removed it as we neared the Vatican, lowering a black veil over her smile. Nineteen fifty was the Anno Santo, and many other pilgrims lined the audience chamber, but my father and the waxen, white-robed ascetic now making his way towards him—two men who had "reached the top" in their respective fields of godliness and finance—eclipsed the rest of us, in my view, like some long-awaited conjunction of Jupiter and Pluto.

To be the son of the founder of the world's largest brokerage firm meant, among many comforts and conveniences, being liable to hear the person I was meeting for the first time say,

"Merrill? Not so fast—any relation . . . ?" and having to decide in a split second whether my cross-examiner was someone I could fool by pretending to go along with the joke ("Oh sure!") or whether I must hang my head and confess. With members of the world I grew up in, it cost nothing to tell the truth. Their sense of how to live was neither mine nor, I suspected, my father's, who, as the son of a crusty but credit-extending doctor in Green Cove Springs, had taken jobs to get through college and never left a room without switching off the lights. "Thank goodness I come from poor parents," I once said, to the hilarity of my companions. But I meant that my parents' values had been formed long before they had money. Finally there was a world teeming with people who'd never heard of my father or the Firm, people like the girl from the hospital corridor or the models of Tsarouchis, and I yearned to know them, to be mistaken by them for their own kind. In these fantasies it had yet to strike me that my unlikeness to their own kind was precisely what made them look twice at me. I went on trusting that some yet-to-be-achieved incognito would save me from exposure until—faint as the chances were—I should have "made a name for myself."

Florence came next. Alas, Rome had so glutted us with sights that it is more the gleams and glooms of our shuttered hotel than the Duomo or the Uffizi that evoke our week there. The Maggio Musicale was mounting, in the Boboli Gardens, two thrillingly rare operas—Gluck's *Iphigénie en Aulide* and Weber's *Oberon*—which I insisted we attend. But opera out of doors, it transpired to my grief and to my father's uncomplaining somnolence, gave up its strongest claims. Gone were the effects I cherished most: the dimming of pineal baubles at the auditorium's inner zenith, the gasp of stale backstage air on my face when the gold or crimson curtains parted, the sense, all evening, of sheltered communion and psychodrama. One touch of nature routed such illusions; Agamemnon's soldiery

39

swarmed down the real hillside like a glee club of ants, and
Teresa Stich-Randall as she sang swimming into view—in the
moat's real water—came closer to Mack Sennett than to the
naiads of folklore.

The weather turned summery. In that same heat, under the
sun of this same June, I would be meeting Claude; the days were
now countable on fingers. It was time to collect Tony's and my
Citroën, in Venice. There for a day, I recall little but inhibitive
waterways and wrong turnings. Tony had settled into a famous
old *pensione* on the Zattere, his room enhanced with pictures
and ornaments, a green-and-white-striped coverlet, extra pillows, a bowl of anemones. The trip to Spain had been a trial,
nearly literally so. There'd been a "sort of accident" in a remote
village. He'd hit someone—a child—not seriously: he'd seen it
in the rearview mirror, getting to its feet. Should he have
stopped? The thought of a night—or a month—in a provincial
Spanish jail spurred him onward to Madrid. There the French
ambassador—Martine's husband, if I remembered Martine—
had said a word to the right person. But no sooner were Tony's
nerves mending in Venice than a worse blow fell: a column
drunkenly leaned into from a moving New York subway train
had split open Bill Cannastra's head. One of the several ensu-
ing elegies likened this death to the great god Pan's. Ah, it had
been a horrendous season. . . .

But not entirely a waste. For all his languid manner, Tony
had the phenomenal energy of a Cellini, able to jump six feet
in air from a standing position. When I saw him he'd just had
a pamphlet of poems printed by the monks on San Lazzaro in
the lagoon, where Byron spent mornings learning Armenian.
I had to admit the book was handsome. It looked French;
motifs from a disk of black jade Tony kept on his desk decorated front and back covers; a single sonnet ran over onto the
next page. There were ten short lyrics in all, too hushed and
aesthetic even for me, though certain effects had a simple oddity I pondered the making of:

40

When the snow falls in a wet March
And we wear our velvet collars up,
Silence, a silent figure on the Marble Arch,
Breaks from her broken pedestal and rises UP.

Tony was elated that day by the perceptive things "someone" had said to him about these poems, a few nights before, in a gondola. Who? Oh, a new friend, he offered vaguely, a Princess. . . . My heart sank; princesses *were* poetry if he liked, but what could they make of it on the page?

Tony had discovered photography as well. Together we picked up his latest prints, which pleased him so much he ordered them bound into a Venetian-paper album stamped with his initials. To anyone with an identity problem the camera is a godsend, each shot proving (if nothing else) that the photographer has composed *himself* for the split second needed to press the shutter. It is also a way to make quick raids on life while keeping it at arm's length; you look at things no longer quietly, for their own sake, but greedily, for the images they yield. Studied later, if the rainy day ever comes, their historical present inspires an emotion not always felt at the time. I bought my camera on the spot and before driving to France photographed my father.

It is after lunch. He is sitting in the hotel room, nicely dressed as usual. Miss Beltrami, leaning forward like a fortune-teller, is taking his blood pressure. At his elbow, half eaten, the crème caramel he orders at every meal. Beyond it, a tray of medicines: cough syrup, thyroid extract, sleeping pills, nitroglycerin, to name the few I remember. As I haven't learned to coordinate the lens opening with the light meter, these beginner's images suffer from melodrama. My father looks ancient, ravaged by shadows, deprived of natural light or a flash of humor from me. One picture, though, by accident, is of professional quality: a half-full goblet of water set on the window ledge between open shutters. Bleached and sunstruck, the city blurs off into background—but no, the glass, a lens within a lens, contains it: a tiny topsy-turvy Florence, there alone in magical focus, its values true. My next subject will be Claude.

Not long ago Robin gave me a fat autobiographical typescript to read. Here I found the story of his being shown, in our Roman hotel, pages from my novel—an incident otherwise forgotten. Writing more or less overtly about his life became my nephew's calling. Ever since that night? I can almost think so. Through the years I've watched him, from woman to woman, in Greek taverns, in Zen gardens, his agile frame clothed vividly as a bird's, younger than his children, his script still cramped as a boy's, taking patient, at times hallucinated, note. Poems, annals of bicycling, travels to Madagascar or Turkestan. The things one can be held answerable for . . .

My father, in 1950, had six years to live. To this day he remains an almost perversely mild and undemanding presence in my thoughts, triggering none of the imaginary confrontations I have with my mother. His company, by those last years, was an end in itself. As part of his entourage, I no longer questioned how to improve the hour. I didn't care if I ever wrote another poem; I lay back, contented, in the very arms of Time. It was a contentment I strove again and again to recapture. A risky project, since one of its elements was an almost limitless boredom. It would be the wise lover who by dint of scenes or séances kept my spirit on its toes. Surely this bland diet, this custard on the emotional menu, cost more than it was worth. My father had disciplined me conventionally as a child, here a spanking, there a blue eye darting fire, but once I no longer lived under his roof, any such showdown came to seem unthinkable. A four-page letter in his beautiful, rounded hand documents a ripple in the too-smooth surface we'd arrived at. Naturally, he wrote, it disappointed him that I didn't care to join the Amherst fraternity whose national president he was. Still, he understood and respected my choice. What left him puzzled was the violent tone of my letter saying so. Knowing how vital it was that he avoid stress after his latest heart attack, couldn't I have tempered my refusal? Evidently not. It was a stab, however ill timed, at restoring the dynamics proper to the discourse of fathers and sons, forfeited by our years of living apart.

It is 1986 and I am again in Rome. This wet Sunday morning has been uncommonly trying. I left my passport in a taxi the night before. Since Peter Hooten is tied up with the producer of the thriller he has just starred in, I've invited a dull American friend to lunch. The police station where one registers the loss of a passport is conveniently on the way to our restaurant, but the officer I speak to shakes his head. Taxi drivers don't, by and large, return lost passports; at best they drop them in a mailbox. Let the Signore come back in two hours and talk to the head of that department. Once at table, it turns out that my guest takes his Sunday lunch very seriously indeed. Aperitif, antipasto, piccata, salad, dessert, coffee, grappa . . . Mainly to keep him company, I too order dessert—something simple, anything, a crème caramel? But how delicious it is! I scrape my plate clean. Parting from my friend in a glow of well-being, I return to the police station, and there, on the desk of the man I was told to see, my passport awaits me. Next, it is brilliant late afternoon. Peter and I are overlooking the city from the terrace of the Aventine. Peter grew up in Florida, an easy drive from my father's birthplace; sometimes I pretend that he is my father as a young man, before my birth. The light deepens. Now only do I recall that crème caramel was my father's great weakness, often ordered twice a day, during our long-ago time in Italy. Today, moreover, this very Sunday, October 19, is his birthday. He would be one hundred and one years old.

IV *The lovers reunited.*
Last hour with Hans.

Homey and unremarkable by morning light, the Hôtel des Roches Blanches at Cassis on the Côte d'Azur had seemed, at the end of my fifteen hours at the wheel, a blazing palace. Claude himself, closing his Herbert or Traherne, rising so abruptly that his chair fell over, for a long moment answered fully to the ardent phantom he'd become during our separation. I gasped to see him once more in flesh and blood. He looked the way I felt: stunned with relief, at peace because we were together at last, off balance because we would now have to face the fact, not the fantasy, of being so. Was his frame limber and powerful enough to receive the likeness I'd made of him? In the lens of my new camera, his chin was weaker than I recalled, and his hands stronger; his hair less golden, his gaze more intense. Those hands and that gaze humbled me. From them had issued a flow of such letters!—pages marveled over in Paris and Poros and Rome, earlier ones wrapped in silk at the back of a drawer in my empty apartment—letters of an eloquence and spontaneity I hoped one day to rise to, though my efforts seemed a schoolboy's by comparison. No matter; the long term apart had ended. From letters I was graduating into life.

What with separate lodgings at Amherst and the rare, guilty weekend at a New York hotel, Kimon and I had hardly ever spent nights together. Now with Claude came unlimited, unprecedented bounty. For as far into the future as I could see,

44

my lover and I were free to sleep and wake side by side. Through an infinity of days and nights ahead, each would have—what greater blessing?—open access to the other's body. So deep and pent-up was my craving for blind flesh-and-blood reassurance, it once or twice crossed my mind that almost anybody might have— No, banish the thought! It was Claude I had chosen, Claude I loved, Claude I would cleave to.

Neither of us had sunned on a shingle beach, or tasted sea urchins, or visited so many little towns in an afternoon's drive. It was early in the season—the hotels half full, the Mediterranean cold—when a walk down the empty beach at St Tropez led us into hot water. Far off, two other bathers could be made out, squirming irritably back into their briefs at our approach. Fifty meters later, cries of amazed recognition. It was Barney Crop and his lover Hubert. Barney!—once cute and catchable as a tadpole but now, after a couple of years in Paris, painting still lifes and society women, well on his way to adult froghood. We'd lived together—how else but platonically?—during the months before his departure and had kept up; he knew all about the love of my life. I tried not to see, over the carafe we shared on the waterfront, a glaze of withheld comment settle upon his naughty, grinning face. At Claude's expense? What impudence! But no matter, I said to myself again; Barney was a shallow vessel; I was graduating from him too.

As we drove back to Cassis, after a long silence, "You were once in love with Barney," Claude said.

"Claude! I was in love with everybody! And why? Because I didn't have a lover. *I do now.* That's the difference—don't you see?"

"You'd had Kimon."

Oh dear, this was awful. "Weren't there other people in your life?" I whispered.

Claude took my hand. We both intensely hoped no more faces would loom up out of the past.

The hope wasn't to be realized. We'd planned to drive

across northern Italy to Salzburg, our destination for the summer. A phone call changed our itinerary. Hans Lodeizen was dying of leukemia in Lausanne. Thus this chapter—which ought to have been, like my honeymoon with Claude, devoted to *him*—has a Dutch poet as its central figure.

Hans was a graduate student at Amherst when we met in 1946, five months after Kimon had sailed for Greece. True to form, I fell in love. Just as certain words—like "naked" or "muscular"—would leap from the page I was reading to stimulate an erotic nerve end, so this Cherubino had but to think "love" and every problem dissolved, light filled him, he knew why he'd been born. A variety of religious experience? I hadn't yet come across Borges's definition of the lover as founder of a religion with a fallible god, but I was nothing if not devout. Devout and fickle. Between my eighteenth and twenty-fourth birthdays there must have been ten or twelve young men *en fleurs*—like Barney—whom I was smitten by in succession, or two or three at a time. Of these, Hans was by far the most meaningful. The affairs, true to some grand renunciatory model, tended not to be consummated in any usual sense of the term. Rather, they gave rise to *poems* about love—a sorry substitute, I feared, for the real thing. Whether those young men divined from the start that I would be made happier by a poem than by lying in their arms, or that *they* would be, I cannot say. Perhaps it was a simple case of that curious but widespread law whereby people instinctively withhold what you want from them.

But what exactly did I want, or think I wanted, from a lover? To be undressed of my affectations, clothed afresh in passion's more convincing wardrobe? Out of childhood comes a bluntly scissored memory of paper dolls, over whose all but genderless undergarments new selves—hunter or peasant, soldier or man about town—could be affixed by tabs at shoulders and hips. If at present the garb of an aesthete seemed cut out for me, it was because poetry and grand opera were the only keys I possessed

46

to the heart's innermost chamber and the psychic nudity permitted there. Alas, the heart's innermost chamber, to judge by the reaction of those I paid suit to, was all too often a suffocating hole.

I didn't think of *them* as paper dolls, no; but . . . postage stamps? I could spend hours, at ten or eleven, with my album, attaching new finds by means of little gummed hinges, calculating the ever-increasing value from my catalog. Not otherwise did I catch myself, at twenty or twenty-one, gloating over bygone names and faces. I took pains to distinguish between the uncanceled idealization of that year's crown prince and the far more precious rarity of a timed and dated "conquest," which (soaked in advance by one cocktail too many) had slid into my care, summoning up foreign parts, dark-skinned couriers, intimacies scrawled on lost pages addressed hardly ever to a person I knew. How thrilled I'd been to obtain my first stamp from Siam or the Orange Free State! Now, with Hans's profile already in the engraver's hands, and my presses thundering yet again into action, I could look forward to filling in my first window on the blank page of "Holland."

Hans wanted, sensibly enough, a love that kept his spirit intact. He was first of all a young man of the Old World, whose blue sunbeam eye, purling Dutch voice, and friendly sketch of a bow on meeting or parting functioned by reflex at times when my compatriots would have been tearing their hair. However vital to him the writing of poetry, good manners made him treat it as something that simply "happened," as if a tree should say with a rueful shrug, "Look, these little pink what-d'you-call-'ems have broken out all along my branches." Indeed, Hans was blossoming here in the New World, and not only as a poet. He was tasting the freedom and anonymity felt by Americans abroad. For the first time in his life he had escaped his large, influential family; the last thing he needed was to have his style cramped by a possessive friend. Yet he was

47

drawn to me. The time I spent on poems and term papers impressed him in spite of himself. The atomic age had begun, and I still favored the cumbersome old cotton gins of Art and Scholarship? Next to mine, Hans's mental furnishings were streamlined, eclectic. He expounded the Existentialists. He held forth on Plato's vision, on Nietzsche's, calling the latter "terrible, terrible" with a smile and a shiver, as if speaking of a tale by Poe. In the biology lab he showed me the scarlet pulse of a fertilized egg. He wanted me to read Chamfort's maxims, look at a mask from the Congo, hear the violin sonatas of Beethoven.

One autumn afternoon we left the music library with a borrowed album. I was coming down with a cold, and midway to my rooms, feeling a nip in the air, Hans took off his scarf and put it round my neck. I lived off campus that year, in the town barber's house. We lit a fire and sat on the floor with sherry, while the ravishing "Spring" Sonata, interrupted every four minutes by having to change the record, burgeoned around us. When it ended, Hans asked if I knew the Henriette episodes in Casanova's *Memoirs*—of course I did not—and began to tell, delighting in every detail, that infinitely romantic story. It begins with the laugh of an unseen woman at a roadside inn; shows her to us first disguised as a soldier, then in Rome at Casanova's expense, refusing to tell him who she is but playing the cello so passionately that her lover stumbles from the room to bury his face in the lilacs outside; and ends years later with words scratched by her diamond on a windowpane in the Alps. My cold, however, just when I might have glowed with joy, was ripening fast. In the face of Hans's concern—he offered to come back with soup from the dining hall—I protested that it was nothing, that I needed no mothering, without ever pausing to reflect until the downstairs door shut quietly behind him how welcome *his* mothering would have been. The moment was like a sprain; henceforth our intimacy would limp somewhat.

48

I'd had another crush at Amherst, on a shy, black-haired American from Argentina named Seldon James. We roomed together the summer following my demobilization. (During my eight months in the army—basic training, then office work—the war had been virtually won. Clerks with bad eyesight, like me, were being returned to civilian life.) But Seldon left college at term's end for the navy, and I'm afraid I barely noticed his reappearance on campus a year later, so taken up was I by my feelings for Hans. There came a painful evening nevertheless. Maggie Teyte, then my favorite singer, miraculously turned up in Amherst with a program of Debussy and Fauré. Those songs were charms I tried to keep always within reach. Many of them I'd sung under my breath on marches in the army; they dissolved pain and made boredom sparkle like wine. At intermission, throwing on my Oscar Wilde overcoat, I went out into the chilly dark. Seldon stood nearby; so did Hans, wearing only a jacket and shirt. "But you're not warmly dressed; you'll catch cold," I cried. "Here—" And remembering the scarf he had once put round my neck, I took mine off and insisted that he wear it. People were watching; I felt Hans's discomfort but couldn't drop this parody of what he himself had done so gently and impulsively a few weeks earlier. He might have shamed me by handing the scarf back. Instead he sketched his little bow and moved away. Indoors, just as the lights dimmed, I noticed to my dismay that he was sitting with Seldon. They'd come to hear Maggie Teyte together; they were friends! Pangs reserved exclusively for the gay shot through me—I was jealous of both parties at once. From the stage a third love produced her ageless, lilting summary:

> C'est l'histoire des oiseaux
> Dans les arbres.

Two years later, in New York, my heart must have been engaged elsewhere: I spent an afternoon with Hans, and even heard that he was meeting Seldon for dinner, without a trace of those old palpitations. Yet when word reached me in Cassis that he was ill and wanted to see me, I knew only how much he had always meant to me and that we must travel by way of Lausanne. Claude hugged me and agreed.

The clinic might have passed for a luxurious Swiss hotel. Pacing the corridor on Hans's floor was our college friend Ray, who had traced me to Cassis by phoning my mother in New York. He told me things I preferred not to register. Hans's parents—I'd met them once at Amherst—joined us, thanked me for coming, but added that it would be a kindness if I stayed under an hour. I went in. The large, lived-in room, full of books and records, overlooked the lake. Hans lay cranked up in bed, a picture of health thanks to his daily transfusion. He had asked, he said, blushing as if confessing to a clandestine love, to meet his principal donor, and shaken hands with that great strapping fellow whose blood was keeping him alive. But soon, he added solicitously, lest I grow too alarmed, his condition would stabilize. He'd thought of Italy for his convalescence; if I was there in the fall we could perhaps spend some weeks together? Nothing, I swore, would make me happier. (And Claude?) Among the books on the bed were George Sand's memoirs, which Hans praised in the same terms—"She sends me floating up and up like a balloon"—he used to describe the nurse's nightly injection that put him to sleep like a baby.

He then drew from the bedclothes, diffidently, his book of poems, *Het Innerlijk Behang* (*The Wallpaper Within*), published just that month in Holland. A prompt reviewer had already hailed its freshness and assurance. Although I knew no Dutch, the work indeed appeared daringly up-to-date—short, unrhymed lines, free of capitals and punctuation. As we turned the pages together, I saw that Hans had inscribed the book to me and that it was dedicated to Seldon. "Seldon and I were both displaced in America," he said with a slow, candid look. "It was natural for us to gravitate toward each other. Yours was the friendship I wanted, but Seldon's the one I needed." He next found a poem whose epigraph was a line I'd written, then a few sly stanzas about a party at my mother's in New York, finally the two poems dedicated to me. One by one he read them out in English. The last of the four was no more than a quatrain, but it brought back a certain midnight amble through the campus together, an hour I'd forgotten precisely for its having unsheathed, like a Euclidean proof, the clash of temperament that divided us:

> the stars & the incurable
> moment of the two crossed beams.
> Orion discovered & in his hand
> o fate in his hand the sword.

When word of Hans's death not long afterwards reached me in Salzburg, a poem began to take form—or rather, for once, *not* to. Lines varied in length, end words rhymed or didn't. The phrases, like river stones, learned their own shape and smoothness from the current of grief that swept through me. I'd had no brush with death so close as this. The experience merged for my poem's purposes with that of Europe, of Switzerland in particular, where

> The glittering neutrality
> Of clock and chocolate and lake and cloud
> Made every morning somewhat
> Less than you could bear;
>
> And makes me cry aloud
> At the old masters of disease
> Who dangling high above you on a hair
> The sword that, never falling, kills

—for it seemed to me that Hans had died cheated of his "real" death, that death to the very last remained his sword of Damocles, never falling, always out of reach. This was pure poetic doubletalk, meaning, if it meant anything, that I as survivor remained incapable, and would for months and months, of deeply realizing what had befallen my poor friend. The hanging sword as an image of deferral appeared from out of the blue—or so I thought. But in a flash that winter I recognized it as the sword from Hans's quatrain, *his* image and the image of his youthful valor, which on his deathbed he had put into my hands.

We were no longer alone when I took my leave. Our friend Ray—well named, his pleasant features abeam—had returned with flowers and magazines. A nurse came in to ready Hans for his dinner tray; or was there to be a transfusion appetizer? Looking back, half out of the room, I caught my breath. A brilliant stripe of late sun ran down the left side of his glowing, rosy-brown face. Why didn't he shift, or squint? A blood vessel had burst when he bent over a few weeks earlier, and Hans was already blind in that eye.

My erotic activity in those early years between seeing Kimon off to Greece and saying hello to Claude at Freddy's party was rare and seldom involved the person I happened to be "in love with" at the time. Neither was it much pleasure to look back upon. This was due partly to the insecurity more or less guaranteed by the odd sexual athlete who saw in me a novel challenge, and overwhelmingly to my own naïveté. Finding someone willing to spend the night seemed of itself such a miracle that I would start before daybreak sending out tendrils to bind my companion to me forever, despite the scant affection or trust I felt. (Why did I need someone to spend the night in the first place? Because I had no Inner Resources and feared being alone. Because, as in Auden's tongue-in-cheek Utopia, what was no longer forbidden was compulsory. Because in a

few years I would be an old man of thirty and no one would ever look at me again.) Needless to say, my gambits frightened off creep and charmer alike. If by any remote chance a second meeting came about, I would arrange to bring to it so much uneasiness that the rendezvous ended before it had properly begun. Some such mechanism underlay my break with Kimon. In my guilty view—for which I had, if not my mother, "society" to thank—the reprieve he offered took on the aspect of a sentence. Like the colt that, genetically programmed to be broken, nevertheless throws its first riders, I shied away from being saddled with a lover capable of seeing into my heart, for would he not then despise the confusion he saw there? Far better the unrequited pangs I knew so well, which guaranteed me "no little innocent bliss," as Tonio Kröger put it, and could always be used as fuel for a poem. Regarding those platonic crushes, it should be added that back then—before such matters were codified by the color and placement of a pocket handkerchief—I was pretty much in the dark as to sexual "roles" and "types" and may (for all I knew) have been sleepwalking on the brink of incompatibilities all too apparent to my beloved.

Long after his death, I heard that Hans, without any help from me or Seldon, had found love in America: a young Puerto Rican dancer living in a Harlem apartment crowded with family. When Hans returned to Holland he told Ignacio (if that was his name) to write him not at home but in care of a friend who knew the story. A day came when this friend had to write a letter himself, breaking the news that there would be no others. It was read in angry disbelief. Ignacio knew—knew—that Hans couldn't have died; this was all a plot, on the part of those (as he must have pictured them) cinematically bourgeois parents across the ocean, to thwart his love. It took a Dutch go-between's visit to New York, and a folder of newspaper tributes, to convince the boy.

The story, had I heard it during Hans's lifetime, would have

53

filled me with jealousy. Forty years later—like "Tu oublieras Henriette" etched on an icy windowpane or the "Spring" Sonata heard by chance on Public Radio—it stops me in my tracks. I smile, I shake my head. With passions like that, for instinct's beautiful children, there could have been no question of competing. I am old enough to have survived one or two similar loves, know what they bring to a sedentary, overcultivated type, and am glad that life granted Hans this particular deep enchantment.

V
Flagstad in Salzburg.
Alison on the picnic.
Vira's romance.
Mallorcan finches.

I<small>N</small> <small>SALZBURG</small>, Claude and I rented an apartment crammed with the owners' books and furniture. A tiny cement balcony permitted a view of the mountain. A great feather-quilted bed gave rise to dreams and their fulfillment. At the street door began the cafés, the chocolate shops, the souvenirs imprinted in gold with silhouettes of Mozart. Much of the town lay in ruins. Fountains, façades, sidewalks, the cathedral dome were all undergoing repairs. After dark a great night-watchman searchlight from the Café Winkler uphill checked on their progress. The Festival had just begun. We'd booked a few performances in advance, but as we pored over the complete prospectus it seemed that something irresistible was being offered at every turning: tomorrow's concert of Dittersdorf trios in the salon of a genuine *Schloss*, or the next afternoon's marionette version of *Faust*. In the weeks ahead we spent hours every day wangling rehearsal passes, offering coffee and pastry to a *Frau Philharmoniker* (the wife, that is, of an orchestra member—even *she* had a title!) whose friend had tickets to sell, begging our landlady to rack her brains for another contact when the original one fell through. Reading magazine articles many years later about the agony and expense of sustaining a drug habit, I would be reminded of that summer's quest for tickets to the Salzburg Festival.

The rehearsal we attended was of the second act of *Fidelio*. That day I would be hearing Kirsten Flagstad for the first time since 1941. With our entry into the war, it became unpatriotic to admire Wagner, yet Flagstad's singing of his heroines had overwhelmed me as a boy. Single-handed she proved by her noble presence and the clarion tenderness of her voice that opera, risen above the sorrows of consumptive harlots or seam-stresses, left also the Greek dramatists in the dust and Shake-speare in the shade. Here she came now, my idol, as Leonora, one of the few irreproachable roles in the entire repertoire. A matron disguised as a beardless youth, wearing homespun knee-britches and holding a little lantern, she descended the dungeon stair. Time stopped at her first, spoken words. In my emotion I simply didn't hear the other singers. Only at a later perform-ance did Julius Patzak, the Florestan, with his sweet, tarnished tenor, emerge as a perfect wonder. To the American press many of these European artists gave off a distinct sheen of "collabora-tion." Flagstad herself was said to have sung for the Nazis in her native Norway; the same accusing finger pointed to Elisa-beth Schwarzkopf (our Marzelline); while the Festival's reign-ing maestro, the great Furtwängler, conducted both the or-chestra and himself in visionary, white-haired disdain of such petty rumors. True, we were here on "enemy territory," an easy drive from Berchtesgaden, yet in my innocence I tried to re-joice at how much people had thrust behind them.

But was this not, Claude darkly suggested, a mere entr'acte in some nonstop theater of war? For the so-called Korean Crisis was making headlines that summer. Our mothers, never think-ing international escape routes might differ from one war to the next, wrote identical letters urging us to open bank accounts in Portugal, so that if Americans were suddenly obliged, etc. We smiled, but panic was in the air. Must the world be put through it all again? Wallace Stevens had called for a poet "capable of resisting or evading the pressure of reality." Now in dead earnest Claude and I talked of moving for the rest of our lives to Liberia. Even a few years of grace were a lot to ask and would only grudgingly be wrung from Washington and the Kremlin. Our hopes and fears came back to us from the stage of the Felsenreitschule as Josef Greindl, across footlights, directly addressing an audience so musical, so sober, and so cosmopolitan that they would surely, the next morning, be able to bear his message to the heads of state it most concerned, sang Sarastro's noble plea for brotherly love.

One afternoon Claude returned excited from the post office, where he had run into a Harvard friend. We'd been asked on a picnic the following day. We were six: Claude's friend and his wife, and another young couple, recently married. The husband of this second couple, whom Claude had also known at college, was the son of the poet John Peale Bishop. Meeting friends of Claude's for the first time—he had already met most of mine—I was relieved to note that they looked and behaved like anyone else. There would have been hundreds more of us in Europe that summer—young, educated, "nice" Americans whose discovery of the Continent, in the footsteps of Hawthorne and Henry James, had been deferred by the war. Many were on grants to study abroad. In a new city we headed straight for the museum, for the churches starred in the Guide, for *Schloss* and *Denkmal*. If our choice excluded, as choices will, broad realms of experience—so be it. The events of the past decade had spoiled any appetite we might have had for public life. It was Culture's turn now, and we meant to get as much as we could. With, of course, breaks for fun, like today. Claude and I having spent the past weeks wholly among foreigners, these compatriot faces, shy though I felt in their presence, refreshed us like the little meadow pond we splashed about in after the first glasses of white wine had been drunk.

57

Jonathan Bishop's wife, Alison, cut a striking figure in her swimsuit: blonde, white-skinned, elongated, with the cat face of a Cranach Venus. One waited for her to purr. Out came instead a voice at once hollow and assertive, like an oracle's; Claude whispered that she was a writer, and deaf in one ear. Over our sandwiches she began telling an unpleasant story. Somebody they'd known at Harvard, while driving through a Spanish village a few months earlier, had struck and killed a child. Unfeelingly, unthinkingly, this person sped on, never stopping, to Madrid, where influential friends pulled strings. I realized at once that the driver in question was Tony Harwood and, when Alison had finished, remarked loyally that hers wasn't quite the story I'd heard from him—although, even secondhand, it exhaled the airy hubris that woke my original pity and terror. Alison gave me a shrewd look. "Oh, if he's such a friend of yours," she said in her odd voice, "why didn't you stop me when I began the story?" After that, I hoped never to see her again.

The car that struck the child was of course the same black Citroën Claude and I drove away from the picnic and in which we would soon set off from Salzburg. The Festival was ending. We contrived to hear a *Don Giovanni* with Ljuba Welitsch as Donna Anna, a role she'd sung in New York the previous winter. But the heroin that, unknown to her fans at the time, made for those electrifying performances—the tiny Ottavio sucked dry by his Black Widow—had taken its toll. Here in Salzburg, only months later, she was unable to get through her last great aria. Schwarzkopf sang Elvira in this production, and Irmgard Seefried Zerlina. These two sopranos had over the summer come to stand in our eyes for polar opposites: Schwarzkopf all airs and artifice, effects so fine as to be virtually detachable from the score; Seefried at her most lyrical, still somehow *speaking* the music in her human concern for directness and clarity. How could they bear one another? Yet at the end, astoundingly, they took their curtain calls hand in hand.

* * *

A high sunny road leads into Italy. "Verona, Vicenza, Padova," Claude chants in ecstasy as the roadsigns fly past. "Ferrara, Firenze, Ferrovia!" By evening we've returned the tainted car to Tony's Venetian garage—let it be his from now on—and settled ourselves above him in the historic *pensione*. Mosquito nets draping the beds give our room the air of a colonial hospital ward. It is rather Mrs Humphry Ward that Tony's room, more so even than in May, evokes. White-and-red Fortuny curtains of sheer silk, weighted with colored beads, float inward from the balcony doors. A sandstone Khmer head is flanked by two pictures framed in blond tortoiseshell. I recognize his unhappy, wisecracking mother, but who on earth is that other siren, equally striking in her sultry ripeness? Is *that* his poetry-loving Princess? At my question he rolls his eyes and utters an indrawn, Jamesian "Ah . . . !"

Claude's mother has herself decided that Europe is safe enough for a month or two of sightseeing. A tough cookie, bossy and independent, Vira nevertheless warms my heart as the kind of mother—in my book there are two kinds only—who seems resigned if not indifferent to her child's private life. She knows enough to leave unsaid a number of things whose saying all but severed the lines of communication between my mother and me. Well, perhaps we're always at our best with mothers not our own. If Vira's presence strains Claude's patience, I slip happily into the role of a difficult son's "nice friend," who eases the tensions and takes up the slack—now in the sumptuous hotel at the Lido, where Vira treats us to lobster and roulette, now in shops full of costly things we despise, now in the railway carriage where, after a scene with the porter, Claude pointedly withdraws into Meister Eckhart. When we reach Florence, Vira decides to go off by herself to Capri. Whether a romantic encounter is in the back of her mind or subliminally invited by her gait and perfume, within ten days she has met a well-spoken, suitably mature Saudi Arabian businessman and re-

59

vised her entire future. A grand villa with servants awaits her on the Persian Gulf. Her fiancé has already gone ahead to make the arrangements; the wedding is set for next June in Missouri, where Vira lives. Claude is presented to his prospective step-father over lunch in Rome. What's he like? "Oh, dapper, emphatic, sure of himself . . . ," says Claude, looking troubled.

"Dependable?"

"How would I know? I've never met an Arab before. Neither has she."

"Shouldn't you—what is it the men in a family are supposed to do—have him investigated?"

"Where would one begin? Besides," Claude resumes after a silence, "what right have I to interfere? We don't let our mothers run *our* lives."

This is my good strong-minded Claude. I still picture the "rights" between parent and child as one-sided.

With Vira we proceed to Naples and sail for Barcelona in early October. A few days later we have settled—Claude and I for the winter—on Mallorca, in the Hotel Maricel, above the sea, a long walk or pleasant tramride from Palma. The hotel is new and two-thirds empty. A few other Americans linger on, among them a Hollywood scriptwriter, bitter and broken, who late one night following our brandies at the bar taps on Vira's door, groaning her name. Over breakfast he will cringe to hear it told with a laugh in the acoustically merciless dining-room. Europe has so served its purpose that Vira goes home sooner than planned. The writer departs for Rome, like the penitent Tannhäuser. We aren't lonely. In December, Freddy comes to spend a fortnight at the hotel. Thanks to our single letter of introduction, we meet the foreign colony. Lunch with Robert Graves is a failure. Claude expresses doubts about the White Goddess; shown to the bathroom, I perceive too late that I should have asked for the loo and am obliged to pee in the basin; we aren't asked back. More congenial are the Bowdens,

60

a retired American couple who off and on throughout the winter have us for tea and music. Accompanied by her husband, Mrs Bowden sings Schubert songs we can't hear often enough. She would have turned eighteen in the early 1900s. Beneath a clubwoman's camouflage—tailored jacket of blue wool, permanent wave in her white hair—her psyche wears trailing skirts and speaks in symbols. She gives a dinner for us in town; on my plate lies a laurel wreath. But my sense is mainly of being alone with Claude. We spend mornings reading and writing in our connecting rooms, pausing to stare out at the sea or down at the little uniformed bellboys acting their age on the terrace. Late afternoons we walk along the coast, or in to Palma for an aperitif before dining back at the hotel. We've talked it over and decided not to acquire Spanish lest it "spoil our Italian." Yet something gets through, because one day the young barber who comes to our rooms with his scissors and lotions is prattling away and I break into laughter. "How marvelous that you are poets," he has just said unmistakably. "Nothing comes out of *my* head but hair!"

Mornings at work, local color, the sea . . . "It's Georgetown with plumbing and servants," said Freddy, meaning the summer we'd spent in Maine together. I nodded nostalgically. There was no need to point out the major difference, that I was now (another Spanish word slipping through the blockade) *casado*—housed; that is, "married." Yet I couldn't help noticing, alone with Freddy at his visit's end, how much more freely my tongue wagged and my mind worked than they did with Claude. It wasn't that I'd made the wrong choice. Friendship's chattering stream simply came as a relief from the uncharted waters of love, though it was to these that I'd committed myself. As other friends were doing. Returning from our walk, we were met by the little bellboy with an envelope addressed in Tony's impulsive cuneiform. He was leaving Venice for Geneva—a prolonged stay—this great change had taken place in his life—he could say no more at present. Freddy jotted down the name of our friend's hotel. He had cousins in Geneva and planned to look them up later in the spring, unless his publisher's advance ran out before then.

Freddy left behind a typescript of his new novel, *The Seasons' Difference*. He and I figured in it as a pair of secretive, inseparable teenagers. Countless touches I knew by heart brought "Harry" and "Rufus" to life and measured the inches we had grown in the seven years since our graduation from Lawrenceville. Hadn't every cell in our bodies changed? The message of Freddy's book, however, seemed to be that none of his characters, young or old, was going to change in any profound sense without the help of Christ. My head swerved aside from this spoonful of bitter syrup. If, as I kept fancying, my homosexuality was driving a wedge between us, so was Freddy's piety, and nothing either of us could do would change our ways. My eventual letter about his novel brimmed with things unsaid, and he must have felt its inadequacy as sorely as I did.

These reservations notwithstanding, on Christmas Eve Claude and I attended midnight service in the cathedral. At its climax a surpliced choirboy climbed into the pulpit and holding upright before him an angel's flashing sword sang, unaccompanied, a Catalan hymn for the Last Judgment. Mrs Bowden tracked down words and music; I learned to play the haunting song on my recorder, which sounded almost like a boy soprano. (Recorder duets were one of Claude's and my sedate entertainments.) On Christmas morning Claude gave me a pair of *rouge-gorges*. The little brown finches—the male with a band of crimson at his throat, as if he'd just then slit it—built a nest, laid eggs, neurotically destroyed them. We named the birds Ralph and Ivy. Released from their cage, they would hover for long minutes in midair before the closet door's oval mirror, enthralled by selves they could never be sure were their own.

From my publisher in New York came a present that allowed for even greater self-absorption than the finches': my first book. I looked at it in every conceivable light. What impression would it make upon my old teachers? upon Randall Jarrell? upon the youth of Liberia? upon a future world from which English had disappeared? The edition was limited to 990 numbered copies. Had I known onto whose shelves these books would go I might well have set about examining the text afresh through the eyes of each new owner in turn. But it was life-threatening to learn that my father had ordered a hundred copies for his friends and business associates, people to whom a page of verse, were it ever to confront them, would be speckled forbiddingly with stanza-shaped reefs and treacherous, variable soundings. So—one tenth of the tiny edition doomed to oblivion, at a single stroke! (Two years later my book had not sold out. I'd hoped for a small, select readership? I was getting my wish.)

Spring came early. One morning a taxi drove us twenty-five kilometers into the countryside, to a point from which we could hike back to the hotel through almond-blossom fragrances that buzzed and stung like bees. Another day we saw folk-dancing in an inland village. A Scarlatti-like melody for pipes and drums that sometimes comes over me in the course of a sleepless night will have to be surgically removed from my brain if I am ever to be free of it. One afternoon I let the finches out of their cage without remembering that the window was open. Before I could shut it, Ralph had flown, not for once to the mirror, but to a tree in the garden below. He and Ivy (safely behind bars) called back and forth heartrendingly. It was sadder than the *Trovatore* "Miserere." I ran downstairs with the cage, set it outdoors where he could see his mate. It did no good. His cries, as evening fell, came from farther and farther away. A bird used to captivity makes little sense of the greater world, falling prey easily to owl or hawk. We replaced Ralph, but the new finch lacked spirit, failed to ingratiate himself with Ivy or with us, and we gave them both away without bothering to name him.

※

     "Isn't it lovely here?" my companion is saying. "After so many stoic winters with Jonathan in the cold. Look at those palm trees, feel the air."

Thirty years have passed since our first, unfortunate meeting. Alison Lurie and I are sitting by starlight on the steps of a boarded-up shack halfway between her house and David Jackson's. We became friends with Alison and her husband (now amicably divorced) not long after Salzburg, when I was Jonathan Bishop's colleague in the Amherst English Department.

"Who would have thought we'd end up like this?" she marvels in her odd, off-key voice, which has come to delight me. *"In 1950 there seemed to be thousands of other young people just like you and David, or Jonathan and me—full of talent and ambition. But so few of us kept at it. And now those who did have readers and reputations. The rest . . ."*

The rest married, raised their children, voted for the wrong candidate, sold products nobody much wanted (including ideas), took to the bottle, had heart attacks, went south for the winter. Over the years it hasn't been beyond us to do some of these things ourselves. What made the difference?

"I used to think," I say, *"that deep down, all the other boys at school with me were just as clever and imaginative as I was. Even the bullies. We were Americans after all, we'd been created equal. The only difference was that they'd learned, and I hadn't, how to disguise this fact in order to be popular."*

"With other clever little boys pretending to be dumb? I see," Alison laughs. *"What age did the truth dawn on you?"*

"Oh, thirty-five . . . forty? Has it dawned?"

"It's true," she goes on after a pause. *"Back then we hadn't*

64

done anything yet. Not that we were completely interchange-able either; this was before the campgrounds and the discos. We were just young, like everyone else, and in Europe for the first time. Starry-eyed, dying to feel at home there."

"Remember Tony Harwood?"

"Of course. Jonathan liked him. He said it wasn't given to just anyone to emerge full-grown from the brain of Evelyn Waugh. He had that accident in Spain. What became of him? Are you still friends?"

"He died three years ago."

"Oh, I'm sorry," says Alison. "What of?"

I sketch in the marriage, the drugs, the delusions. The un-written masterpieces, the Tibetan child. The life in hotels. The life his example taught me not to live. The leather, the lawsuits. One night his heart simply stopped while he was ranting. I'd kept—in spite of so much nonsense—a kind of faith in him, in his being able one day to write something amazing.

"But he went mad instead. Was he a pure product of Amer-ica?" Alison muses. "The kind that Europe stains beyond re-demption? Americans are meant to resist the wicked influence, like Scotchgarded fabric. Especially writers. If our novelists want to live in Paris, they've got to drink a lot and act extra tough. Have you been to the Hemingway House yet? It's worth the five dollars. Look at the faces, listen to the comments. They've never read a line he wrote, but he's Papa, he's a fer-tility symbol. You and I are viewed with suspicion: we're 'mid-Atlantic,' we're 'genteel.' "

"It's not fair. We're as American as lemon chiffon pie."

"Speak for yourself," Alison says. "I just meant it must show in our sentence structure that I have a flat in London and that you spent all those years in Athens or listening to foreign operas. Perhaps we'd be taken more seriously—and Tony Harwood would be alive and famous today—if none of us had ever left home in the first place. But then who would you want to be taken seriously by, who doesn't take you seriously already?"

65

I suppose she's right. She is certainly right about Key West. After "all those years in Athens," this return to a world I've known from infancy moves me in mysterious ways. It is the America that shaped my parents. Here are the same black families on porches, the same root-cracked sidewalks and giant smooth-torsoed trees I knew from visits to my grandmother in Jacksonville. Nothing surprises, everything delights. Often, before daybreak, the rooster next door utters a cry so like Norma's piteous "Io non posso!" as sung by the late Florence Foster-Jenkins that my own laughter wakes me; and down the street from us a cemetery, sugar white and wholly above ground, makes dying seem like a piece of cake.

VI
Romanesque buildings.
The science of love.
My sister in Rome.
Music in Paris.
Named by Alice.

Brick by brick, the color of dried blood, a molecular mystery took shapes that echoed the body's own. Lobes and groins stretched off into murk. Only later would come those Gothic "miracles" of engineering, psychic spaces pierced by gemlight. At St Sernin in Toulouse, weird creatures, small as parasites, glared through drilled eye-holes from capitals supporting a weight of architectural dogma. The cold pink of cherry blossoms lightened Albi's fortress church, and the Tarn moved on tiptoe eddies. The eponymous heresy, with its "dualist doctrines" for which thousands perished, seemed harmless enough by now, like brick structures massive against clouds but, once reflected, going to pieces in the slow green river. We heard Palm Sunday service in the old church at Elne, its gloom shot through by chocolate fish, dolls, stars, all wrapped in multi-colored foil and dangling from the tips of laurel boughs, so that the congregation appeared to inhabit a huge, supinely fragrant Christmas tree. Joining the children's procession through the cloister, we mouthed the words of the dismal anthem:

> *Chrétien, j'entends à haute voix:*
> *Vive Jésus, vive Sa Croix!*

67

Now by bus, now by local train, we and our ton of luggage zigzagged slowly north. We went to Moissac and Carcassonne. We saw Lascaux. After only minutes in the caves, our guide told us that our presence was killing the wall paintings and expelled us from those numinous animal presences to the Arcadian woodland overhead. We did well to pay for a second look, for within a year or so the whole affair closed down, like an injured bivalve; eventually a replica was built for tourists. But if my poor human breath was harmful here, something in this vernal France was taking its revenge. Night after night I lay propped up in bed, gasping till daybreak. The initial thrill of being a famous asthmatic soon wore off. Like Proust, however, once inside the *cordon sanitaire* of the great boulevards I found my symptoms abating.

Alice Toklas had booked us into the Hôtel Récamier in Place St Sulpice. Our two rooms this time were small and connected by a length of public corridor. What had happened to our great love? Back in a city after months of isolation, we found difficulties springing into relief. Claude was companionable but restless, taken up with other friends. In self-defense I had lunch with Barney Crop, who then guided me through a very large, serious shop crammed with the crystals and iridescent beetles he loved to paint—sitters demonstrably more brilliant than Mrs Bemberg or Christian Dior. I had dinner with the cleverest of Freddy's Princeton girls; she hung her head to one side and said how lonely she was in Paris. I agreed. Used to Claude's presence, I was unequal to these hours without him. The more cripplingly dependent I grew, the more I felt him puzzled, holding back. One cause for our troubles was plain: I hadn't learned how to love. Like the young person who yearns to "be a writer" without putting himself through the blind alleys, the fears and rebuffs impossible to sidestep if the lifework is to be truly accomplished, I had counted on "being a lover" with no credentials beyond a certain expectant footlit intensity. That my feelings were childish I might have guessed from how quickly

68

they changed—Cinderella slipping into her rags after the ball—
into hurt feelings. But we'd invested too much in each other to
dream of parting.

It troubled me most that my intensity wasn't up to Claude's.
From my old "unrequited passions" I had come to believe that
the lover had certain sacred privileges. In those Provençal
courts we'd missed visiting by less than a millennium, the love-
crazed troubadour like Peire Vidal was *owed something*—if
only pity and high consideration—by the lady who listened
without yielding to his suit. Yet there must have been hours
when that lady would have preferred smalltalk to romance.
Claude's love, like his taste in music or art, abashed me. Where
I was content to "find myself" in a Fauré song or a Degas interior, he identified manfully with a Zen scroll or the *St John
Passion*. We weren't of course competing, yet how not to feel
superficial next to him? I was enough in touch with the amateur
psychology of my time to assume that the nastier the insight,
the truer it was. High spirits must be downplayed; the fanged
uglies of the ocean floor were more fundamental than the
dolphins and flying fish.

How had Claude learned to love? For one thing, he studied
the handbooks every morning: Plato, Augustine, St Francis,
Freud. (In my room I read Mallarmé—page upon page that
almost completely resisted the understanding—or Bachelard's
elemental, unpeopled reveries.) More to the point, Claude
had learned how to live. He rose impatiently above boredom
and unhappiness, the better to grasp what the world offered.
He set aside hours of the day for chores, for study, for medi-
tation. He knew the rounds of labor and diversion proper
to city or countryside. The journal he'd been keeping almost
since mastering the alphabet served him as both judge and
guardian angel, for even the wasted day bore fruit, once confessed to at due analytical length. During seasons of solitude
and introspection Claude thought nothing of leaving a party
early or a concert at the intermission; by staying on he would

merely have encountered more raw experience than his journal could process without fudging. Despite his example, I sat for hours inhaling the wallpaper's hypnotic poppies and thought well spent the morning given to repunctuating a poem months old.

One of that winter's poems described the implacable European hotel room—I wrote it holed up in one—among whose "six walls" a faceless traveler or a fictive "we" recurred, materializing and dissolving like the room's own dreams. It had the obligatory note of sadness struck without exception by my early poems, regardless of my state of mind during their composition. (Hadn't someone said that all poems were elegies?) In short, I was highly pleased with it. Not Claude. "Look what you've called it," he said. " 'Hotel de l'Univers et Portugal.' "

"Yes; remember," I said hastily, as over me an awful realization began to creep, "I showed you the ad on the ship to Barcelona, in a travel magazine? Such an exquisitely silly name—"

"But Portugal? What 'Portugal' meant to us last spring? Didn't you think of that when you wrote these lines?" And he read aloud:

> "Bleakly with ever fewer belongings we watch
> And have never, it each time seems, so coldly before
> Steeped the infant membrane of our clinging
> In a strange city's clear grave acids . . .

Or this," Claude added in his gentlest voice, as I hung my head. "Think what this says about our faith in one another:

> The lovers' speech from cool walls peeling
> To the white bed, whose dream they were."

It did not occur to me to protest that these last lines owed more to a poem Freddy had written seven years earlier than to my feelings about a real lover. Poems were made out of words, as Mallarmé told Degas—a bit of wisdom that readers like Claude kept obstinately brushing aside. But he was right about the title; why hadn't I thought to change it before showing him the poem? Now the harm was done, I'd betrayed part of our lovers' code for the sake of mere art and had nothing to offer in my defense.

My sister wrote announcing a trip to Rome in April and hoped I might feel like joining Bobby and her there for a few days. Claude urged me to go. When I made a face, he pointed out that it had been nearly a year since I'd seen any of my family. What if I was homesick, nothing else? Very well, I groaned, it was worth a try. And indeed my spirits began to lift in the plane, revived at the hotel, bubbled like *spumante* throughout dinner. Robin's spring holiday—he was the fourth at table—had given his parents a pretext, but another reason for their Roman holiday soon emerged. Our father wanted Doris to consult Dr Simeons about her headaches.

It came out with the rueful merriment she called upon in all but the gravest emergency. Headaches were headaches, nothing more. On days when they didn't keep her prostrate in a dim room, she went on blithely about her business. Wife, mother, daughter, hostess, board member, wrapper of presents and runner of households, throughout it all as much a joy for the eyes as her midsummer flower arrangements, Doris was the wonder if not exactly the envy of her friends. One paid for a life so given over to claims and duties. If she couldn't explain her headaches, others could. My father, who returned from Italy a convert to the psychosomatic view of illness, had been dropping Dr Simeons' name at regular intervals. "In case you haven't heard," Bobby interposed, "your father's gone through a hell of a time with Kinta these last months." Doris reached protectively for Robin's hand—wasn't he too young for these adult topics? The boy himself settled her doubts. He already knew from his younger brother that Grandpa wanted a divorce.

I made a rapid calculation: yes, it was time. Our father's

first two marriages—to Doris and Charles's mother, and to mine—had each lasted thirteen years. Kinta's term had expired exactly a month ago. "Do you mean," I hazarded, "that twenty pairs of shoes from Capri failed to bring happiness?" We all began laughing, as family members will at stories lost on the outsider. Daddy might have known, said Doris, wiping her eyes, those shoes for Kinta would misfire. When the first pair she tried on didn't fit, out they were thrown, the whole lot, without further ado. "I thought she could have donated them to the Salvation Army," Doris went on, "but Kinta didn't appreciate the suggestion." "Tell Jimmy what she said." "Oh, that was funny," said Doris, putting on her idea of a vexed New Orleans accent: " 'Why, Doris dear, what a thought— twenty indigents in the Hamptons, all wearin' *my shoes!* ' " The episode contributed to my father's growing sense of being yoked to a perfectly impossible woman. The realization that she might survive him and inherit houses he loved, paintings and furniture he had collected, filled him with life-giving rage. Robin had been well informed: divorce was in the cards. By the same token, given the old man, so was remarriage. Past and future loves, flames not exactly pentecostal, were already descending upon the guest-rooms of Palm Beach and Southampton. "Your sister and I'll have our hands full, just keeping him single for the rest of his life," and Bobby laughed, mirthlessly now, lighting his pipe.

I brought a copy of Tony's Venetian book of poems for Robin. As he read it in the next bed before we turned out our lights, his murmurs of pleasure took me by surprise. "It's so fresh, so simple!" he kept marveling. I bit my tongue. Any "simplicity" of Tony's would have to be the purest artifice, a Petit Trianon of titled milkmaids and silver churns. According to Kimon, poetry in our complex age was *meant* to be ambiguous, allusive, hard to read. Still, one had to begin somewhere, and my nephew had plenty of time to ripen—but wait. Wasn't I judging his taste with the same high-handedness that Claude, had he wished to do so, might have brought to bear upon those "lesser" writers and composers I preferred to Homer or Bach? I closed my Cocteau play with a grimace, wished Robin sweet dreams, and switched off the pink-shaded bedside lamp.

It was a pleasure to see Dr Simeons again. After examining Doris he sat down with us both to discuss her symptoms. They were, he thought, due largely to stress. He and his psychiatrist colleague, a Dr Detre, could do her a world of good, if she in turn would consider staying in Rome for two months. My sister went through the motions, but I knew before the question was out what her answer would be. She couldn't possibly spare the time, no matter how tempting the goal. Nor was it simply a matter of time, I understood without her saying. What of the usual mortifying incidents and feelings that everybody knew were apt to surface under the analytic eye? And if the treatment didn't work? "I guess I'll just have to make the best of it," she said with a little silvery laugh, pressing Dr Simeons' hand and glancing my way for support. Life made claims, the glance conveyed; we had others beside ourselves to think of. But Doris' decision helped me to one of my own. Before leaving his office I asked her to wait and had a few words alone with the doctor. I mentioned my asthma attacks. As for those injections he had spoken of last year, just what would they do for me? Dr Simeons was eloquent. Doris had slipped through his fingers; I did not. On the basis of his reply I returned to Paris glowing with anticipation.

We hear a piano recital by Solomon that wittily includes perhaps the easiest sonata by Haydn ("Why, I play *that*," says Claude) and the Beethoven Opus 111, difficult both to play and to hear, Schnabel having omitted it from his complete 78 r.p.m. recording. We know it largely from its description in *Doktor Faustus*. Tonight's performance—the trills of that last variation drawing a fluttering curtain across green chasms and misty heights—leaves us both gasping. "He is the *only* composer," Claude says, and for once I agree. Another evening Flagstad bids farewell to the Paris Opera. I've not heard her as Brünnhilde since 1941. Although it is sung in German, all the elements of this French *Götterdämmerung*—scenery, direction, the very texture of the orchestra—lend an indefinable silliness to the sacred work, as when the Bible is read in the language of Marivaux and Voltaire. Noble, vindictive, radiant, Flagstad alone is proof against trivialization. "You can tell she has a very great soul," a strange voice once proclaimed in the crush between acts of *Tristan*—meaning, I suppose, the singer's access to feelings and actions that sprang not at all from what we knew of her private life as a Norwegian housewife. I think of the remark as Flagstad, making her final entrance, prepares to set heaven and earth on fire. Is being "true to oneself" such a virtue after all? Aren't there passages whereby the psyche climbs into far, high-ceilinged chambers, then returns safely from the escapade? At evening's end, in any event, Brünnhilde's last flames leapt skyward, and the good-natured log, uncharred as always, came out to receive a standing ovation.

Claude took me, on our first arriving in Paris, to call upon Miss Toklas in rue Christine. He and Alice had corresponded for several years before they met. That spring he'd stayed on in Vermont to hand-set, print, and oversee the binding of Gertrude Stein's *Things as They Are*. Plain, even governessy on the outside, all passionate turmoil within, the finished book (Claude had given me its first numbered copy in Cassis) lay on the drawing-room table, at one now with the Picassos, the needlepoint chairs and plum-glossy horsehair sofa, the high windows illuminating the clutter of two exemplary lives. It was here, Claude told me, that his hostess joined him a thoughtful half-hour late on his initial visit, allowing him time to look through the prominently placed handful of letters I'd sent in her care, while he was crossing the Atlantic.

Alice and Gertrude had always kept a special fondness for male couples, if literary so much the better, and Alice's welcome, when she joined us, was the warmer for decades of practice. Many pilgrims had described her. One knew about the tiny stature, the sandals, the mustache, the eyes. Like Max Beerbohm or the young Truman Capote, she might have been something created by a dollmaker for a fastidious child. News to me, however, was the enchantment of her speaking voice— like "a viola at dusk," as a critic in the thirties had written of Flagstad's quieter moments; the phrase suited Alice equally well. She had no traceable accent, no affectation; the voice was quiet, pitched low, and of a kind of homespun suavity that kept slightly puckering her mouth, as though it, too, in its way, were savoring the charm of her diction. (Gertrude's voice was beautiful also, to judge from recordings. Imagine hearing the two antiphonally!) The big white poodle Basket, the original Basket's replacement but still the most famous animal I've ever met, lay at her feet. His manners were plain, even perfunctory, like an old countrified nobleman's; as man of the house, he clearly had his share of nonsense to put up with.

"I grew up in San Francisco," said Alice on my second visit. "My father was a Pole, an army officer. I remember being made to dance on a tabletop, at nine or ten, for a crowd of uniforms— and loving it! Ten years later music was still my passion. I and my San Francisco friends awaited the new piano pieces by Debussy much as New Yorkers had the death of Little Nell. But Gertrude decided our life was already so full of writers and painters that there was no room left for another art, so that was that."

Going with Claude to a Ravel opera had been her first musical outing in decades. I was surprised that Alice, having known (and judged so stringently) all those famous people, should be refreshed by the likes of us, until Claude pointed out the obvious: she'd buried most of the others. We were asked back, to lunch, to tea. Early on, she decided that "Jimmy," as my friends called me, wouldn't do. Neither would "Jim," my grandmother's choice, which made me sound "all boy" and was adopted without question by every Southerner I met, as well as my teachers and fund-raising classmates. No, Alice would call me Jamie. She told us which stationer to patronize and took us in person to her barber for haircuts. We were presented to the painter Francis Rose, Gertrude's and her last enthusiasm and their only mistaken one. It may well be that she thirsted for *any* company now that she was alone. Yet she gave a good account of her solitude—rereading that year the New York Edition of Henry James—and I timidly concluded, by the time we left Paris, that she'd accepted us as friends.

We were going to Rome. I'd arranged with Dr Simeons to take his course of injections and persuaded myself (and Claude?) that this would turn me into a new and muscular person, happier, more self-reliant. We would return to Paris at summer's end, under which mistaken impression we left our two largest suitcases and some boxes of books in the Hôtel Récamier's baggage room and boarded the night train relatively disencumbered.

I liked Alice's calling me Jamie; it lent me the win-some air of a lover in a ballad. A decade later, also in Paris, Daryl Hine and I were strolling about after our first lunch together. He was twenty-four and wore a cape. Mended spectacles flashed beneath a forehead Victor Hugo's mother would not have disowned. "Quel joli papillon," purred a fallen woman from her doorway. "We'll pretend she means your bow tie," said Daryl, then cleared his throat hesitantly to ask, "Shall I call you James—"

"Oh, please do," said the gracious elder poet.

"—or Jimmy?" Embarrassed, I let my answer stand. But as others took up the name, I found that I quite liked it; "James" makes me sound in control of my life, as by now, surely, I am.

Still others who've known me first from reading The Changing Light at Sandover feel easier with the semifictional "JM," and I respond accordingly. The only nuisance is the hour spent unearthing a letter in order not to sign the wrong name to my reply.

Alice also had her own fond and funny name for David Jackson, based on an initial misconception she clung to long after it was cleared up. To her he would always be David Livingstone, as though in order to find him I'd had to brave, like Stanley, some remote and uncharted "interior." Which was, after all, one way of looking at it.

Nor was it hard to hear in Alice's name for David—with his gift for good-natured, self-forgetful response—an allusion to the very timbre of life. Living's tone. Next to me, who out of fear or pride held back from experience, David greeted it with open arms. Whether responding to the quizzical looks at our first massive Stonington party (the liquor store owner's ruby anniversary) or running singing and laughing down a green mountain in Japan, he treated the whole world as a friend. Even his marriage's failure left him on happier terms with his wife than ever before; he had the golden touch.

It showed in his writing as well. When we first met, David was finishing a novel remarkable for its flexible prose and wide-ranging sensibility. There was no character, however remote from himself, to whom his quickening imagination didn't extend. His single fault as a novelist was an unwillingness either to revise or to plan ahead in more than the vaguest terms. As time passed and book after book didn't quite get accepted by a publisher, David stopped writing. The untended garden turned to peat, to tar, and eventually fueled our séances at the Ouija Board. Here the problem of shaping the material into an intricate, balanced whole was out of our conscious hands. Peering like teenage grease monkeys into the celestial machinery, we had to trust it to hang together. Its revision into a poem, or play of voices, would be my affair. Of us two, David was the

77

medium: a cinch to hypnotize, reacting with tears to messages that had yet to be spelled out. He was born with a caul—a rag of membrane, pressed stiff and brown in the family Bible— and this, according to the South Dakota midwife who attended his mother, usually meant psychic powers. Everyone who met him was drawn to the warm, eager tone of his living. For better or worse, the powers behind Sandover were no exception.

VII

Settling down?
Kimon and Mina pass through.
A picnic at Nemi.
Dr Simeons tries his hand.

T HE RAVISHMENT OF ROME in early summer! It must have eluded me the previous year, when my father's presence, like one of the tinted monocles I'd acquired for my camera, bathed whatever subject I focused upon in invalid yellow or a kind of harmless Oedipal crimson. Here at last was the city, if not in its true colors, then filtered capably through the eyes of Corot and Hubert Robert. Domes glowing with health rose above drowsy green thunderheads (the famous pines), walls forgave the wistaria that dragged them down, the Spanish Steps uplifted their descender, and a new light so loved the world that it edged my shadow with gold and braided itself over and over into the fountains' crystal fringes.

My euphoria came in part from those daily injections of what turned out to be the hormone ACTH, extracted from the urine of pregnant women. Dr Simeons, summoning his only male patient from the waiting-room packed with plump, voluble society women, whom the treatment allowed to subsist on a caloric pittance of 1500 a day, administered it jovially. He asked how I felt, how my work was going. And on these cool, radiant mornings, walking back to the hotel from his clinic, hearing the cries of tennis-playing monks, not quite meeting the eyes of the young flower-vendor in the shadow of an ancient

79

wall, I could imagine no place—and more to the point, no person—I would rather be.

At a fussy little writing-table in the hotel, I went on with the novel I'd shown Robin the opening of. Strange as it sounds, I really believed I knew something about the human heart, as if a few romantic comeuppances (like Seldon James or Barney Crop), together with a taste for opera, sufficed to give me Stendhalian credentials. The project got nowhere. I kept retyping its handful of chapters, each time with fewer lines and wider margins to increase the number of pages and make it look like a book Tony would want to read. Finally it foundered and sank; the surviving characters, more dead than alive, crawled aboard my next piece of fiction. Well, I could always go back to poetry—or could I? Week after week, whatever I began led nowhere. I was reduced to dear life, dipping into it uneasily, like a widow into capital.

Claude, too, felt the diminishing returns of deskwork in these new and beautiful surroundings. Before lunch he and I would visit the small, sleepy American Express office in the Piazza di Spagna, to collect our letters. Upright green-and-black taxis sailed round the fountain, and the periodic bus, leashed to a system of electric cables overhead—which spat out harmless fireworks whenever the connection broke—wheezed to a halt at the foot of the great flower-banked staircase. Some days we'd skip our prepaid lunch at the hotel in favor of a vine-roofed courtyard nearby, where the waiter let us go through our mail in peace. "Listen to this," I said, reading from my mother's letter. "'. . . I know I've reached the age where such things happen, but it's hard to believe, Son, that in the past two weeks *three* of my oldest and dearest friends have died. . . .'"

"Snap! crackle! pop!" Claude twinkled irreverently, quoting the classic Rice Krispies ad. I loved his rare fits of silliness. We were so young after all; I could see no connection between the

80

deaths of my mother's sexagenarian cronies and the tears I had shed for Hans.

Hotel life wears thin. Claude decides he must go to Ravenna. Resentful of my injections, which keep me in Rome, I will myself to write a poem imagining Claude alone and happy among the mosaics I perhaps shall never see. That weekend, at least, I'm free to meet the dazzled sightseer in Florence for Haydn's recently unearthed *Orfeo ed Euridice*. (A detail missing from Gluck's version fascinates us: the death of Eurydice by snakebite. "Trust Haydn to be specific," says Claude.) Back in Rome, we move into three high, cool tiled rooms in Via Gregoriana, a perfect refuge from the summer's heat. With it comes the use, at hours when the dressmaker's fitting rooms that give on it are idle, of a verdant courtyard downstairs. At last we can cook and eat at home.

Such a refuge, I hope, will help me fend off the kind of invitation I received from some friends of my mother's. "Floyd and I just bet you're starved for a real American meal," said Eula Baker on the telephone. "Do you want to bring a friend? Fine. It'll be just us and the children." Floyd was an army major. Both he and Eula were from Jacksonville. We must have known a hundred people in common.

Their neighborhood of squat stucco villas and small gardens looked, in fact, not unlike parts of Jacksonville, minus the broken sidewalks and the Spanish moss. Their two mannerly little girls (who as our talk swirled round them greeted each surfacing name with the single question "Are they kin?") went to a Bible-oriented school for officers' children. All four gasped at how "Uncle Jimmy" lived. I had an apartment, spoke Italian, ate where the Romans themselves did? I might have gone native on some coral isle. Eula feared the salami, the shellfish, the salads. Did I realize that the Italian cheeses weren't pasteurized? Aside from a nightclub or two, they hadn't set foot in a restaurant all year; she and Floyd ate in American homes. It was amazing how quickly the Italian housekeepers learned what the family liked. The Bakers hadn't taken to pasta. "You know how we Southerners feel about rice!"

Grace was said over food of dreamlike familiarity: glazed ham with pineapple, rice, sweet potatoes, frozen string beans, biscuits, homemade coleslaw, vanilla ice cream and coconut layer cake. Plates thus laden had to be cleaned. Claude had a theory that unwanted food didn't put weight on. But Dr Simeons' scales, the next morning, showed exactly how much the meal had meant to me. In its course I was made to realize what it had cost, in both time and taxpayers' money, to bring to table. For none of these things could be found in *Rome*, said Eula with affectionate condescension, as if talking of a small town upriver from Jacksonville. No, no; Italy still counted as a "hardship zone." Eula and some of the other wives took a military plane to Germany twice a month and shopped for food at the central PX. "They must be mad," said Claude, hearing about it. "I could eat Roman food for the rest of my life."

I savored the Bakers more than I did their dinner. Their idiom soothed my ears like once-popular songs. Henry James would have prized them as cameo performers in the comedy of Americans abroad. Still, to enjoy such evenings wasn't my reason for leaving home. I hinted as much in a letter to my mother, who wrote back that "we never know" when friends like these might come in handy. Priority seating on the last plane out before the Reds took over? The thought appalled me. Nothing must stand in the way of my expatriation.

Now Kimon and Mina arrive (on their way to New York, where I've offered them my apartment), with gifts impossible to live up to—a Byzantine wooden cross, a cigarette-holder of red amber that belonged to Mina's husband, and his amber worry beads. The last two are presented in boxes of molded leather; Rome is full of them: Kimon found these in a shop near his hotel. By unhappy coincidence I've bought the same kind of box to give *him*, for cufflinks or trinkets, but haven't thought to put anything in it. Finding it empty, he looks up, bewildered.

Kimon has never been to Rome and wants to see Keats's grave. Mina, who hasn't left Greece for thirty years, will see anything we like. Of all the art Claude and I have conscientiously "done," the piece I keep returning to and most care to show them is a large Etruscan sarcophagus in the Villa Giulia. Two gleaming terra-cotta figures recline on its lid, gazing off in the single direction of the afterlife—man and wife, no doubt, though they could as easily be brother and sister. Their identical smiles recall those of archaic Greece, only shyer, more full of wonder. As we study them, bewilderment again crosses Kimon's face. I know what he is thinking. Why, with all the splendors of Rome to choose from, have I wanted him to see these hollow effigies? Do he and Mina resemble them, in my view? I wished things didn't always have to be taken so *personally*. True, the terra-cotta man, in these last moments, has begun to look dreadfully like Kimon. But what if it's the placid, sensuous accord of the couple that moves me most? And where do I fit in? I picture Kimon and Mina waking in my New York apartment next week, answering each other from room to room, raising blinds upon possessions the sunlight ransacks; it will be like the looting of a tomb. I decide on the spot to give the hero of my unfinishable novel a purpose in life. Let him be writing a monograph on Etruscan funeral sculpture.

Irma Brandeis is the next to pass through. Twenty years my senior, she made up the entire Italian Department at Bard College the year I taught there. She has the lofty bearing and principles of those ladies with garlands or a musical instrument, to whom sestinas were written in the *dolce stil nuovo*, ladies quick to chastise the unvirtuous, stern in spirit, gentle in heart and speech. Though allowed to meet her mother and some of her friends—Barbara Deming, Joseph Campbell and

Jean Erdman, an old Chinese gentleman—and though we talked freely about a thousand and one subjects, I divined that her story was to be heard only gradually, if at all. I matched my reticence to hers. We'd spent one of my last days in New York together, having lunch, going to see the Richard Lippold *Sun*—a huge and diaphanous rhombus of gold wires quivering in space—at the Metropolitan Museum. Before parting she said, "So I'm not to hear about that ring you're wearing?" It was a plain wedding band from Claude, engraved on the inside "J.M. from C.F." I'd given him in exchange a signet ring from my mother, flashing the Merrill crest to the world and also engraved inside, but with her initials and mine. I glanced at Claude's ring as if I had never seen it before. "Oh yes," I said, blushing. "My hand was beginning to look awfully bare, so I bought this for myself."

Irma comes to lunch in Rome, bringing us a book by a poet whose name neither Claude nor I have heard—Eugenio Montale. She reads aloud the opening poem to us before the book leaves her hands. *"Le trombe d'oro della solarità,"* it resonantly ends, calling to mind the *Sun* we saw on our last day together. Leafing through its pages, I notice that the book is dedicated "to I. B." but after all, countless people bear the same initials, and even supposing these point to my friend, it isn't for me to comment—a lapse that Irma may well find supremely tactful instead of what it is, my shyness amounting almost to indifference when faced with the treasure of someone else's life. That same shyness underlies my chronic anxiety in the realm of ideas—theology, critical theory, Plato *vs.* Aristotle, and so on. Shaped by ideas like everyone else, I nevertheless avert my eyes from them as from the sight of a nude grandparent, not presentable, indeed taboo, until robed in images. "A mind so fine that no idea could violate it"—Eliot's famous phrase, suggesting the elfin tissue from which such robes are spun— will eventually, I trust, flatter and justify my fastidiousness. Meanwhile how to get by in the company of friends like Claude and Irma, to whom ideas are paramount? Their immediate pleasure in each other lifts that burden from my shoulders; I can be silent if they want to talk about Aquinas or "difficult ornament" in medieval rhetoric.

Irma joined us for a picnic at Lake Nemi, called Diana's mirror in antiquity, whose circular beauty outshone its historical—or prehistorical—associations. With us was someone Claude knew, and I knew of, from New York: Robert Isaacson. This bizarrely handsome young man, olive-skinned and heavy-lidded, with manners derived from a close reading of Firbank, had once studied the harpsichord at Black Mountain and was now in Rome for an indefinite stay. I could see that Claude was attracted to him, and masochistically assumed the attraction to be mutual. Sure of us both, Claude led Irma into a long allusive discussion. We listened for a while; then, as counterpoint, or in order not to be silent, Robert and I discovered a number of "common friends" and made light of them while our companions went on drawing Virgil and Caligula and *The Golden Bough* up from the depths of the reputedly bottomless lake. We swam, drank our Frascati, ate our sandwiches. I took photographs, but the camera failed to catch the day's blur of fellowship; each of us looked distinctly harried, ready for a bath and another set of friends.

Irma's high-mindedness didn't prevent us from asking her an outrageous favor. Since she was on her way to Paris, and since we had decided to stay on in Rome, would she mind "just stopping by" the Hôtel Récamier and arranging for the suitcases and boxes in storage there to be shipped to us? The maneuver turned out to involve their transport by taxi to a distant station, where paperwork took up most of the day, but she never reproached us, and in due time we and our tyrannical possessions were reunited.

It was now, in this charming summer apartment, with so much for once neatly unpacked and in place, that things at last fell apart. Claude, not surprisingly, had the wit to take charge of his own life. He sought out a psychiatrist—Dr Simeons' colleague, in fact. At a joint consultation they had given him sodium amytal or, as it was popularly known, the "truth drug." Claude couldn't recall, by evening, what truths emerged, only that the doctors had exchanged glances and agreed that he should be helped.

I envied him. What would *I* do, now that my course of injections had ended? There were no flare-ups between us, just a sense of Claude's dogged need to break away and my own loveless clinging. One day I took out my recorder and started to pick out the opening theme of a late Beethoven quartet, a favorite of Claude's. He asked me curtly to stop. One evening he said he was going out to dinner by himself as respite from too much silent tension and the "diminishing voltage," as he put it, of our shared hours. Alone in the twilit rooms, I felt abandoned, paralyzed. I poured a drink, unable to think where to have my own meal. Forty minutes later I happened into the vine-roofed courtyard where we had gone more than once together. There sat Claude, peacefully attacking his antipasto. He didn't see me; I had time to find another table, another restaurant. But making my presence known, I croaked self-consciously, "Well, since I'm here, can I sit down?" So the meal was a misery for us both.

Freddy wrote from Geneva about a dinner with Tony and his Princess. This lady was Russian, or Georgian, a sister of the "marrying Mdivanis"—three brothers known for their successful courtship of American heiresses. Nina herself was married to Denis Conan Doyle, Sir Arthur's son, presently in Ceylon. She appeared, said Freddy, both old and corpulent enough to be Tony's mother. Her lifestyle—the awful word might have been coined just to describe it—was grand to the point of suffocation: dachshund, chauffeur, maid, Bentley, hotel suite. Yet Tony struck him, Freddy went on, as being

86

wholly in his element, if an element were indeed what titles and vain ornaments, Theosophy and hovering waiters, combined to make. Not that Tony's weakness for unlikely women came as a surprise—surely I remembered the *sage-femme*. How could I forget her? (As a soldier late in the war, Tony had found himself prowling the streets of a mean little Norman town. His then limited French didn't deter him from ringing a fortune-teller's doorbell and boldly extending, to the hag who opened, his palm: *lisez*—read it! It took her a while to get him off her steps, and him longer yet to grasp her calling: not a "wise woman" at all—a midwife. Telling the story on himself, its hero struck us as exulting in this proof of an innocence never to be wholly tarnished.) Dear Tony. Now he and his Princess, figures on still another Etruscan sarcophagus, were together gazing off in a single direction, as Rilke said lovers should, and I was in no position to make fun of them.

Dr Simeons had urged me to keep in touch. His injections left me feeling fit, if not exactly transformed in body. Where were those muscles? "Get some exercise," he suggested at our last meeting. "Go to a gym." As if the tennis and swimming urged upon me as a child hadn't been enough for a whole lifetime. Now, inspired by Claude's therapy, jealous of it as well, I made an appointment and volunteered, in reply to the doctor's usual questions, that both my life and my work left something to be desired. Dr Simeons listened closely, then acted with undreamed-of kindness and dispatch. "Come with me," he said, in a flash ushering me out of his downtown office—was it lunch hour?—and onto the back seat of a smart little pale-green motor-scooter. I put my arms, as instructed, about his stout, gray-suited person, and off we went in sunlight, through traffic, under trees, past architecture, over the muddy river, and up to "his" hospital, the Salvator Mundi on the crest of the Janiculum. Here we settled ourselves, both slightly panting, in an impersonal white cubbyhole. With Claude's experience in mind, I was looking forward to the truth drug. Instead we got right down to business. I needed psychiatric help, the doctor thought. Under normal circumstances he would have referred me to his gifted colleague, but Claude was already Dr Detre's patient, and I could see, couldn't I, that a conflict of interests might arise? He himself (Dr Simeons went on, a glow of anticipation overspreading his face), while not a trained psychiatrist, had sufficient clinical experience to feel sure that he could do me some good. Would I let him try? We'd know soon enough if we got into waters too deep for him. I grasped eagerly at the straw.

It was a step toward independence, if independence was what I wanted. Claude seemed to want it *for* me, and must have tried—he was too sensible and articulate not to—to bring some of our difficulties into the open. But I, like all three of the proverbial monkeys at once, cared neither to hear nor see nor speak to him about what we were going through. I presently found myself taking a second step. A young man I'd been seeing during the year at whose end I met Claude—seeing if not believing, and never bedding after the first couple of times—rose up from the pavement late one afternoon. He, too, had come to Rome for an indefinite stay. Was Via Veneto turning into MacDougal Street? With the red-gold curls, the perfect profile and spoiled mouth of a shop-window mannequin, Wayne had remained as tenderhearted as his flighty nature permitted. When I told him my troubles he broke a date, gave me dinner, and took me back to his rented room. My blue-and-red silk neckerchief was scorched, I noted happily, from having been draped over the bedside lamp. We spent the next afternoon at Ostia, on the oily sand, in the dirty sea. A Roman boy on the train back to town caught Wayne's eye; we parted at the station without making plans. But I felt better about life in general.

88

❊

That early novel was a self-defeating venture for two reasons. One was language itself. Given metrical facility, poems are far easier to write than prose. Shaw dashed off a three-act verse play in as many weeks; it would have taken him six months to cast it in his usual closely argued, painstakingly unmetered simulacrum of human speech. And Shaw had had the grounding in Latin that allows one to write correct prose without undue difficulty. I, on the other hand, like most American writers, must either make do without a style or patch one together from a dozen imperfectly assimilated models. The second problem was my simple youth. A young poet's ignorance of life will go unnoticed. Meter, rhyme, felicitous phrases, and what not mask the underlying weakness or banality. With fiction, where dissimilar characters suffer and grow and interact, there is no place to hide. One either knows what people go through or doesn't.

I'd had a brush with psychotherapy in New York four years earlier, soon after my break with Kimon. The theory in those days was that homosexuality was an illness, hence curable. At my mother's earnest wish I agreed to consult a doctor her doctor had recommended. My mother flatly dismissed the life I dreamed of living. "Society will not condone it," she more than once told me in her soft, reasonable voice; but if society meant the kind of people who, before the divorce, spent weekends with us in Southampton and Palm Beach, I longed for the day when I should be safely beyond the pale. My father had broached the forbidden topic once only, years before. He was recovering from a heart attack when I went to say goodbye on the eve of my induction into the army (and prompt surrender to an opera buff with chevrons). His advice from his hospital bed was brief and practical, more like folk wisdom than an un-

89

canny reading of my mind: "Never let another man put his hand on you." I begged him not to worry.

As expressions of mid-twentieth-century prejudice go, these of my mother and father seem harmless enough. Hundreds of thousands of parents—not just mine—must have spent the forties and fifties urging secrecy and repression upon their queer sons. So I am surprised to hear from Jerl (a young, politically correct friend who digs me like an archaeological trench of outmoded notions) that he and his "support group" view such meddling as a form of verbal sexual abuse. He has to be joking! But no, he assures me; a single shame-producing word can be as traumatic as an incestuous caress. I nod soothingly. Jerl and I represent the difference between classic psychotherapy—that constricting and expensive underwear once made-to-order in Vienna—and its postmodern evolution toward letting our lives hang out in vivid, one-size-fits-all attitudes cheaply available at Benetton or The Gap.

However. My first psychiatrist turned out to be large and motherly, thus precluding on the spot any confessional ease. At twenty-one, did I even have a self to disclose? Still, we kept at it doggedly for several months, until my evasions and general listlessness got through to her. A year or so later I met Louise. She was my "advisee" at Bard, this bright, funny, tiny tomboy from Memphis, who brought a villanelle to our first conference. At a roadhouse one evening she asked me to dance. Back in my room she began undressing me. Any "cure" was all at once beside the point; what we found ourselves doing proved to be a thrilling discovery—at least until Louise broke off, pleading pain and fear, and fled. Like Faust upon his first glimpse of Marguerite—"O belle enfant, je t'aime!"—I was in love. In the days ahead I slipped pleading messages into her campus mailbox, bought prophylactics, sought to waylay her on the paths between dormitory and classroom. For her part she avoided me, left the notes unanswered, changed her major from Contemporary Literature to Child Psychology, and moved in with the lesbian head of that department. So much for heterosexuality. Louise and I met on my return from Europe and liked each other all over again. We even went to bed one sunny, tipsy dusk, but were by then so set in our ways that nothing came of it. Instead we made do with lifelong friendship.

VIII *Mothers on their own.*
A new sister.
The rings.
Scenes from married life.

V IRA'S MATRIMONIAL bubble burst. Only weeks before her wedding, with hundreds of friends invited to a reception at the country club in Missouri, came a telephone call from
the bridegroom in his sea-girt villa full (we indignantly fancied)
of houris and loukoums. It was Vira's first clue that things were
amiss. Sweet talk over the crackling wire failed to sugar the pill:
he was backing out. Claude returned white-faced from the sto-
ically brief call, his worst fears confirmed. I wondered if his
mother wanted him to come home.

"I don't think so—she's too humiliated." He gave a mourn-
ful laugh. "Fifty years ago I'd have challenged the cad to a duel.
Mother would have been rid of us both. . . ."

"At least she's come through in one piece," I said. "Not like
the woman in your story." Our previous talks about Vira's romance had carefully skirted any mention of a fable Claude had
written in Salzburg, months before the Saudi Arabian. In it a
divorced American woman traveling abroad meets Death per-
sonified as a sinister foreign gentleman. I couldn't help but feel
Vira's not dissimilar experience had been shaped in part by the
power of her son's word.

"Remember," said Claude, "poetry makes nothing happen."

His tight smile closed the subject. "Let's hope your mother's luckier."

For by the kind of counterpoint dear to Victorian novelists *my* mother was getting married at summer's end. Each week two or three letters kept me abreast of the latest arrangements. Something told me (though I refrained from passing it on to Claude) that my mother wasn't about to make Vira's kind of mistake. The snapshot I received of Colonel William Plummer in his air force uniform showed him to be lean and sandy-haired, with a look of the utmost probity. He himself had written— telling of a daughter nearly my age—and sent presents, a book he thought I'd enjoy, a two-pound box of guava paste. Although I'd never heard his name until the previous fall, he and my mother having lost touch for a quarter century, their friendship "went back" to World War I. Bill was then a young air force pilot at Pensacola. On weekends in Jacksonville, her hometown, he knew Hellen Ingram as one of the pretty girls who went to dance under the Japanese lanterns on the roof of the new George Mason Hotel.

By 1950 Bill's first wife had divorced him and his second had died; he was close to retirement. My mother, single for thirteen years, charming to her suitors but not looking for a change, suddenly letting herself be persuaded . . . ? "The sons cross the ocean," said Claude gloomily, "and leave them with no one to turn to." Whether or not he was right, I approved of this autumnal courtship. The fact that my mother and Bill remembered each other in blossom-time seemed to ensure their happiness. The ocean between us, however, diluted the reality of her decision. It took a letter announcing the arrival in Rome of Bill's daughter to jolt me into full awareness. I hadn't thought so far ahead. From now on there would be these new, flesh-and-blood family members to have and to hold, to love and to lie to—for if I'd understood anything from my mother since 1946, it was that my "life," while I'd now reached legal age to pursue it, must not be rubbed in the faces of right-thinking people. Betty Plummer was coming with three friends, all of them fresh from Southern women's colleges. My mother knew *my* kind of male friend better than to suggest that I supply "dates" for the whole party. But naturally I would want, said her letter, to do as much as my schedule allowed for Betty and her friends during their brief stay.

The doing took some thought. Those sharp-eyed ambassadresses couldn't be asked to Via Gregoriana. They would want to explore every inch of the apartment. Although by July Claude was sleeping no longer in the bedroom but on an austere couch in the *salone*, the big incriminating double bed spoke for itself. It crossed my mind to dissociate Claude from the project altogether. Wayne would have thrown himself happily into a night on the town with Betty and the others. But I feared that his vivid looks and manner would give him—and by association me—away. Claude, with his intellectual dignity, plus a new mustache, which lent him the air of a young Flaubert, was the obvious choice to impersonate exactly the friend he was, for that matter, on his way to becoming: sober, reliable, a Good Influence, as Betty might say when questioned. Not that my mother was likely to change her tune where Claude was concerned. I decided to keep him offstage until the eve of Betty's departure. Before then I should have taken my new sister on a moonlit carriage ride past the Forum to the Colosseum, and the entire party for a day at Tivoli and the Villa d'Este.

Dr Simeons pretended to think my qualms worth hearing about and advised me, not for the first time, to spare myself as much stress as I could. Lately there'd been a narrow escape. A pleasant older woman, whom we'd met the previous fall on the ship to Mallorca, asked us to Positano for a weekend. Claude declined almost angrily; I thought it might be fun to go—wasn't it time we saw a few Italians? "Don't forget," Dr Simeons urged me, "that if you're not enjoying it you needn't stay. Come straight back to Rome and give me a call." I stayed; but it wasn't easy. Having let fly the one joke I'd prepared—something to do with my arrival from the Amalfi station in a carriage, like *mozzarella in carrozza* (a tasty Roman specialty)— I fell prey to an anxiety known till then chiefly in dreams. My hostess and her lover did their best, in vain: I might have been seated naked all evening before an instrument I could not play. Next morning, after a hushed telephone call, they deposited me at the villa of a fat expatriate American, perfectly nice, no doubt, but to me that day an evil cartoon of everything I dreaded turning into. Tense and silent, I sat with him on a concrete bathing platform, until he gave up trying to be friendly and excused himself. Why didn't I rally my forces, phone Dr Simeons, return to Rome? A fly stung me; the sun weighed like lead. Do something, God! I implored. Whereupon a white-capped head popped out of the sea, a lipsticked mouth began chatting: "Aren't you coming in? What's the matter, can't you swim? The water's divine even if the fishermen do make ka-ka in it. Twenty years ago I had a hygiene complex, but my analyst got rid of that." Within moments I was up to my neck in intimate (if faintly shitty) sapphire. My savior was a Russian sculptor named Guitou Knoop, who lived exultantly by her wits and whose work—conventional busts and Arp-like abstractions—was collected by discerning millionaires she proceeded to name, along with the well-known artists and musicians whose mistress she had been. We dined together that night. "Well, you landed on your feet, didn't you?" said Dr Simeons approvingly, when he heard about my weekend.

Now here I was once more *in carrozza*, clopping with Betty Plummer through the city she thought I was at home in. The other, less fortunate girls were writing postcards and "rinsing out their things" at the hotel, while before us the soot-and-silver monuments loomed and pivoted and receded beneath a full moon in "unpavilioned heaven." Nothing was easier than to like Betty. An only child who didn't act the part, relaxed yet pert, with blonde bobbed hair, slender waist, and responses that bubbled from her like an enthusiastic meadow spring, she was a young version of women I'd known from babyhood, "Aunt" Lalla or "Aunt" Mil, Jacksonville friends of my mother's, into whose laps I'd crawled, whose voices I could distinguish in the dark. From that single hour I began to guess how much Betty and my mother would come to mean, over the years, to each other, the joys and misgivings exchanged, the snapshots of children and anniversaries, the whole lifelong tissue of trust to be woven between them. She would give my mother—without even realizing she was giving—the very things I withheld. In return she would treasure the love I kept at arm's length, not to mention the sound advice on everything under the sun, from setting a luncheon table to conducting a life, that I would be following less and less in the future.

My mother's efforts to make me into a different person had led her to open letters not addressed to her, to consult lawyers and doctors—behavior that appalled her even as she confessed it. Her latest move, however, I found hard to forgive. Packing to leave New York for Atlanta, where she and Bill would live after their marriage, she came upon some boxes in the cellar, full of letters to me, and wrote asking my permission to destroy them. Time was precious, the mails slow; if I agreed, I had only to send her a couple of words by cable. Otherwise she'd have them put in my apartment, to which she had a set of keys. I recalled the boxes in question; they contained letters brought home from the army, nothing I greatly cared to save. Freddy's and Tony's letters from that period I had already stored safely in my desk, many blocks away, along with Kimon's and Claude's. I sent off my thrifty cable: DESTROY LETTERS. In due course my mother wrote saying that she knew I would be relieved to hear that *all* letters had been destroyed—those under her roof and those under mine. I wrote back in shock. Freddy's letters alone meant "an incalculable loss to posterity." In the context of Claude's and my deteriorating love, her action struck a crippling blow. It left me with little evidence of having been loved by anyone, except her. What was the poor woman thinking of? I knew well enough. As postwar vegetation overcame many an ancient stronghold, the arguments among people her age against sexual or political irregularity were shrinking to a single mean-spirited fear. Publicity would render you unemployable, a "security risk." Your former partners would come forward, with letters and so forth as evidence, to blackmail you. With so many "mysterious young men" in the picture—my mother's case went—those "awful" letters could vanish overnight, and I would live under the "threat of exposure" for the rest of my days. (Had she read the letters, or was she just imagining their awfulness? Either thought led to misery.) It never occurred to the alarmists that a person who made no secret of his life was a sorry target for blackmail. The discretion my mother urged was the *sine qua non* for the scandal she dreaded. But so fine a point eluded me at the time, as it did Dr Simeons.

All the above figured prominently in my sessions with him. One day, feeling I'd painted too cheerless a portrait, I was inspired to illustrate my mother's lighter side with a little story. After their marriage, in February 1925, my parents lived in New York, in a brownstone on West Eleventh Street. By autumn my mother was, as people used to say, "expecting"— her close friends already knew the thrilling news. One of these friends, an ex-beau named Frank Huckins, finding himself in New York prior to his own marriage, came to tea. When the butler showed him in, my mother rose awkwardly; Frank hadn't realized how advanced her pregnancy was. "Oh, Frank, isn't it exciting!" she cried, taking his hand and pressing it against her swollen belly. As his palm sank into a deep unnatural softness, he stared at my mother in horror and concern—whereupon, mischievously smiling (being barely three months preg-

97

nant at the time), she removed the down pillow she'd stuffed into her dress as a joke. "I always thought I'd write a Japanese 'pillow book' one day," I said, looking at Dr Simeons for corroboration of my mother's zany wit. His face was a study, his laugh reluctant.

Betty and her friends, all unawares, shed a gentler light upon my mother's nature. We had a beautiful day for our excursion, and it had been an inspiration to hire Marcello—my father's driver, whose telephone number I'd kept—to take us. His ten words of English were now several hundred. In his pearl-gray slacks and powder-blue sport shirt, he looked as certifiably Roman as any tourist, dropping a coin into the Trevi Fountain's quivering reticule of light, could wish. I felt an extra degree of credit beamed my way for having produced so genuine an article. The girls, like blossoms in the presence of a bee, seemed to grow lovelier and more animated as the day wore on. Whatever lay in wait for us—brickwork and vista, fountain and muddy path, the herb in the sauce and the ice in the wine— they greeted with cries of wonder. With questions too. Who on earth dreamed this up, and when? How in Heaven's name was it built? Was there a book on the subject? Would the cook part with his recipe? Why was the sky so blue? Marcello, whose English was giving out, threw back his head and laughed. After a few attempts at replying, I saw his point, saw—from the girls' too-rapid nods of comprehension—that facts would only clutter their lively minds unnecessarily, like a full basket on a racing bicycle. Their Confederate pennants fluttered, their spokes flashed and hummed. How easy life would be if my mother's curiosity were like theirs, an aimless reflex called into play, so many laps on an oval track. But in her view, inquiry *led somewhere*. To letters in a drawer, to the torso among ferns. It was the cross she bore. She'd been a journalist—in this chapter we've seen her blue pencil at work—and had spent half of her life up North.

One of Betty's friends—dark-haired, magnolia-skinned Grace—struck me as holding back in a cloud of irony faint and provocative as scent. Had *she* lived up North, I wondered, or was she simply more grown up, closer to marriage, than the others? "I thought," said Betty, reading my mind and taking my arm, her words masked by the sound of plashing water, "that Grace might be fun to ask out to dinner with you and Claude. She's a little more grown up than the others. If that's all right?"—finishing on a smiling, hesitant note because Southern men must imagine, however mistakenly, that the final decision is theirs.

Everything went smoothly. We collected Betty and Grace at their hotel and gave them a Campari on Via Veneto. I cannot remember where we dined, but a photographer making the rounds of the restaurants passed through ours, so I know even today what an attractive foursome we made—the girls in their smartest dresses, Claude and I in the lightweight cotton suits that were the inexpensive height of fashion that summer. (Claude's was palest buff and mine a whitish olive, but the variety seemed endless. Robert Isaacson had found one of electric blue closely threaded with crimson.) Only late in the long and merry meal did an awkward moment arise. "I'm going to ask Jimmy about his ring," Betty announced gaily. And turning to me: "Rings have to have a story, I always think."

My fielding of the same question from Irma a year earlier stood me in good stead. "Oh, it's just a ring I wear. I've had it for ages."

"May I see it?" Betty held out her hand.

"If only I could get it off . . . !" I grimaced, making a show of trying.

"May I see yours?" said Grace to Claude with a smile, holding out *her* hand. Horrified, I watched him obediently remove his ring—my ring, rather, with my initials and my mother's on the inner band—and surrender it. By the time I collected myself enough to kick him under the table, Grace was turning the

99

ring this way and that, trying to read the inscription. Claude gave a little pleading chuckle and got it back from her. Too late. Meeting my eyes across the empty glasses and crumpled napkins—with no trace of hostility, more as if (or so it reaches me today) we could at last, now that the All Clear had sounded, be the best of friends—she mouthed, for me alone, a petrifying two-word sentence:

"I saw."

Speaking of marriages, a couple of my mother's stories illustrate the lights and darks of hers to my father. On an early trip to Paris, the incorrigible man, who never hid anything from her, even the truths likeliest to cause pain, took my mother to a kind of nightclub-brothel, which he and his partner, Mr Lynch, had patronized as bachelors. Only when seated at a table with a bottle of champagne did my father learn that "his" girl had chosen marriage and respectability far from the capital. This was reported by "Eddie's" now middle-aged playmate, in her backless dress and marcelled hair, who sat with them sipping and smoking, perfectly indifferent to my father's winning ways. Was she only pretending to remember him? He redoubled his efforts; it stung him to be seen in so bleak a light. Presently the band finished their cigarettes and struck up a sultry tango. The Frenchwoman turned to my mother and asked if she cared to dance.

"What did you do?" I gasped.

"I said I'd be delighted. You should have seen Daddy's face. That was the last time he tried to impress me with his old girl-friends."

The second story shows my parents twelve years later. They are dining at "21" in New York; once again—as Jerl nods thoughtfully in the back of my mind—my father has ordered champagne. He wants my mother to know that he means to break with Kinta and turn over a new leaf. (But Kinta's winning cards—the false pregnancy, the threatened suicide—have yet to be played.) As always, my father believes his words. So does my mother. Alas, in the car back to their apartment he goes too far. The worst is over, they're going to be closer than ever, he tells her—falling silent before the glowing embers of his unburdened spirit at last. My mother presses his hand. Then, with an amazed headshake, he breathes as if to himself:

"But God, I sure do love that little girl."

"My heart simply turned to ice," said my mother, ending her narrative. "When we got home I collapsed, I fell to the floor. He had to call a doctor."

Late in life, hearing this story, I tried to distance it by recalling a line from my poem "The Broken Home": "How intensely people used to feel!" Used to feel? In fact these parental tendencies—his to give pain by confessing, hers to suffer it in silence—were alive and well in my own nature.

At least no extremes of irony or anguish marked my mother's marriage to Bill Plummer. An incident dating from their early friendship would seem to assign it to the genre of those Hollywood screwball comedies so popular a decade later. In 1925 my mother, by then publisher of her own society newspaper, was spending a week at a new Miami Beach hotel free of charge in exchange for future mention in her columns. Bill, in town overnight, took her to a downtown restaurant. He was already safely married, and my mother safely engaged, though wearing the ring on a chain round her neck rather than on her finger. My father's divorce was still pending, and scandal, in that age of innocence, could ruin your life. Driving back from dinner, Bill failed to see the sharp, never-again-unlit left turn onto a bridge; before they knew it, both young people found themselves in deep water. They surfaced, dripping, then had to fend off a succession of Samaritan drivers stopping with offers of help. "Bill, the publicity!" my mother hissed each time he seemed to waver. (Publicity—dreaded with reason, now that it was hers to dispense?) Finally a taxi picked her up, leaving Bill to wait for the salvage crew. Over the telephone the next morning my father admitted that, seized by a premonition, he had fallen to his knees and prayed for her safety. "You mean last night?" marveled my mother, who all too soon would see my father's amorous antennae tuned to other wavelengths, and learned that it had been at the precise moment when the bay's water stopped her watch.

Why these compulsive vignettes? Perhaps their heroine lends herself more readily to anecdote than to any firsthand account. Or is it that her behavior—like the Muse's own—keeps crystallizing into verse or narrative? Readers impatient for the real thing will be rewarded soon enough. My mother is already making plans to visit me in Rome.

Two years after our meeting in the sea at Positano, Guitou Knoop began work on a head of my father, which I had commissioned thinking they'd take to each other. The scheme misfired. Southampton wasn't equal to this "interloper," this "adventuress." In family mythology Guitou joined my ever-swelling ranks of friends "unworthy of your least attention," as both my mother and my sister, revealingly, phrased it in their letters. Still, I got a novel out of Guitou's profitable summer. And she had a crucial part to play in my life with David Jackson, for it was her account of Stonington that led us to rent the top floor of an old building there: "You'll feel right at home—it's a tiny Mediterranean port, full of beautiful young Portuguese fishermen." In her eyes, perhaps. In ours it was a New England village on the Sound, full of clever wrinkled semi-famous people whom by the end of our second season we couldn't live without. We hardly missed Guitou when she broke with her local lover and moved away. I'm afraid my portrait of her in The Seraglio didn't please her. But those are all different stories.

IX
A room of my own.
Streetwalking.
A literary soirée.
Making friends with the natives.

OUR SUMMER LEASE was up. Wearily, sadly—
but relieved, too, that the stalemate had been broken—Claude
and I moved into separate apartments; we'd lived together not
quite fifteen months. He found a high sunny studio overlooking Piazza di Spagna. I took the first place I was shown, at the
top of a big ugly turn-of-the-century building in Via Quattro
Novembre. For its height it was singularly viewless, and I have
never lived anywhere quieter: a big bare parqueted room with
so generous an alcove for sleeping that it had a fireplace and
could double as my study. There was a glassed-in galley for
cooking, and above the bathroom tub an antique *scaldabagno*,
whose great roaring grid of blue flames produced hot water in
a trice and a trickle. I lit it with alarm no familiarity could dis-
pel. My actual landlord, a Count Bracci, I met when I signed
the lease and saw only once again—by comic accident—at the
end of my stay. I would hand my monthly envelope to his son
or daughter-in-law. The young count and countess made a show
of consulting me, before I moved in, as to the re-covering of
the armchair and sofa, which—along with a bed and a lamp
and some kitchen things—turned the bare apartment into a
furnished one. From shop to shop they took me, wanting to be
sure both that I liked the fabric and that it would be extremely

103

cheap. Late in the day we agreed on something green-and-white. Praising my frugal tastes, they then sent me to a nearby carpenter for a worktable and a bookcase, which I could further economize by painting (green-and-black) myself. To get even, I bought two more lamps, expensive ones, and four elegant straight chairs. But my greatest luxury—sent by airmail at unthinkable cost from Aunt Mil in Jacksonville—was a down pillow. After the inert slabs of wadding I'd endured for months, here was such stuff as dreams were made on.

To Claude and me, on alternate days, came Quinta, a slender gray-haired *cameriera* who kept our modest lodgings as if they were palace apartments. Quinta's homemaking IQ was at genius level. In my coffin of a kitchen she cooked delicious roasts and vegetables, having begun the day by shopping for them. She braved the *scaldabagno* for my laundry, stringing sheets and shirts out of a back window before ironing them— where? And never in all her comings and goings did she cross the wide wooden floor without shuffling underfoot a collection of cloths so soft and waxy that her paths gleamed like canals at twilight.

Along with Quinta, Claude and I would be sharing another key figure: Dr Thomas Detre. A month before we gave up Via Gregoriana I had a dream identifying Dr Simeons with my father. The former heaved a sigh and confessed that he'd bitten off more than he could chew. He'd never pretended to be a psychiatrist. For one thing, we were already friends. For another, he had far too much personality of his own. He spent "my" hours elaborating, out of a genuine wish to help, such roseate metaphors for the therapeutic process that I left his office walking on air. Unhappily it was from what the sufferer, not the healer, found himself saying that help would come in the long run, and I was grateful to Dr Simeons for acting on this truth as soon as it had dawned upon him. Any objection to my becoming Dr Detre's patient seemed to have vanished with Claude's and my resolve to separate. A schedule of appointments was set up at our initial meeting—the usual fifty minutes a day, five days a week. Thus while Claude and I no longer had a common roof over our heads, we would soon (at different hours) free-associate on the same couch.

I had to wait for a departing patient to make room. "Two or three weeks at most," Dr Detre said in his precise Hungarian voice. "We are winding up our work together." As I knew of cases where going to an analyst had become a lifetime's occupation, part of me was relieved that the doctor foresaw—he did, didn't he?—some kind of time limit to our own "work." He assured me matter-of-factly that ten months or a year would suffice for our purposes: I was young enough, and healthy enough, not to require prolonged treatment. Another part of me had been looking forward to a career as a concert psychotic. Now it emerged I needed little more than to have, as it were, my clumsy fingering of "The Happy Farmer" corrected. But of course getting on with life was the main thing. Why, by next July I might be free!

Dr Detre's office, actually the sitting-room of his apartment, was out in Parioli. Allowing for a thirty-minute bus ride to and from our sessions, I calculated that they would take care of over two hours each day—as if time were a restless child in need of supervision, instead of the old, impassive guardian. Meanwhile how to get through the weeks before we started? I might conceivably work at something of my own, though my papers were dusty and yellowing, but who would I spend my evenings with?

I went out into the streets, hoping to find my answer there. From Via Quattro Novembre's noise and fumes I could escape to the Quirinale in one direction or (crossing Piazza Venezia) to the Campidoglio and the Forum in the other. My favorite route to Piazza di Spagna—where the American Express office or the English bookshop a few blocks away relieved the pangs of homesickness—took me down the narrow Via

Pilotta, under the limestone buttresses that shored up the hanging gardens of the Palazzo Colonna, past furniture makers, junkshops, every imaginable kind of artisan. I paused longest at the "windows"—two narrow glassed cabinets taken indoors at night—of an engraver patronized, it would seem, exclusively by the College of Cardinals. His specialty was a round paper label, an inch or two across, just the thing for a debutante's bookplate or for sealing up a cellophane packet of sweets, against whose contrasting ground (red on white, red on lavender, red on paler red) a flamboyant ecclesiastical hat stood out, dripping tassels of varying lengths that forked and multiplied like antlers or a family tree. Within sat the old man, at a workspace no bigger than his two huge hands, scrutinizing through a jeweler's loupe some latest triumph of two-dimensional millinery. I hoped for courage to step inside one day. At another shop, photographs of grim old people had been transferred onto white enamel ovals, evidently a popular form of tombstone decoration. Why not go in and arrange for the photographs I'd been taking of Betty and Irma, my father and Freddy, to be made into shower-stall tiles? What better audience for my steamy renditions of "Nell" or "Le Spectre de la Rose"?

Often I lingered at these shop windows so as not to be caught scanning faces in the street. Seeing the reflection of a jaunty young man, I took care to let him pass before turning to study his back. If ever, feeling my eyes, one of these boys looked round, ready to smile, I went through a whole charade of preoccupied indifference that sent him, smiling now for other reasons, on his way. A few further steps brought me to the Trevi Fountain, where one could appear to be idly enjoying the play of waterlight upon baroque gods and horses while peripheral vision took in the workmen already half turned by marble dust into overalled statues, seated together at a wineshop I would sooner have turned to stone myself than enter. The kind of encounter I looked for depended on acting with the speed of a camera—a "click" of intelligence between two perfect strangers. Wayne, to hear him talk, brought it off several times a day. But the people my cumbersome time exposures were set up to attract vanished into a ghostly blur, as behind sheet after sheet of water, until I was the only figure left standing among the thousands whom the great fountain refreshed.

If my wanderings lasted until evening, I took care to avoid the Colosseum, the banks of the Tiber, or the Borghese Gardens, places recommended by Wayne, where I pictured furtive persons like myself congregating in order to meet emancipated ones like him. I kept to the thronged streets. As the starlings, chirring like crickets, settled in the trees and the shopkeepers lowered their iron curtains, would there be among these crowds no single young man to be struck dumb, like Des Grieux in Act I, by my noble demeanor and sweet face? There would not. Each was headed for a meal at home. Later, perhaps, answering the call of pleasure . . . ? But I would be asleep by then. I'd found a restaurant I kept returning to. Although the food was indifferent and the lights too bright, it had the virtue of being so near my apartment that I ran no risk of attracting company on my tipsy way to bed. Some anonymous verse on the menu charmed me at first with its Da Ponte–like fluency:

> Sè l'Albergo da Raimondo
> Ricercato è dagli sposi,
> Ciò vuol dir che deliziosi
> Sanno i giorni qui passar!

Yet by the fifth or sixth visit the words had grown callous and mocking, and a night came when I walked past the unctuous proprietor with the coolest of nods. Perhaps for once I had somewhere else to go.

Two poems I'd written in Mallorca were being printed in *Botteghe Oscure*, edited in Rome by Marguerite Caetani— a princess (not as hard to come by, evidently, as Tony made them sound) and an American to boot. Soon after my move

I went to a large evening party at the *palazzo* in the street that gave its name to the magazine. I knew not a soul and was about to leave when a gaunt bespectacled man with a dragging foot limped up to me. He said my name, took my hand in both of his, and introduced himself in a melodious drone: "I am Morra. We live at the same address." It was hard, in the talk-filled dimness, either to hear or to see as much as I would have liked, but I told him I had a good cook and offered to give him lunch. After agreeing on Friday he led me across the room to meet a couple of black writers and their wives. The idea had come to him that one of them, a poet named Ben Johnson, might help me translate a few poems by— had I heard of a living poet named Montale? I could say truthfully that I had. With the smile of confirmed intuition, Mr Morra now excused himself. I stayed on talking to my fellow Americans, drank another glass or two of wine, and made a second lunch date before saying goodnight. No one at the princess's party resembled the kind of person I longed to meet in Rome. But anything was better than another whole day left to my own devices.

My stock went up when Quinta, who must have checked with the *portiere* downstairs, learned that she would be serving lunch to *Count* Morra. Ah, Signor Jim, this was a personage of great distinction, a Resistance hero, intimately allied with the House of Savoy! I had never known her so voluble. At the sight of my guest by daylight, in his shabby jacket and old-fashioned shoes laced above the ankle—the sole built up a good three inches beneath his lame foot—I automatically dismissed her report as gossip. ("Discounted," I nearly wrote; but he could keep his title—who *wasn't* a count in Italy?) Umberto, as I would gradually learn to call him over the months to come, accepted a finger's-breadth of wine and set about putting me at ease. His face, at once goatish and austere under a high brow from which sparse reddish hair had been slicked straight back, hardly moved as he talked; his hands, however, were restless as a satyr's. I caught myself trying to see how far up his cuffs the glinting red-gold wrist-hair went. His English put mine to shame. His manners were natural, even humble, like the hut of forest boughs that shelters a great wizard. At fifty-five he seemed both very old and of no age at all; his mind kept him young, as did an adorable innocence of spirit. It wasn't just that he was a bachelor; he might have been a virgin. In his company, conversation was always taking a turn that left him blushing, whether from shock or amusement one could never say. It would then be for Umberto, fingers sinuously interlaced, to sound his characteristic drone, a deprecatory note long as a lifeline, and haul the endangered topic back to respectability.

This virginity, if that is what it was, gave him a good deal of license, especially (it seemed to me) in his friendships with young men. I didn't suppose that my being *literary* made Umberto seek me out, though it helped. Later, when he met some of my friends, I was able to tell in advance which ones he was likely to take to. Claude, for instance, with his cogitator's brow and fierce mustache, he found too deliberate, too much what he would be for the rest of his days; by contrast, Robert Isaacson's hesitant, emotional temperament drew him like a candle's glancing flame. These judgments, to be sure, were never put into words. Neither were the "ideas" he embodied. Was he a saint? a socialist? *He* wouldn't say. I thought of Kimon, unable to get through an hour without verbally reminding himself and his listeners of the meaning of Life. In Umberto, by contrast, it was the life of Meaning that showed, in his gait, in his speech, in his scholarly habits and his restless hands. Part of me longed to seduce him, part of me despaired of ever living up to him.

There was food left over for Ben Johnson and me that Sunday. After lunch we lit our cigarettes and turned to the two Montale poems he had brought along. Until that moment I had been proud of my Italian; now, faced with line after line

I did well to decipher a word of, I realized my folly. I'd scarcely passed the level of fluency enjoyed in English by a youth I met years later on Crete. "English is a much simpler language than Greek," he informed me complacently. "You have only the single word 'stone,' while *we* have . . ." (proceeding to rattle off the Greek for rock, boulder, pebble, etc.). Ben suggested I get a serious dictionary before we went any further. It was a beautiful warm day, his wife had gone to the movies—why not take a walk?

We tried the Forum. I might have waxed sentimental over the ruins of Catullus's *garçonnière*, but places that "breathe History" have always left me cold. The chalk-and-blackboard ghosts of "great" (that is, ideologically inspired) human deeds deaden the very air between stroller and scene. Shakespeare's play in which I had acted Casca to Freddy's Cassius at Lawrenceville was already more than I cared to know about ancient Rome. I hoped to learn instead something about Umberto, how he and Ben had met, what form their friendship took. The tale I heard was simple to the point of drabness, involving a committee, a fellowship, an intercultural institution that Umberto helped to run. Ben made it—made culture itself—sound prosaic and depressing, like a branch of civil service. I wondered for an instant if I'd been mistaken in my enthusiasm for Umberto, then concluded that the drabness came from my companion's view of these matters, the dreary "forum" of faction and opinion I found so suffocating in American intellectual circles. Or not only American: the following year Umberto had me to lunch with a Serbian literary critic. Afterwards my fellow guest and I walked as far as the Trevi Fountain. Knowing that I was a poet, he asked, "*Quelles sont vos recherches?*" I changed the subject in alarm. I didn't want to talk shop, and while I suspected that his question meant nothing more intimidating than "What are you after?" or "What are you trying to accomplish?" the word *recherches* with its overtone of "research," of archives and institutional backing, set me gasping for fresh air. Or was it, finally, that both the Serbian critic and Ben Johnson were straight and saw no point in trying to charm another male?

We had followed some of the Sunday crowds into the catacombs, the cool dim underground chambers a relief from the swelter aboveground. As we emerged I realized that we were being followed. A handsome, rather dreamy-eyed policeman in uniform had kept us in sight for some time, turning where we turned, pausing when we paused. I mentioned the fact to Ben, who reacted—like any man with a clear conscience—by looking round and establishing eye contact. The young policeman came up to us, smiling with relief, and asked if we were Americans, where we were from, how we liked Rome. He was just now off duty; could he treat us to a coffee? Emboldened by Ben's chaperonage, I suggested we return to my apartment for a glass of wine.

Luigi Valentini came from a village fifty kilometers south of Rome. After Ben took his leave, we sat on, with our wine and, unless I was greatly mistaken, greatly liking each other. Luigi's pistol lay in its holster across the room. I'd dreamed of an Italian lover; now was the time to act. "It's child's play," Wayne had told me. "You just lean over and nuzzle them." But what would Luigi think of me then? Besides, in my fantasy, now so close to realization, it was he who leaned over. Why hadn't he? Well, no doubt his finer feelings prevented him. My opera-going self, always my guide in romantic matters, cast him in the role of a modest boy, reluctant to aspire beyond his station. Out of the question to disenchant him by making a vulgar pass. No, no, we must first become friends. Eternal friendship—duets from *Don Carlo* or *The Pearl Fishers*—rose fluently to the lips of my opera-going self. I needed to practice my Italian, a knowledge of English could lead to promotion for him. His eyes glowed, his whole face beamed at the prospect. A different person would have made hay in that sunshine, or written the hour off as a total loss. But knowing no better, I asked him to dinner on his next day off, shook his hand warmly, and sent him on his way.

My opera-going self. It was born in the music room at Southampton during the summer (1937) my parents separated. Picture a huge hushed space hung with red damask. Sun streams through stained-glass escutcheons and spirals up each corner column of carved and gilded wood twenty feet high. I am sitting at one of two grand pianos, next to Mrs Longone, who has just opened the score of Pagliacci and is explaining the dramatic appearance—through the curtains, before the action itself begins—of the hunchback Tonio. Carol Longone is a new friend of my mother's. Originally from Florida, she was once married to an impresario and has Lived Abroad. I will start piano lessons with her in the fall. Meanwhile . . .

The score she plays from shows the singers' words in both Italian and English. Tonio warns the audience that a powerful story is about to be enacted, and not to mistake its interpreters for bloodless puppets. (It may be this morning that I outgrow, once and for all, my marionette theater.) "We have human hearts," Tonio sings, "beating with passion!" Passion? I've been, so far, a happy, sheltered child. Although something terrible is happening to our family, it hasn't been brought home to me in any profound sense. A couple of weeks ago my mother called me into her room and handed me my father's brief and no doubt handsomely phrased letter saying that he was leaving her. Having read it, I was inspired (at eleven) to let it flutter from my fingers to the carpet. "Oh, don't be dramatic," said my mother with some asperity. I knew what she meant—up to a point, beyond which I knew nothing whatever. Tonio's words, sung to a melody I find unspeakably beautiful, puts things in perspective. Just as a child cannot dream of attaining the depth of the woman's feeling as she detaches herself from his arms and goes—like the heartsick clown in Mrs Longone's synopsis—to powder her face at the mirror, so we in the audience must feel less than the actors do; it is as simple as that. Strong feelings are the stuff of art. They belong not in the home but on stage.

Thus opera was from the start an education less musical than sentimental. During performances my eye kept straying to row upon row of us, blank-faced in stagelight, inert, waiting to be moved. We were the puppets! But weren't we learning too? Why else had we paid (or our mothers paid for us) to hear Violetta suffer, Wotan turn upon his wife, and Gilda disobey her father? Against so many all too human figures Flagstad's Brünnhilde stood out larger than life. Her love threw a wrench into the entire celestial machinery; when the flames died down and the Rhine subsided, nothing was left but the elemental powers that prevailed long before the gods (narrow-minded nouveaux riches, like the people we knew in Southampton) sprang up to embody them. Next to the powers of such a woman, all male activity—Siegfried's dragon slaying, Einstein's theorizing, the arcana of password and sweat lodge—seemed tame and puerile. I longed throughout adolescence to lead my own predestined hero, whose face changed every month, into music's radiant abyss.

(Such dreams die hard. "I want this to cost everything," Claude remembers my telling him during our courtship. Strange how the reckoning, when it came, asked not a groan more or less than either of us could afford, given our age, our pretensions, our resilience. At fifteen—at twenty-five, for that matter—I trusted suffering to improve the style, the lover's loss to be the artist's gain. Don't I still? In the final tableau of a recent New York Götterdämmerung, human figures have ventured forth among the wreckage to peer upstage as light breaks over the stilled waters. The director might have illustrated my point by getting these survivors up to look like Mahler and Strauss, Debussy and Stravinsky.)

Week by week, then, those first seasons at the old Met, I pursued my education. I learned what Thaïs inwardly suffered, what mad Lucia, what even her heartless brother and nitwit husband "felt." Surrendering to adult voices in the darkened house or singing along in my room to a drinking-song whose flip side was a prayer, I found myself trying on emotions till then inconceivable, against the day when I should be old enough to wear them in public.

Long before that day dawned, I weighed the morality of interpretation. I'd heard Iago cheered and Desdemona hissed. What, after that, did "good" and "bad" mean? If, as my mother might have said in her own defense, genuine feeling kept one's responses from being dismissed as "dramatic," so did artistry. How to decide at Salzburg, for instance, between Schwarzkopf and Seefried? Their human tempers—the one's iced champagne, the other's flaky strudel—were equally products of the strictest training. Art honored both the reticence my mother recommended in life and her right—or mine, if it came to that—to fall to the floor when nothing else availed. To the degree that the aria's meaning depended on who sang it, the question of how to attack one's own high notes was in no way academic. Throughout the 1960s in Athens I off and on mourned the lengths to which Chester Kallman (Auden's beloved and our neighbor, his life, like all our lives those years, a tissue of passionate betrayals) had modeled himself in boyhood upon the Wrong Soprano—on Zinka Milanov, say, with her queenly airs and clutch-and-stagger reflexes, or on Ljuba Welitsch, incandescent and obsessed, whose last performance at Salzburg haunted me still. (It was in homage to Welitsch, I felt, that Peter Sellars, in his Harlem-slum staging of Don Giovanni, had Donna Anna shoot up on the brink of her final, ecstatic cabaletta.)

For my part, memories of Rosenkavalier with Lotte Lehmann helped me to smile and shrug through the worst. Here was a bittersweet, faintly homosexual, wholly survivable alternative

114

to my dreams of immolation and all-consuming love. Certain doubts arose belatedly when I took Peter Hooten to that opera, which had all but made me who I was, only to see him unconvinced by the Marschallin's "self-sacrifice." He blazed out at her, as we walked home, like a young Chenier or Cavaradossi attacking the corrupt regime. Manipulative, narcissistic—who could swallow such a woman? It came to me that Peter was indirectly attacking certain aspects of my relationship to him, with its own dramatic age difference and offstage Feldmarschall (David Jackson), whose prior claims made the young Octavian's position so intolerable. Listening to him without shrugging, I felt what it had cost the Marschallin to shrug. The hold of art wasn't to be broken that easily.

X *Dr Detre takes over.*
   The Rake *on stage and off.*
   Luigi's hospitality.

OUT OF NERVOUSNESS and a desire to impress
Dr Detre at our initial interview, I brought into play the heavy
red amber cigarette holder that once belonged to Mina's husband. My psychoanalyst and I were sitting face-to-face; the
couch work would come later. To offset his youth—for he was
only a few years my senior—Dr Detre was soberly dressed and
gave out an air of sallow, almost funereal gravity. Midway in
our talk the beautiful holder fell and broke into three pieces on
his tile floor. I pocketed them. Neither of us would ever allude
to the incident. Dr Detre finished what he had begun to say.
While in therapy the patient was urged strongly neither to
marry nor get divorced. Among homosexuals, with no legal ties
between partners, distinctions tended to blur. The principle
was nonetheless worth keeping in mind. The only other "rule"
was relatively trivial: if for any reason I missed an appointment
without giving notice in advance, I would be expected to pay
for it.

"One question now, if I may," he said mildly. "Why are you
consulting me?" I cast about in momentary panic. Wasn't it
enough to be disturbed, or "shattered," even, like my piece of
amber? Then it came to me: I didn't know how to love, I didn't
know how to live, but I did know how to write a poem. Did
once and didn't now—hadn't since leaving Mallorca, months

116

MY MOTHER

MY FATHER

HANS

FREDDY

TONY

CLAUDE, GRACE, BETTY, AND JM

DR DETRE

IRMA

Rolf Tietjens

JM AND ROBERT

HUBBELL   UMBERTO

KIMON AND MINA

before. That was my reason for seeking help. I wrote, therefore I was; if I couldn't write, I was nobody. "You must not expect that situation to change in the near future," said Dr Detre. "Psychotherapy is a full-time job. You will have little energy left for creative work."

Three weeks later our daily sessions began. The first step was to get my "history"; the word called up a vision of the Forum downtown in all its documented dullness. Still, I did my best to keep him entertained: my parents, the Divorce, my beloved Mademoiselle, my stint in the army, teachers and friends and lovers, recurrent dogs and loyal, one-man dreams. "Take your time," the doctor had said. To oblige him I dwelt upon certain climactic moments. At eleven, for instance, following a school-mate's hint, I tracked down a story in the kind of New York newspaper "we" never saw; the caption beneath my photograph read "Pawn in Parents' Fight." I knew my custody was in dispute, but—only a pawn? I suggested to Dr Detre, just to make things easier for him, that my sense of personal unworthiness dated from this incident. But even with such digressions my history was over in four hours, like those half-day bus tours of Rome from which the archaeologist-to-be forms his first vague suspicion of the strata, the sleeping temples and thoroughfares, that underlie the modern city. As I talked Dr Detre sat across from me, silent and receptive as a mirror, now and then meeting my eyes or asking for clarification of a specific point. These were crucial hours. For one thing, we would never again *see* each other. Once I moved to the couch, I would be talking to the blank ceiling or to the brilliant window across the room, while he, in a chair discreetly to one side, made sense of my words.

One dream I reported dated from the summer of 1947, but it had stayed with me. In it I'd become a fish, beslimed and barnacled, making sluggish rounds in the central tank of an old-fashioned municipal aquarium. People were gazing at us—

at me and the *real* fish, that is—through thick glass. Our green-ish waterlight played over their faces. All at once I realized I'd caught someone's eye, a stout middle-aged man in nineteenth-century dress, whom on waking I identified as a bit player in the film *Les Enfants du Paradis,* one of the crowd assembled outside a carnival tent to see Arletty as a naked allegory of Truth. With the limited expressiveness at my command, mainly the intense focusing and flashing of my starboard eye, I tried to signal to this person: *Look! I'm not what I seem, I'm a man like you!* The message got across, but with the wrong results. The stout man broke into smiles and pointed me out to his neighbors—*voyez donc,* a fish who imagined he was human, what next! "So I guess even then," I laughed glumly, "I may have been signaling for help." Dr Detre nodded. My museum of past dreams all at once looked small and shabby.

I never asked Dr Detre what school he belonged to. One of his initial suggestions was that I not, during treatment, read up on psychoanalytical theory, case histories, and all the rest. One day, he hazarded, Freud's *Introductory Lectures* or Jung's *Auto-biography* might interest me, but not now, please. I saw his point—it would be far more valuable to find words for our developing relations than to blunt them in advance by terms like "fixation" or "transference"—and gave thanks that our verbal dealings weren't to be overtechnical. I wondered, though, about Dr Detre's command of English. The undertones and double meanings I sought in my poems were bound, I thought, to reappear in dreams or slips of the tongue; was he up to catch-ing them? But where Dr Simeons had been all nods and ap-preciative chuckles for the odd connection I now and then achieved, Dr Detre's silence took me aback. He showed no interest, furthermore, in my writing, past or future. The im-pulses behind my poems would as a result be expertly blocked and moved, as they say in word-processing circles, into the newly opened file of our joint effort. The goal, I gathered, was

118

to get me back on speaking terms with my psyche, for as in diplomacy, once those "talks broke down," life became progressively more dangerous.

Part of me, of course, went on as if nothing were amiss. Another part, with an energy similar to my mother's in detailing the plans for her wedding, wrote a number of long letters announcing—to both parents, my sister and brother, to Freddy, to Kimon—the contract I had entered into with Dr Detre. The proper volume for self-assertion is hard to gauge at twenty-five; if a whisper goes ignored, try a howl of pain. Whatever the tone level of my manifesto, my correspondents expressed their alarm and affection by return mail, in letters sometimes longer than mine. Clearly I was getting through to them. Clear, too, was the wisdom of having placed myself beyond their reach. Since the "work" of psychotherapy took place subliminally, while the patient was asleep or sunbathing or making a scene at the post office, I, or what was left of me, remained free to lead an ever worldlier life.

I obtained leave from Dr Detre to go with Claude to Venice for the premiere of *The Rake's Progress* at La Fenice. Passing by the theater on the eve, we heard the chorus rehearsing and stood transfixed by these faint, precious hints of what awaited us. We also found the libretto in a music store and within hours knew much of it by heart. Montale, in the Milan paper he wrote for, likened its spare elegance to a bamboo birdcage. The work promised to embody what most attracted us in the collaborators, Stravinsky's neoclassical vein (a cannibal in a top hat, as somebody put it) and Auden's lyrical, cabaret-haunted glamour. People assumed wrongly that Chester Kallman's contribution to the text was nominal; in fact he and Auden wrote alternate scenes. I'd met them both in New York through Kimon, once at the Algonquin bar and again at the Gotham Book Mart party for the Sitwells, whose famous group photograph has Auden perched on top of a ladder. (Chester, Kimon, and I, along with the dozens as yet unpublished in book form, were herded without apology into a back room.) But those long-ago meetings I suffered through mute with shyness weren't to be presumed upon in Venice. Claude and I made do with much loitering in the Piazza, hoping vainly to glimpse the celebrities. For the premiere the world's prettiest theater had been further titivated by a bouquet of red and white roses on the bosom of each box. The house was full; we were all in evening dress—all but a handsome young man who, lest the effect be spoiled, had been made to wait for the lights to dim before marching down the aisle. "There goes Ned Rorem," whispered Claude.

Stravinsky bowed from the podium, the applause swelled and died, the music began. Whatever I'd imagined in advance came out freshly, differently, so much so that after the first scene I suspected the composer of perversely choosing the least plausible setting for the poet's lines. But plausibility—embodied on stage by Nick Shadow—emerged as the wry familiar spirit of the *Rake*, and the score, when finally recorded, grew to enchant me as much for its angelic surprise and invention as for its diabolical way with pastiche. The high point, that first evening, was Anne Truelove's solo scene, which closed Act I with a stirring cabaletta. Here Schwarzkopf came into her own, if not exactly into the role itself. Playing a village maiden unused to pomp, she appeared dressed for London in a great sleeved and cloaked magnificence of gray velvet. (The night before, as we shamelessly eavesdropped, someone in the know, two tables removed from ours, regaled his friends with an account of the dress rehearsal. Doubts had arisen as to that lavish costume; "I'll make the difference with my face," said the diva firmly. And even Stravinsky had been forced to admit, when the curtain fell on a high C bright as the full moon: "She sings well, our little Ilse Koch!") The scene was a triumph notwithstanding. We sat through the remaining acts in a glow of self-congratulation. From this pinnacle the rest of the twentieth century would be all downhill.

Although the Roman opera season hadn't begun, smaller companies were performing one-act rarities by Rossini and Donizetti. Now that Robert Isaacson had left for an October in Venice with the Carpaccios and the Tintorettos, I saw Claude more often and more amicably than I'd expected when we moved apart. He was still courting Robert, doggedly and to no avail. I knew this not from either of them but from Hubbell Pierce, the dearest and most deadpan of my MacDougal Street friends, who'd come to Italy to catch his breath before his London winter. He and Robert were also friends; he refused to believe that we'd never met in New York and scarcely knew each other in Rome. But whom didn't Hubbell know? He bedecked me for, and took me to, a Halloween headdress party at Frederic Prokosch's, introducing me to ten people in as many minutes, including the scion of Jacksonville's most prominent banking family. Here at last was something to put in a letter to my mother, even if I failed to describe my crown of chrysanthemums, Hubbell's navy-blue pillbox, whose brief, businesslike veil concealed not a trace of makeup ("the way we wanted our mothers to look on Parents' Day"), and the young Floridian's bracelet of big emeralds, worn like a bandage across his darting eyes. I began to suspect that, had my concerned friends and relations seen me amid these diversions, for which I might have seemed to give up all thought of writing poetry, they would have felt distinctly shortchanged.

Wayne, too, had left for Venice, with one of his Italian admirers; *he* didn't depend on the foreign colony for companionship. That season found him caught up in the one great winning streak of his life. He could do no wrong. He added gold to his hair and lovers to his list. He actually, like some grand courtesan of the Belle Époque, gallicized his name from Wayne Sheppard to Jean de la Bergerie. The entire world was lined up for his favors, no longer because he was beautiful but because of his fame: he was known throughout Italy as the Boy from Venice. People arrived at our Roman gatherings, gasping like messengers in Sophocles, with his latest exploits on their lips. All at once it was over. He was back in Rome, sitting by my fire, a plate of leftovers on his knees. He'd fallen in love. Who was it this time, I wondered, wearily lifting my eyes—a Milanese businessman, a German prince, a gondolier? "No," said Wayne, his face a wistful rainbow. "An American, a year older than me. But so wonderful! He says he knows you—Robert Isaacson?"

That name again. They'd met just two days ago. "And you left him in Venice to come back *here?*" I asked, captivated, at the tale's end. "Why on earth?"

Wayne shook his head. It didn't make sense, did it? Perhaps they both needed a spell apart, to sort things out. Had Robert said as much? Not really, but . . .

"But you're both serious, you both feel the same way?"

"Oh, I can't tell you—!"

A great certainty filled me; I knew what *I* would do in his place. "You must return to Venice at once. Nothing keeps you here. Show him how much you care."

"You really think . . . ?" Then the light in his face died. "I don't have any money."

This was easily remedied. Wayne thanked me with tears in his eyes, hugged me to his heart, and ran off to book a berth on the midnight train. Was psychotherapy already turning me into a mature person, capable of disinterested kindness? I slept well and woke glowing with satisfaction.

"Tell me now," said Dr Detre a few hours later, upon hearing the full story, "who among the principal characters in this drama are you hoping to impress by your show of generosity?"

I started to say Wayne, but that didn't sound right. Claude? *He* wouldn't thank me for thrusting a person he had designs on into someone else's arms. "Oh," I said aloud, after some further thought. "You mean it's Robert I want?"

"So it would appear," said the doctor.

I took my bus back to the center of town in real perplexity. My quest for a lover—my window-shopping in the streets of Rome—had shown me, if nothing else, the types that appealed to me. I knew also that peerless looks would be of no lasting interest without the invisible psychic musculature, a nervous system trained from the cradle to impart a certain frank, self-assured play to the features, a certain manly swagger to the frame, like youths in Whitman or like Gino the goalie from Trastevere—green grape-blush skin of a Simone Martini Judas and chest like a horsehair mattress ripped open—whom Hubbell had met within hours of settling into a *pensione* where no questions were asked and who was now wearing one of my cast-off shirts to their daily rendezvous. ("Angel," said Hubbell, "shall I give him your telephone number when I leave Rome? He just looks forbidding—underneath he's gentle as the family doctor." Fainting with excitement, I said no, Gino didn't interest me.) Back to Robert, I couldn't deny that Wayne's story put him in a new light. But on neither the physical nor the temperamental level was I aware of being attracted. On the contrary: his striking person was too boyish, his movements too nervous and peremptory. He smiled too quickly, as if passing off an injury or trying to placate his tormentor. I had to conclude that my supposed interest in him came from an altogether different quarter. Here my mind stopped working. Those shadowy corners were for Dr Detre and the fullness of time to illuminate.

A couple of evenings later I lit a fire for Luigi Valentini. We'd dined and drunk; now he was describing his life in the police barracks, how at daybreak he ran from his bunk to splash himself—*torso nudo, così!*—at a barrel of icy water in the

123

courtyard. As if his words enabled me to see him shirtless, I leaned forward and filled his glass. And was there nothing beyond the barracks? I asked. He must be very lonely in Rome, so far from his village. That was true, he replied, *ma c'è sempre la fidanzata.* A fiancée? Yes, a good girl; she had followed him from the village and found a job in Rome as a seamstress. *"La voglio bene,"* he added smoothly. (He "wished her well," did he? Bravo, so did I.) He would see that we met one day soon. I would appreciate her intelligence; she was taking a course in bookkeeping. I felt like Carmen hearing about Micaela. But why, given the *fidanzata,* had he gone out walking alone that Sunday of our meeting? Ah, you know, he said with a wink and a grin, a man sometimes—! He'd brought me something, he went on, looking embarrassed and drawing a paper from his shirt pocket. It was a poem he'd written—long ago, he added quickly, to cover himself. Would I care to hear it?

> *Sognai—e vent' anni non eran—*
> *Sognai la libertà del corpo e dell' amore—*

it began. It was nothing I could think of as a poem, but it touched me like a declaration of love, and I decided to risk an "impulsive gesture." With a great air of—what?—sharing the sentiments of my fellow man, I grasped his hand and spoke my pleasure in our friendship. Our eyes blazed, the iron was hot, but once again Luigi failed to strike. Still hampered, clearly, by his finer feelings. Instead he invited me to come out to his village the following Sunday. After he left I fell into bed. *Torso nudo*—the words ran through my mind, splashing themselves and me until I shivered off to sleep.

Wayne telephoned the next morning. He was back in Rome; the great love had burst like a bubble. Robert had been too busy with other friends to see him, except for a coffee, and they parted acknowledging the sadness and impossibility of it all. "But you must be miserable," I said to Wayne, with equal twinges of guilt and excitement. (Was this brush-off a signal

124

from Robert to me?) "Well, that's life, isn't it?" he said, managing a laugh. If he was free this evening, would he like . . . ? No, he already had a date. (Did I hear sharpness in his tone? Was I going to be blamed?) He thanked me sadly for all I'd done, adding that he was thinking of going to Paris as soon as a certain check arrived. We'd see each other before he left. And after Paris? Back to Rome? "Not on your life. Back to MacDougal Street!"—Wayne's laugh at last a real one of relief and anticipation.

The weather turned nasty. The little local train to Luigi's village dawdled and smelled, but I looked forward to our reunion. For one thing, I'd met his *fidanzata*. A call from Luigi a few nights after our supper by the fire announced that they were together in a coffee bar near my apartment and hoped I was free to join them for a meal. I lied, pretending to be expected at an American friend's, but would stop on my way for a glass of wine. At the sight of the *fidanzata* I didn't know whether to laugh or cry. She was short and fat, with thinning hair and popping eyes. Her handshake felt like a scouring pad. How wise of her to have followed Luigi to Rome; had she stayed behind in the village, he might have let himself be snapped up by the first comer. After ten minutes as the soul of courtliness, I drained my glass and went home in high spirits: my rival posed no threat whatever. Now, from the train window, I studied a wet, hilly bleakness, enlivened here and there by huts of whitewashed stone. Perhaps Luigi lived in one of those, and after our lunch of bread and cheese washed down by some famously intoxicating local wine, we would fall back on sheepskins by *his* fire, drowsy but amorous— Ah! Here was the station. And here stood Luigi in his Sunday best, holding out an extra raincoat for me. "*Ciao*," he beamed. "*Come stai?* Thank you for coming. My mother and grandmother are waiting impatiently to receive you."

The house was indeed little more than a hut. Was there so much as a second room? In the one I entered, a hearth blazed and an improvised banquet table had been laid, but the space, to judge by such other furnishings as a chest of drawers, the unyielding cot drawn up to the table like a bench, and a rack of tools on the wall, lent itself to every purpose. A window transformable somehow into a second door gave onto a wee wet pasture behind the house; here two or three sheep grazed and some chickens pecked. I drank in these details avidly; it was the setting for all the fairy tales I'd ever read. Luigi's mother and grandmother, wrinkled and weathered like the perpetual black they wore, greeted me as guests were greeted in Homeric times. I was made to sit in the one chair. A volley of civilities—except that few of my returns so much as cleared the net—gave way to questions about my journey. Sensing a long afternoon ahead, I gave them my journey in a larger sense, beginning with farewells to my own mother and grandmother, or greatly humbled versions of them, and including my wanderings through Mediterranean lands before being washed up, so to speak, in Rome. Luigi listened with pride, underscoring the chance felicity or glossing, according to his lights, the many that misfired. There was now bread and wine on the table, and real food imminent. Excusing herself, the mother turned to the hearth and heaped two plates with spaghetti in a fragrant sauce for Luigi and me. "Eat, eat!" cried the grandmother. But their own plates—? Never mind, Luigi explained; the women would eat later, as a matter of course.

It was my first experience of the hospitality of the poor. Never stopping to think that pasta merely prefaces a meal, I accepted a second helping. Then—merciful heavens!—came the meat and the potatoes and beans, the salad, the fruit, and the *dolce*. Our every forkful, our every swallow of wine, was scrutinized; the grandmother cheered us on like athletes. Hours passed. There was no further question of conversation. A single joke—about the quantity of wine I'd seen their wretched paragon consume in a wholly fictive Roman tavern—"did" for the whole afternoon. *"Sì, sì, è un gran' ubriaco!"* I kept assuring them, as they rocked and crowed with delight. As man of the house, Luigi positively gleamed; but the medal's reverse side depicted a road whose deep ruts of gender it would take an ox to negotiate. He must have given a sign, for the women reluctantly served themselves, and the heavy food quieted them. Meeting my eye, Luigi rose. We would walk down to the "center" *per divertirsi* before I caught my train. My hostesses didn't protest—men had their reasons. His mother, dignified as Penelope, took my hand and thanked me for being her son's friend. His grandmother made the sign of the cross over me, nodding sagely as unexpected tears filled my eyes. Then we were walking downhill in the dusk. I was too bursting with food to think of anything but Rome and solitude and the contents of my medicine chest. One more ordeal, however, lay in store: the "club" across from the station, where somber-suited men, refugees like us from hearth and groaning board, were drinking and listening to the radio. "To divert ourselves," Luigi had said, but *we* created the diversion here. Everyone was middle-aged or old, none was good-looking, each had to verify my provenance and degree of expressiveness in his language. Whereupon deciding that I was genuine—or passably so, for surely a single glance from their expert eyes had detected the forgery—these Berensons of the community would clap for little glasses of brandy it was not permitted to refuse. When at length the train choked and staggered into the unlit station and the moment came to thank Luigi, my jaw hung open and no words came out.

Speaking Italian (as later Greek), I used the language at best well enough to say what I meant—a daring departure from the frills and involutions brought out in me by the mother

tongue. Likewise on Dr Detre's couch I found my English adapting itself, somewhat, to his own. Along with everything else, our sessions were teaching me to be intelligible to a foreigner. Out in the world, as my Italian progressed, I found myself learning even more easily from fellow Americans whose mistakes I heard and inwardly corrected than from monoglot Romans using expressions they were at a loss to paraphrase. (Thus, urged by my mother to seek friends worthy of me, I was glad to acquire a minimal fluency in Virtue and Honor from strangers to those tongues, instead of having to communicate solely with the often dull and respectable "natives.") Again and again I've replayed my dialogue with Luigi, that first evening by the fire. Freely rendered into Greek and moved a decade into the future, it would have run little chance of miscarrying, the preliminary understanding behind it having been arrived at through further practice on one or both sides. Yet there was always a first time, and Luigi's crumpled loose-leaf poem kept surfacing among my old manuscripts and letters for many a year.

Victims of brain damage unable to speak but asked to set their needs to a familiar tune—"Greensleeves" or "Santa Lucia"—have uttered what they couldn't otherwise. In much the same way a foreign language frees the speaker. Once he has learned his first five hundred words and mastered a few idioms and tenses, he is ready for action. He has added to his Greek Nai ("Yes") the slow headshake meaning assent, to his Italian exasperation the pursed bud of emphatic fingertips already caught in a second-century mosaic of a fishwife in the Naples museum. He is on his way to embodying, however crudely and clumsily, that local divinity, the language. The process teaches him to speak a mind far less individual than he had once thought it. Among friends we are no doubt free to be "ourselves"—giddy, vague, sullen, unforthcoming. We can say what we don't mean, and still be understood. Or we can say nothing, like couples long married who speak hardly at all. A stranger's ear and a stranger's grammar, by contrast, keep us at concert pitch. So does a stranger's garb.

In 1950, before cheap sportswear became uniform worldwide, it was harder than it is today for the American to look European (or vice versa). Yet I prided myself upon melting into the Roman pot. One morning I realized that everything I had on had been acquired in Italy—underwear, jacket, shoes—and exulted, as when I'd dressed for the Paris Party some friends and I gave in our senior year at Amherst. We held it in a romantic empty house once owned by the author of the *Uncle Wiggly* books. Our invitations told you who to come as. Tom Howkins played Diaghilev to Bill Burford's Nijinsky; Ben and Helen Brower came as Mallarmé and Berthe Morisot, and Bill and Nancy Gibson as George Moore and the Folies-Bergères barmaid (both by Manet). Seldon was a hollow-eyed, dope-crazed apache. Hans, on a cane, with a blood-stained bandage round his head—in reality he still had three years to live—was Apollinaire. Greasepaint mustache and Monday-night-at-the-opera tailcoat sufficed to turn me into a Proust athletic enough to stand on a table and recite Don Pasquito's Tango from *Façade*. We had strong punch, a small combo, a moonlit garden. It ended badly—with Hemingway (a student none of us knew, invited for his looks) pistol-whipping our poor drunken Somerset Maugham under a blossoming tree—but what was an ointment without flies? In memory the party shimmers and resounds like a *Fête* by Debussy. Freedom to be oneself is all very well; the greater freedom is not to be oneself.

XI *Mademoiselle.*
Claude's dinner party.
Robert and his friends.
The Michelangelo Pietà.

I DREAMED THAT NIGHT of my beloved Mademoi-
selle, from whom (as I reminded Dr Detre) I'd been separated
at the age of eleven, just when I needed her most. She was the
oldest and simplest of three all-but-generic sisters who'd somehow made it through World War I with their civilities intact.
Her title was purely professional. Mademoiselle had been married and widowed. She wasn't even French but a guilty mixture
of Prussian and English. Among her forebears she was proudest
of the explorer Fanning: we found on my globe the specklike
islands named for him. At nine and ten, when my mother's
troubles gave her scant time for me, I transferred, day by day,
more and more love to this good soul. Such was my need for
her love that I drew with my compass the kind of neat statisti-
cal pie plate that embellished the financial pages my father
threw aside in frustration, and each night before our prayers—
I knew the Hail Mary in four languages, thanks to her—asked
Mademoiselle how much more of it I'd earned that day.
Whereupon the shading in of another slender wedge allowed
me to fall asleep proportionately fulfilled. One night I got carried away and told her I loved her more than I did my mother.
Mademoiselle recoiled, scandalized. That was the end of our
chart and my first taste of a love that dared not speak its name.

130

The second promptly followed. When my parents separated it was felt that I could do with masculine supervision. But the rugged young Irishman my mother hired—handsome as Flash Gordon—didn't work out. It wasn't his fault. He helped me with my math, took me to a gym on weekends, slept in the next bed. Watching him undress through slitted eyes, I ached to lie in his arms, as I sometimes had in Mademoiselle's after she'd signed my forehead with a goodnight cross, but of course this was unthinkable *between men.* So I spurned his efforts to be friends, teased, pouted, ran away from him in the subway until he gave up, quitting at the end of his second month. How lonely he must have been, stuck day and night with a minor who appeared to despise him, and how badly in that Depression year he must have needed the job. But if sides had to be taken, my loyalties were to the discarded, long-suffering, irreproachable woman he had supplanted—to Mademoiselle, I added, in case I wasn't being clear.

"Do not forget," said Dr Detre, "that Mademoiselle was originally hired to supplant your mother, so that *she* would have more time to attend to your father's needs."

Say no more—I was off. My father had supplanted my mother *twice*, not only with Mademoiselle but with Kinta. By seeking custody of me, hadn't he aimed at taking my mother's place himself? ("We're getting warm!" Dr Simeons would have exclaimed; Dr Detre let me find my own footholds.) No wonder tears had filled my eyes when Luigi's mother thanked me for my loyalty and his grandmother made the sign of the cross over my head. This was the mothering I missed: ignorant, reliable as rock. My poor plain pious Mademoiselle, who'd boarded-out her daughter in East Hampton the better to care for— But wait: didn't that turn *me* into a supplanter? According to an appendix in *Webster's Collegiate Dictionary,* my very name, James, meant "the supplanter." Luigi himself—wasn't he, in this cat's-cradle fantasy, supplanting my father? the young Irishman? any man I loved but couldn't attain? Or had I made sure, loyal to injured womanhood, that the men I loved should *be* unattainable?

Reaction set in on the bus home. How deeply, how unspeakably, such perceptions bored me. They shot up like vines overnight, a strangling jungle growth, at absolute odds with that clean spare cabin of the achieved self waiting at the heart of so much pathlessness. But maybe the achieved self wasn't clean and spare at all, was rather a sprawling temple of volcanic stone, quarried from bygone outbursts, the uppermost blocks carved with huge satisfied heads facing in every direction. Having seen friends in analysis grow into "monuments of selfishness," I very much hoped to avoid the fate. The different person I meant to become would be more receptive to others than I had been thus far, more conscious of their needs than greedy for his own fulfillment. When I reached my apartment Quinta told me to call Signor Claudio. I did; it seemed that Robert had returned from Venice, they were having dinner two nights later, would I care to join them? I hesitated over the right tone to take. "It was Robert's idea," Claude added with a trace of irony. "He said he wanted to know you better."

The weather had changed; it felt like summer again. I wore a pale cotton jacket and a green bow-tie. Robert, asked elsewhere for drinks, wanted to meet us at the restaurant. So Claude and I had an hour to ourselves beforehand. Dr Detre was never mentioned; we'd agreed from the start not to compare notes. I told him about my day with Luigi, he described the concert I'd missed as a result. What did he hear from his mother? Mine was coming to Rome—yes, yes, in less than two weeks—then taking me to Paris to meet my new stepfather. Claude shook his head sympathetically: I'd really had to face quite a parade of passers-through. Irma, Wayne, Betty, Hubbell. . . . Was no one content to stay quietly at home and let us get on with it? "With our Emancipation," I put in wryly, "our Metamorphosis." "I've been noticing, though, from keeping my journal," said Claude, "how linear, how elegant, one's experience is over here—don't you agree?—after the busy weave of life in America." (I stole a look at his tweed jacket, in which he was beginning to perspire.) "Living at such a remove," he went on, "we're able to confront these figures one by one, in the full glow of what they mean to us. They don't overlap or interact. We can see them coming from far off and prepare ourselves. It's like a marble frieze, or a Greek play. That was Creon's scene, now comes Jocasta's." I nodded, impressed by his overview; of course, Claude was further along in analysis than I was.

We dined, I seem to recall, in a kind of Hungarian basement—unless this detail is merely the product of my wish to go deeper into things, in fanciful conjunction with Dr Detre's nationality. We were the first to arrive. We sat down, ordered wine, and said we expected *un altro signore*. Claude frowned at his watch, a trio struck up *Zigeunermusik*, at which point—and there had never been anything quite so strange—I myself came hurrying into the restaurant, wearing a pale cotton jacket and red bow-tie, looking distraught without my glasses, and hoping I hadn't kept us waiting. This newcomer, that is, while plainly Robert Isaacson, was dressed like me, had the same haircut, the same turn of the head, was someone I knew with more than intimacy. I knew him from inside the skin, the way I knew myself—not that that was saying a great deal at the time. He sat down next to Claude, smiling across at me with the same mollifying smile I'd produced on such occasions from early boyhood. I looked away.

Far from being elated, I felt let down, as by some elaborate practical joke. That the joke, its sartorial aspect at least, hadn't been planned cut no ice with our host, who looked hurt and excluded. The story of Wayne that Robert and I shared—stamped though it was *for future reference*—set up vibrations Claude must have sensed without being able to identify. Or identified wrongly as sexual, since I, for my part, felt nothing of the sort. As the evening wore on, however, our complicity showed in fits of infectious silliness, and Claude's discomfiture grew; his every remark, so reasonable and intelligent, urged us back to his level, which we proceeded to deface with conversational graffiti. The meal lurched toward its end. It would still take a good half-hour to finish the Tokay Claude had ordered with our pastry, but thinking the least I could do was to leave him alone with Robert, I rose and thanked him, said I'd slept badly the night before, and would have to be getting home. Like a shadow taken by surprise, Robert leapt to his feet, protesting he had to be up very early the next morning. Together we left Claude in the Hungarian basement.

Our respective ways led down the Spanish Steps, at whose foot we would part. Robert had a room in Via del Babuino. But no sooner had we begun our descent than "Ouf!" he groaned. "It was so hot in there. Could we sit here for a minute?"—dropping onto the cool stone. We smoked awhile in silence. It was nearly eleven o'clock. From where we sat, façades glowed faintly all over town, like box-holders in the light from the orchestra pit, while the domes of a dozen churches, floodlit earlier in the evening, could now barely be told from purple sky. "This is very nice," said Robert softly. My heart turned over. It was no more than I'd begun to expect, but his directness caught me off guard. Before I knew it, a surpassingly naïve question rose to my startled lips: "Are you in love with me?" Robert gave a murmur of protest, as if he'd been seized too roughly. Had I spoiled everything as usual? Then, *"Cosa fate qui?"* new, official voices were demanding. We blinked up into eyes inscrutable beneath visors: a pair of *carabinieri*. As we set about stringing together some few lame words, *"Stranieri,"* said the second policeman, in a contemptuous undertone. (Was no Italian capable of the iniquities he had in mind?) His partner, the bright one, put out a restraining hand. *"Somigliano,"* he observed, *"guarda. Sembrano fratelli."* And to us, indicating our upturned faces, our matching summer jackets and bow-ties:

"You a-re brrothers, no? *Gemelli*—touins?" Yes, yes! we excessively nodded, still trembling but relieved; amused, too, by his acumen. Or was he slyly letting us off the hook? "*Adesso a casa*," he smiled. "*Dormire, hanno capito?*" We understood, and thanked them. The splendid figures saluted in unison— maybe *they* were twins too—and marched briskly down the steps.

"We'd better do what he said," Robert whispered. "I can't ask you to my place. The landlady's wired it for sound."

"Come to mine."

The next morning, after Robert had gone back to his room, promising to meet me for lunch, Claude telephoned. (He would already have heard from the landlady that her tenant had slept elsewhere.) "I have only one thing to say," he said in a low furious voice. "I hope never to see you again."

And for the second time in twelve hours I was startled by the words I found myself uttering: "Thank you . . . thank you . . ."

"You have been wanting to establish your independence of Claude for several months now," said Dr Detre. "This move was long overdue."

"But *thanking* him? Thanking him for what?"

"Well, since you are as yet incapable of breaking with someone you once loved—something the rest of the world does every three weeks—you took your time and found a sure way to make him do it for you. Do not forget, you were raised in a house full of servants."

My feelings for Robert were so profuse and bewildered that I feared Dr Detre would discourage them, or at the very least remind me of his stricture against "marrying" while in therapy. But he kept mercifully silent, and I began over the following weeks to suspect that my behavior made sense to him, if not altogether to myself. Knowing my mother's visit was imminent, Robert and I spent as much time together as we could. By comparison with Claude, who had a pronounced hermit gene, my new love was sociability itself. His friends in Rome were fun to be with, and he shared them with me—as I in turn, who had no circle to speak of, took pains to have him meet Umberto—with perfect openness. Each accordingly grew to know the other not just from intense tête-à-têtes, or sleepy ones, but from the no less telling standpoint of his behavior in company.

Robert came from St Louis. His parents were divorced. He had been raised by his mother and grandfather. His father, remarried and living beyond the Rockies, kept his distance. There was money on his mother's side of the family—how much or how acquired I never wanted to know, since wealth robbed him of the kind of "reality" I conferred unhesitatingly upon Luigi or Gino the goalie. Love couldn't be kept in a golden bowl, said Blake. And sex, as a cynical Frenchman put it, was the theater of the poor? If so, I wanted a seat in that theater. Money was just one of the disadvantages under which Robert and I labored. That I had greatly enjoyed our lovemaking puzzled me no end. Robert himself seemed blissfully relieved to have exchanged a series of "vulgar" or "tiresome" lovers for someone whose manners and education approached his own. Wayne had been the last straw: "That day he reappeared—before breakfast!—'Death in Venice' took on new meaning."

"Poor Wayne. He thought you were his great love."

"Rubbish. I'd sent him packing; I didn't care if I ever saw him again."

"But you knew I'd hear about it from him?"

Robert blushed as if I were extorting a confession from him. "I told him, if he had to talk about it, I didn't mind your knowing."

Although he kept his room in Via del Babuino, my apartment allowed us greater privacy and comfort. Quinta washed and ironed his shirts along with mine. We liked to wear each other's clothes. We rented an upright piano and bought—in a shop around the corner—a cherrywood virginal made in East Germany, complete with gold-and-black label above the keyboard giving us the manufacturer's telephone number in case of emergency. For all his diffidence and airs of the salon, Robert was an accomplished musician. My great pleasure was to sit beside him, studying the brown aplomb of his hands and turning the pages as he played. Much of his repertoire was new to me: Rameau, Couperin, Scarlatti, Haydn, Byrd. I asked again and again for a grumpy little Telemann bourrée with the melody in the bass, until finally—shades of Albertine made to keep pedaling the same piano roll—there was one less piece of music in the world and one more truth. But even with pieces I did know, like the Mozart sonatas or the "Italian" Concerto, the delight of hearing them unmediated by phonograph or concert hall never wore off. It was the difference between the bread one had baked oneself and a packaged loaf. Robert's very limitations along with the instrument's, the impurities of volume or a mordent's unexpected crunch, seemed to make the music wholesomer, less forbidding. I began to spend time alone at the keyboard, trying to approximate Robert's style by dotting the rhythm as with raisins or adding like so much ornamental sugar the trills and *appoggiature* licensed by Baroque convention. I saw that piano practice, prison fare in childhood, could become a staple of adult life.

The brightest and nicest of Robert's friends was an art historian named Marilyn Aronberg. From St Louis like Robert, she knew, unlike him, quite clearly where she wanted her life to lead and was fully equipped to get there. Exploring Rome with the two of them, or with Marilyn alone, pausing for long minutes to analyze a fresco I wouldn't, by myself, have wasted a second glance on, seeking entry to famously inaccessible churches—San Giovanni in Restauro or Santa Maria Sempre Chiusa, as we nicknamed them in our vexation—I began to see what a given school or period might imply beyond a handful of masterpieces and a few world-famous names. The least promising picture, under Marilyn's expert eye and Robert's intuitive one, showed ways of "handling space" that a later master had learned from. Barocci's "boudoir pinks" anticipated Fragonard. Afternoon sun through Carlo Dolci's leaded windows made light of figures borrowed from Raphael. Objects told stories, drapery billowed and glistened with emotion. The stage lighting of Caravaggio, the body language of Bellini's infant Christs, the buried geometry in Piero della Francesca, revered and misunderstood by otherwise negligible men, testified to a vitality, a unity of effort, that crisscrossed the map of Italy with magnetic currents. Here was a history that didn't, for once, rise up from old, bloodthirsty stones. The power it chronicled, however warped by fashion and patronage, was comparatively clean, selfless, conferred by surrender to the craft itself, part of a proud calling and a long tradition that left me dazzled, though to a serious dilettante like Robert these were truths that went without saying.

Besides Marilyn and her circle he had two older friends: a spidery Italian art collector who knew Mario Praz—who in turn had the evil eye!—and a fat English diplomat who for next to nothing rented St Philip Neri's vast apartment in the Palazzo Massimo. (The hitch was having to move out each year on the Saint's day—along with every last trace of tenancy: papers, clothes, toothbrush—for the Pope to say mass on the spot and in the proper spirit.) These two men might have been put on earth as warnings to a tasteful young person not to overdo it. But culture, for Robert, was a lighted house full of wit and feuds and cooking smells, where he would always be welcome. The family received him, so to speak, in their dressing-gowns. There was even a chapel for his worst moments. Outside that haven raged the emotional life, his previous taste of which— the year with Rolf, a German photographer in New York—had left him "all but dead from exposure. Time exposure," he added contritely when I looked startled. It was odd and not unpleasant

138

for a change to feel stronger, more reliable, than the person I loved; and I resolved to use my advantage with caution.

Michelangelo's great abandoned *Pietà* (now in Milan) could, in those years, be seen on the last Monday of every month in a banal thirties' villa at the edge of town. We were the only callers that afternoon. The sculpture stood in the curving well of a small staircase. Inert, narrow-chested, Christ sags to his knees, utterly dependent—as, to judge from his frailty, he must have been in life—upon his upright mother. Both figures are unfinished afterthoughts, scarred all over by the same chisel. But broken free, just inches to one side of them, dangles a splendid muscular arm, grimily veined under its polish: the arm of the solar god who might have towered above all comers, had the stone been sound. (When did *my* marble split? Snapshots from years before the divorce tell how something had already turned one brave, unlettered little boy astride a gigantic stallion into a sissy of six, posed, hands folded and ankles crossed, at the slide's foot.) Faced with the *Pietà* as with an athlete doomed by injury to spend his youth in a wheelchair, reading law or Sanskrit beneath photographs of a self in glorious action, the visitor feels both loss and gain. Without that flaw in the original marble, this inward, famished understudy for creative Love would never have come to light.

"The prince and I think it's an allegory of the Dark Ages," said Robert in the inane voice of a hostess. But I guessed that to us both the sculpture spoke more troublingly than either wanted to admit.

Therapy has its fashions, like everything else. Had my break with Claude come thirty years later, Dr Detre might

have urged me to discover and "release my aggressions." In the famously mild 1950s, however, breaking through to some idealized core of anger wasn't the obligatory gesture it later became for lovers on the outs. Towards Claude I felt no lurking ambivalence. If taking up with Robert answered to a somewhat bitchy impulse of mine to get even—why not? But there it ended. Schooled respectively by Senecan forbearance and Mimi's crystalline "senza rancor," and on both sides by a mother's dignity in the face of rejection, Claude and I spared ourselves no little fruitless havoc.

Life with Robert was a far richer immediate source of unexplored feelings. With it came a certain blurring of identity and gender, as when lovers wear each other's clothes or adopt each other's mannerisms, and the solitary reader looks up in sudden doubt as to who he or she might have become under the spell of a seductive book. Proust had broken this difficult ground for our time, but at such exhaustive analytical length as to put the entire subject off limits. A few years after my return from Rome, however, a poem by Elizabeth Bishop appeared in a little magazine and pointed to new strategies, while summoning up with a pang those joyous months when Robert wore my jackets and I his shirts without thinking twice about it. "Exchanging Hats" was a mere eight tetrameter quatrains long, neatly rhymed, lighthearted. But like the White Rock nymph, it smiled down at its reflection in depths so refreshing that I read it a second, a third, a tenth time.

The poem begins by evoking the behavior of grownups—clownish uncles and spinster aunts—at a beach picnic, but through a number of delicate modulations, changes of tense and meter and tone, these figures grow ghostly, other- or underworldly, wise as that Ovidian Tiresias who at a more genital level than Miss Bishop's also explored (in her phrase) "the headgear of the other sex." The poem ends:

140

Unfunny uncle, you who wore a
Hat too big (or one too many),
Tell us, can't you, are there any
Stars inside your black fedora?

Aunt exemplary and slim,
With avernal eyes, we wonder
What slow changes they see under
Their vast, shady, turned-down brim.

I never doubted that almost any poem I wrote owed some of its difficulty to the need to conceal my feelings, and their objects. Genderless as a figleaf, the pronoun "you" served to protect the latter, but one couldn't be too careful. Whatever helped to complicate the texture—double meanings, syntax that William Empson would have approved—was all to the good. Here, though, was a poet addressing herself with open good humor to the forbidden topic of transsexual impulses, simply by having invented a familiar, "harmless" situation to dramatize them. I was enthralled.

People keep talking about man's "search for a father," the importance of a male paradigm for the growing boy. Hence the young Irishman my mother hired to teach me manhood, little dreaming he would turn out to be an object of desire instead. But how about that child's need for a female role model, lacking whom, conceivably, the grown man's psyche or anima (always envisioned as feminine) might well remain pinched and mean? To this end I've always had an eye out for "the right woman," someone my spirit could aspire to resemble or, put less ponderously, to whose turn of mind and way with emotion I felt attuned. Neither Brünnhilde nor the Marschallin had turned out to be much of a help in day-to-day living. Over the years Elizabeth kept filling the bill. Like her I had no graduate degree, didn't feel called upon to teach, preferred to New York's literary circus the camouflage of another culture. My accord with the author of "Exchanging Hats" came to a head, as it were, one day in Brazil, when she and I were being driven through sunny red-and-green hillsides sparkling from a recent downpour. Just ahead squatted a small intense rainbow we seemed about to collide with before, leaping out of our path, it reappeared round the next bend. Something Elizabeth said in Portuguese set the fat black driver shaking with laughter. "In one of the northern provinces," she explained, "they have this superstition: if you pass under a rainbow you change your sex."

XII

Psychosomatic behavior.
Paternal tact and maternal
prejudice.
Revelations.

THE DAY BEFORE my mother arrived I lay on Dr
Detre's couch, repeating a familiar litany. She couldn't endure
my "life," I must practice the utmost discretion, it would kill
my father if he ever found out, and this in turn paralyzed my
relations with *him* to the point where—

"If I may interrupt," said Dr Detre, "we are wasting time.
Whether you know it or not, last May your father asked Dr
Simeons and me for a joint interview. He told us then that he
believed you were homosexual and asked what, if anything, he
personally could do about it. We said there was nothing. He
thanked us, he paid us, and that was that."

It figured. My father had always been a great one for seeking
expert opinion. Dr Detre's story, with its instant ring of truth,
overwhelmed me. My mother was mistaken: my father knew!
Better yet, whether as man of the world or merely as compas-
sionate parent, he'd had the tact to keep silent. How long had
he known? How did he find out? (Not that I would ever put
such questions to him.) Tenderness and gratitude flooded me.
He loved me intelligently, without wanting to change me into
somebody I wasn't.

This revelation brought my mother—too often blurred by
excessive closeness if not by the trembling of the hand-held

camera—into sharper focus than usual. Her dread of scandal or blackmail, which for lack of experience I was unable to dismiss, struck me next to my father's behavior as an old-fashioned, provincial reflex. She had been named for her grandmother, a formidable woman, born in the North, an educator and historian who showed her designs for an early wagon-lit at the Chicago world's fair of 1893, who "nearly" saw the connection between malaria and mosquitos, and whose medical researches led her to publish a long paper "proving" the biological superiority of whites to blacks. The benign side of this heritage underlay my mother's intelligence and resourcefulness, her newspaper work, the maiden voyage to Europe paid for by her savings. Rather than give in to idle self-pity when my father left her, she started a small business in New York, made her own circle of friends, and attended as best she could to her mother and her increasingly operatic child. At the end of World War II— I had already been demobilized—she was serving with the Red Cross on Guam. A touchier legacy showed in a couple of passionate biases, one of which was maternal.

I was what mattered most, I was "all she had." A single look into my eyes awoke in her the blind instincts of the partridge or the she-wolf. She marked with despair my lack of protective coloring, my inability to lie low in a world rife with danger. True to the values of her time and place, my mother knew chiefly how happy she would be if my terrible tendencies were "just a phase," to be swept sooner or later under the rug for good. In practice, my father's forbearance amounted to the same unspoken wish. But as a man living more widely in it than any woman of that world could or would—hadn't his boyhood paper route included the red-light district of Jacksonville?— *his* rug was a positive Aubusson next to the sensible, narrow, braided-rag affair laid down like a law by the prettiest girl on the other side of town.

I too had instincts, and my answer to my mother's arrival in Rome was to get sick. I'd met her plane, settled her into the hotel where my flowers awaited her, taken her to a famous old restaurant at the foot of the Spanish Steps. We had plenty to eat and plenty to discuss. Untouched on the banquette beside her lay a work in progress; ever since I could remember she'd resorted to needlepoint when bored or under stress. Out instead came photographs of her wedding for study and commentary. I was shown my grandmother, Betty, *her* grandmother, friends I'd scarcely thought of for a year and a half. After dinner we climbed the steps by easy stages. Before kissing me goodnight in the hotel lobby, she took my face in her hands, searching it for signs of change or simple reassurance. I managed to smile and nod. Outside, I retraced our route. I sat for a moment on Robert's and my step overlooking the footlit domes and palaces; but no feelings came, and I walked home like an automaton. The next morning's first sip of tea and taste of bread and honey awoke a dry, grinding pain at the center of my being. Had my mother recovered from her ulcer only to pass it on to me? I telephoned Dr Simeons, who told me to come right over. I broke my appointment with Dr Detre, then called my mother to unmake our plans for the day. After examining me, Dr Simeons, bursting with delight and interest—here, if ever he had seen one, was a classic psychosomatic complaint—declared that my gastric juices had ceased to flow and that I could digest not so much as a biscuit without first swallowing a substitute for the truant fluid, available at any pharmacy. So mine was a common complaint? Oh dear me, yes, said Dr Simeons; one out of every five Italians had trouble stomaching family life.

"Your point is made," said Dr Detre the next day. "She cannot fail to take you seriously now."

Or I her. Back on my feet two nights later, I escorted my mother to the opening gala (*Nabucco*) at the opera. The best seats I could get were in the second balcony. Even here our neighbors struck us as sumptuously turned out, their satins and uniforms pure Stendhal. A life in tune with the senses had burnished these Romans to perfect physical types. Peachbloom youth and the proud ivory of age met here as equals. In her improvised evening dress, its chief elements a choker of big false pearls and a low-cut black cardigan, my mother alone emitted mixed signals, managing to look at once joyless and girlish, widowed and provocative. Had she forgotten how a married woman dressed? Yet against the intermission's chattering crush, to whom the madness of a biblical king might have been their hall-porter's latest tantrum, she stood out with such mute unflinching rectitude that I led her to the bar defiantly, ready to challenge the first quizzical glance shot her way.

I invited Floyd and Eula Baker that Sunday, along with some of my new friends—Umberto, Dr Simeons, Robert and Marilyn, Ben Johnson and his wife, three or four others—for drinks and canapés. Such occasions brought out the best in my mother. Her doctrines and sermons were little help to me nowadays; as in the churches I visited with Marilyn, it was art alone that made the excursion worthwhile. But the light of my lost faith shone brightly in the faces of other members of the congregation. Guest after guest sat beside her, drawn into the smiling communion I took, as host, some indirect credit for. Thus, after the party, by ourselves at last, I wasn't prepared for the sudden dropping of the mask. Out came her needlepoint.

"What are you working on now?" I asked cordially, as if to a fellow writer.

"Something for you," she said, meeting my eyes. "The Merrill and the Ingram crests. To remind you of the kind of people you come from. At the rate I'm going, it'll have to be for *next* Christmas. I'll have them stretched and framed in any case, and you can hang them or not, as you see fit."

"Oh, what a very . . ." The words stuck in my throat. It felt like a great burden disguised as a gift.

146

"Tell me just one thing, son." My mother spoke in dry, exhausted tones. "Would you have asked your father to meet these friends of yours?"

What was she getting at? "I think so; yes. Why not?"

"Do you know that this is the first time in my entire life that I've had to meet colored people socially? If I wrote home that you'd done this to me, no one would believe me. You didn't see the look on Eula Baker's face. And I can promise you that your father wouldn't have taken it as well as I did. Can you answer my question? Would you have asked the Johnsons to a party for him?"

"If I shared my friends with him as fully as I do with you," I said pointedly, "yes. Besides, I've heard all my life about parties you and he went to in New York. At one of them you met the whole cast of *Porgy and Bess*."

"Those were *entertainers*," she sighed. Was I unable to grasp this basic distinction?

"Well, Ben Johnson's creative too." It was maddening to defend a person for whom I felt so little enthusiasm. "A writer. Probably a notch above somebody who sang and danced on Broadway twenty-five years ago."

"How can I explain? People just milled around at those big parties. We never had to *sit down* with the Negroes."

Her frank distress, however conventional in a Southern woman of my mother's vintage, puzzled me, for the attacks I was used to came from a different quarter. Was it simply beyond her to cope with any "minority" at all, including the one I belonged to? "You grew up among Negroes in Jacksonville," I ventured. "Didn't you ever sit down in the kitchen with Old Jane?"

"We're not *talking* about *servants*, son. I loved Old Jane more than anyone in the whole wide world. I'd have thrown my arms around her and kissed her if she'd risen from the grave and walked in on us today. I'd have sat her down in my own

147

place on this sofa. But never"—and here my mother's fixed gaze heightened the eerie gentleness of her tone—"never would you have seen me shake her hand."

So the Civil War continued to reverberate in odd corners of the planet, far from Antietam or Gettysburg, and a decade before Rosa Parks sat down with white folks in the front of the bus. I thought of bringing up my father and his colored valet dining peacefully at a first-class table for two on the old *Queen Elizabeth*. But I was saving his example for ammunition in a skirmish closer to home than this one. Besides, my mother would just have repeated her line: We weren't talking about servants.

And yet, thanks to her quarter century in the North, she passed for a farsighted, iconoclastic sibyl among her Jacksonville friends. One of these, lately widowed, had moved to a brick bungalow suitable for the third Little Pig and stuffed it with the suffocating furniture of her prime. One day after giving us lunch, the dear woman complained, "Hellen, no one ever sets foot in this living room. Tell me, with your good sense, how can I make it more attractive?" My mother had lots of ideas. Down with the heavy drapes, out with the silk flowers, never hang a chandelier from such a low ceiling, get rid of those glass-front whatnots full of eggcups and china puppies— oh, and while you're at it, bring the *chairs* into some sort of inviting relation to one another, not just all witlessly lined up against the wall! Our hostess, who had been looking about in wild surmise, on this last point stood her ground. "Hellen precious," she reminded her lifelong friend, "the chairs were against the wall at Versailles."

Dr Detre asked what had been my own feelings about the Negro servants I grew up among. I painted a few rapid idealized portraits—Emma the maid, James the chauffeur. What had I especially loved about them? Well, that they had time for me, that they were physically warm, instinctive, *real*. Less fierce than the models of Tsarouchis, more relaxed than the girl from

148

the hospital corridor. "Children themselves, in a sense?" the doctor suggested. I shook my head; it wasn't that simple. Bribed by my father's lawyers, Emma lived with us like a secret agent, reading my mother's mail, taking note of her telephone calls. All this she confessed with tear-stained dignity after the divorce. Yet I felt that Emma would have been incapable of betraying *me*. Why? Well, for one thing she'd have to *see into* me, understand what she saw—

"And you could trust her not to see," said Dr Detre. "From the givers of physical tenderness no evaluating insight is to be feared. While from those who appreciate your creative gifts, love is the last thing you are able to accept."

Hmm. . . . But in an instant, dreamlike transition I found myself talking about my writing and defending my sense that a poem too easy to read was without value. Not that I aimed at total impenetrability. My difficult surfaces were rather a kind of . . . mask, an invitation to . . . to the right reader who would have fought through to the poem's emotional core. Could I accept love from such a reader? I wasn't at all sure that I could.

"Do you remember a fairy tale," Dr Detre asked, "about the princess, comatose for a hundred years, closed in by thorns? What is it called in English?"

" 'Sleeping Beauty,' " I smiled, blinking up from his couch. The child put to sleep, I went on, by the prick of a woman's embroidery needle—and here we were back to my mother. I failed to make out why my poetics had to be so mixed up with her; but as Dr Detre remarked before dismissing me, there was no hurry.

My mother and I sit in a rented car in the parking lot at Hadrian's Villa. We've walked about in the early December sunlight, admiring the brickwork, the colonnade, the vistas. No need to name Antinoüs, to call up the emperor's deifying love for a shepherd boy from Asia Minor, in order to feel how

149

languorous, how beautiful, how secure the setting has grown over the centuries. Yet on our way back to the car a tall evergreen hedge makes me think of Southampton, and I take this idyllic moment to say I've learned something that may surprise her: my father knows—has known for some time—about my life. From Dr Detre's account of his reaction, it is safe to add that her worst fears have been misplaced; the knowledge hasn't killed him. The honeycomb brick glows, the high hedge sways in confirmation. Now, what has my mother to say to that?

It doesn't seem to surprise her. "How do you suppose he found out?" she asks quietly. That, I shrug, is anybody's guess. She waits for me to open the car door, slides into her seat, and seeks my gaze before proceeding: "No, son. I told him."

Thus we sit side by side in the rented Fiat, while the whole suppressed episode comes to light.

After their divorce and much to Kinta's annoyance, my mother and father stayed on friendly terms. This meant access by telephone, now and then putting their heads together over my welfare, and his rare, flattering afternoon calls upon my grandmother. At first I wanted nothing to do with him—hadn't he Destroyed Our Home? My mother took pains to keep me open-minded. She urged me to go to Southampton or Palm Beach whenever invited. If my manners and appearance gave satisfaction at court, so much the better: this showed *her* in a good light too. Over the years, my father's heart attacks and my ongoing academic honors made him less formidable and me more so. One day I might even be his equal. But when late in 1945 my mother's suspicions drove her to open a certain letter, making plain the extent of my relations with Kimon, she panicked. I was under twenty-one, she had legal custody of me—should she take me out of college, away from the tempter? (I nod grimly; all this I remember. Now comes what I haven't heard before.) Not knowing where else to turn, she went straight to Southampton with her story.

My father's reaction was appalling, my mother says, beyond

anything I could imagine. Why, his first impulse, until she talked sense into him, was to have Kimon killed—"rubbed out" by Murder, Inc. (Surely Czar Lepke and his henchmen were all behind bars by 1945? The question goes unasked; I am listening in pity and terror.) At the very least, my father stormed on, he could have Kimon dismissed from Amherst— a scandal involving us all, as my mother pointed out. Later that afternoon he called a lawyer, who listened intelligently and added his voice to hers. My father simmered down. He had, after all, two other children and the Firm. Emergencies cropping up far and wide shielded me, in the long run, from the full, unwandering glare of his attention. By the time my mother left for New York, the situation had begun to modulate towards comedy: my father was thinking of hiring a prostitute to seduce me into the paradise of sex with women. (Did my mother dissuade him from this too? A little bird tells me not to ask.) Nevertheless, "I thought he was going to have another heart attack that day," says my mother in the car. "That's why I said it would be the death of Daddy if he had to go on hearing things about you. Before you judge me too harshly, please remember, son," she finishes, turning a wet, white face my way, "that I saved Kimon's life."

European parents might have seen the affair otherwise. In their view no particular harm would attend the seduction of a willing nineteen-year-old. Yet disaster (look at "Death in Venice") awaited the susceptible middle-aged man in love with a youth who didn't know his own mind.

Oblivious to his narrow escape, Kimon was summoned to New York, and we were made to promise not to see each other—a promise we didn't try to keep beyond our first twenty-four hours back at Amherst. The following June he sailed for Greece. The lawyer from Southampton who sat in on that secret parental powwow became my lifelong friend and adviser. In the same spirit that would lead him to consult Dr Simeons on sexual matters, my father sought opinions about my poems, and on hearing from the president of Amherst that they met, or even surpassed, "professional standards," gave them from then on his full if never wholly comprehending approval. My mother developed an ulcer but was strong enough to effect the cure whose final step was her remarriage.

In our parked car at Hadrian's Villa my head spins with all she has told me; I feel that I belong to the House of Atreus, that individually programmed Furies have attended me from birth. Utter nonsense in perspective. But as Robert Frost says, the master plan of any sensible god surely entails its being just as hard at every stage in history for people to save their souls. If so, then the obstacles a fortunate young man creates for himself may—must—have some value he cannot conceive at the time. Even my parents' divorce, however painful and mistaken for them, I am already coming to read as a gift of fate. If being the product of a "broken home" means in my case that I will not risk marriage and children, the homework for future joys, some brief, some lifelong, is already being prepared. Time is a great purifier, and many all too natural wrongs that people do to one another can be used, like fortunes made by cutting forests down, by the next generation to open a school.

Not long ago I came upon a little book bound in pink quilted moiré and filled, in my mother's youthful hand, with sentimental lists: my week-by-week weight gain; my first words; important dates, like the day (March 25, 1926) I was brought home from the hospital to a brownstone on West Eleventh Street, which had every reason to think it would last my time. (Little did it know . . .) The most absorbing list of all went on for pages: the gifts I'd received at birth. The "five shares of stock" from my father's partner, the inevitable silver spoons (nine of them), the six pairs of "silver military brushes"

and the upright masculine life these recommended, were lost in an avalanche of dainty apparel and accessories—lace and net pillows; monogrammed carriage robes; embroidered dresses; a "pink crêpe de chine coat"; a "silk shawl and sacque"; caps of organdy or lace; gold diaper pins, blue pins, pink-and-pearl pins; rattles and bootees and yet more dresses. I counted over a hundred such items. The fairy godmother at my cradle must have sported a BORN TO SHOP T-shirt. Not listed were the genetic traits showered with equal lavishness upon the neonate, which, unlike his dresses and bonnets and diaper pins, are with him to this day.

The miraculous gift of life we receive from our parents comes in a package almost impossible to unwrap; often it seems wiser not to try. Inside are the various clues—most of them older than time—to who we are and how we behave. The fresher the clue, the more unnerving it can be. Family stories, for instance, put me to sleep. As Southerners, both my parents had quite a stock of them, priceless no doubt to the sentimentalist, or as oral history. To my ears they wore thin from the start. Even a story originally as full of suspenseful action and as crucial to my life as the one told me at Hadrian's Villa comes, with time, to date. The poster colors of my father's initial outburst fade in the light of his subsequent civilized response. (By the same token, his prompt letter of apology to Dr Detre for a remark made in Rome about "those god-damned Jewish psychiatrists" remains for its recipient a high-water mark of handsome, man-to-man sincerity.) Also my mother's "it would kill your father if he knew" impresses me less powerfully now that I've heard from three or four friends that the very same words were said to them by their mothers on similar occasions. Given the poverty of the dramaturgy, I wonder at its magnetic pull upon us, who late in life start saying and doing things that remind us of our parents, and our parents of theirs. Surely (thinks many a gifted child) a different self, formed in my case by the pages of "The Snow Queen" and W. H. Hudson's A Little Boy Lost, by passions enacted within the Metropolitan Opera's gold proscenium or the Ouija Board's alphabetical one, continues to give that genetic other a run for its money. Surely those fictions draw me closer to truth than—

Steady. For doesn't Sandover end in a ballroom like Southampton's? And what do we hear at the opera if not the unwearying cries of personal history? Sua madre! Padre mio! Why does my father keep appearing in the men I've loved? Not in Kimon or Claude; they were the lovers. Life with them, however absorbing, lacked, in the long run, "theater," that invisible fourth wall of mutual desire easier to act out than to analyze. Putting it far too simply, if my beloveds saw in me a certain power and charm inherited from the old man, in them I found again his enthralling weaknesses: his fiery blue-eyed rages, his way of defusing honest grievance with a joke or an expensive gift, his emotionality like a schoolboy's ever-ready erection.

"Your father," says my young friend Jerl, "sounds like what my group would call a Love and Relationship Addict."

"No, no," I laugh, "that's the story of my life." But even as I speak I think of the "seraglio," as I titled my early novel about a white-haired tycoon serene in a house full of women once or presently loved.

"Perhaps a degree of alcoholism, then?" Jerl suggests respectfully. Drawn to "adult children," he is reassured by seeing me as no less a survivor than himself.

I protest. That people drank to excess in those years between the wars was a rule of the game, and liquor blunted neither my father's professional acumen nor his sociability. For all we knew, it helped him close deal upon deal. Two or three drinks allowed him to reach others while, yes, making it harder for them to reach him. But the glass in his hand, against which he warned me—I was nine—with tears in his eyes, figures in Jerl's somberly appraising ones as a diabolic rival like Dr Miracle in The Tales of Hoffmann, who over the years has crossed my path in various guises and turned my loves dysfunctional. Suppose he's right. Admittedly, in each affair, a day dawns when I resort to the same aloof, injured airs with which my mother foiled— or fueled—"Daddy's temper." (I must, by the way, find the right moment to tell her that the therapist whose insight and good humor have seen me through the past couple of years is a black woman.) As Jerl talks, my father's demon grows ever realer. Is it good to be so impressionable? I glimpse the familiar hoofprint in Strato's gambling, in David's TV set jabbering till dawn, in Peter's long-buried compulsions now coming harrowingly to light. Looking back, I can read into those dear ones' first radiant smiles the promise not only of simple devotion but of an elaborate co-dependency, as it is known in the rooms Jerl frequents. Do I conclude that my life has been less a flight from the Broken Home than a cunning scale model of it? that my heart, far from being the wild untamable bird of Carmen's "Habañera," had its wings clipped while still in the egg?

Let others connect neurosis with creativity. The real point is that something of the kind awaits virtually every child on earth. Call it cruelty, call it culture. These are the extremes of a broad and unbroken spectrum made visible through our being reared by other humans in the first place, rather than by wolves, like l'Enfant Sauvage. Small wonder we honor our father and mother even when we can't obey them. Without their imprint of (imperfect) love, the self is featureless, a snarl of instincts, a puff of stellar dust.

In his letter about the draft I sent him of this chapter, Freddy singles out its last sentences. (I thought he might like them. No longer a schoolmaster, he lives on the edge of a noble and unthreatened forest in Vermont.) Freddy then quotes a couple of sentences from the chapter he's been writing about a painful episode in his own past: "The fearsome blessing of that hard time continues to work itself out in my life the way we're told the universe is still hurtling through outer space under the impact of the great cosmic explosion that brought it into being in the first place. I think grace sometimes explodes into our lives like that—sending our pain, terror, astonishment hurtling through inner space until by grace they become Orion, Cassiopeia, Polaris, to give us our bearings, to bring us into something like full being at last."

I might have said that it's the gradual focus of human vision, intelligence rather than grace, whereby those traumatic stars, like their ancestors in the night sky, acquire names and stories. But why split hairs? Let the mind be, along with countless other things, a landing strip for sacred visitations. When the insurance man whose poems Freddy left unread at twenty wrote that "God and the imagination are one," I could hardly disagree. And now my friend of fifty years, having typed out my words together with his, goes on to shelve all further question of our divergence, while incidentally positing an exchange of hats not covered by Elizabeth Bishop's poem: "I was struck by how I sounded more like you in mine and you more like me in yours."

XIII

With the Plummers at the Ritz.
At the Tour d'Argent with Tony and Nina.

In the months following the liberation of Paris, Colonel William Plummer had been put in charge of the Ritz Hotel, where Allied brass and distinguished civilians were billeted. Now our turn came. Little of the personnel had changed since his heyday six years earlier, and we felt at once the grateful affection in which he was held by the assistant managers, the concierges, the maids and doormen. "*Mon colonel*," the men called him, although upon his recent retirement from active duty Bill had been promoted to general. He, too, retained a fund of gratifying memories. The telegram from Ernest Hemingway announcing his marriage ("We've made an honest inn-keeper of you"). Marlene Dietrich asking in her famous dulcet rasp who she had to sleep with in order to get a hot bath—a moment whose recounting made him flush, mouth drawn downwards in sour and soundless amusement. This slight, barrel-chested man with thin blond hair and ice-blue eyes radiated dependability. As a career officer, spartan himself, Bill knew how to make things easy and comfortable for others. He'd been, for instance, assigned to Winston Churchill during the latter's visit, late in the war, to Miami and Cuba. From our first hour together in Paris I could sense his delight at having at last not a statesman or superior officer to care for, but a woman he loved. In his happiness he'd even quit smoking. In *my* happiness—wasn't she finally off my hands?—Bill struck me as answering the prayer my mother uttered each time she sat down at the piano, plaintive in lamplight, to accompany herself in what had become the theme song of those thirteen years between husbands: "Someone to Watch Over Me."

Bill calls her, instead of Hellen, by a nickname I don't catch right away. It sounds like "Was" but turns out to be the first syllable of *Oiseau.*

"That was my name for your mother long ago, in Jacksonville," he explains. "There was something birdlike about her— I don't know: soft and bright and alert. Not that she's changed in any way," he finishes gallantly. "The name still fits."

Feigning to ignore us, my mother has taken from her purse a dozen postcards. Writing them between courses to friends at home is her sociable refreshment from the introspections of needlework. With the signing of each in her firm vertical script, a beaklike checkmark pecks a name from the master list. Soft as a dove in Bill's eyes, stern as a hawk in mine?

"*Oiseau?* That was very poetic of you," I tell Bill, half to flatter, half in teasing allusion to the letter he wrote me about my book, frankly declaring it beyond his depth. The very format of verse, for Bill and my mother, suffices to obscure forever even the lyrics I've worked longest to make clear, whereas a page of my most devious and artificial prose will be greeted with relief: "Now you've written something I can read!"

"Poetic? If you say so." He coughs, strangled by the notion. "I wouldn't know. I certainly appreciate the time you spent with Betty in Rome."

"I'd give anything to have her with us right now," says my mother, checking off another name and passing me the card addressed to her stepdaughter. "I've left room here for you to

158

write her a line." I take out my pen. So twig by thread the nest of kinship weaves itself.

A day before I left Rome my phone rang. It was Claude. How was I, how was Robert? We were well—not that we'd seen that much of each other, with Mrs Plummer in town. More to the point, how was *he*? (Still angry? I could tell from his voice that he wasn't.) He was well, thank you. He'd heard from Quinta about my trip and wondered if I had room for a little something—an umbrella actually—he wanted Alice to have for Christmas. Could he drop it off with my *portiere*? A weight I'd been living with floated away, I said I'd be delighted, and asked him to the Christmas party Robert and I were planning. With his little laugh of relief, Claude accepted.

A teatime fire burned in rue Christine. Alice, dressed for winter, peeped forth from a chic but bulky woolen suit. At her sandaled, wool-stockinged feet lay Basket, and Claude's vivid Roman umbrella leaned against her armchair. She was anxious, puzzled. She and Gertrude had always grieved when their favorite couples broke up. Such a waste of time and effort for all concerned! One began by knowing two people; suddenly, each having found someone else, there were four. In another year, eight, sixteen . . .

"You wouldn't have to know them all," I suggested.

"Who could!" She smiled from long experience of those evanescent family trees. But Claude and I, she went on, had seemed so well matched, so right for each other. "You would have seen that he had fun, Jamie. He would have seen that you used your mind."

I tried to reassure Alice that Claude and I would probably remain close friends, if not a couple. She was glad to hear it. Ah, but why psychotherapy? It was so Wagnerian—those hours of listening, that suffocating texture of motives. Why couldn't one conduct one's life in the concise, lighthearted spirit of

French music, of Ravel or Poulenc, instead? Of the enigmatic rose-period Picasso girl, hand raised as though too much had already been said, in profile on the wall behind me? Of the dwarf Louis XV chairs whose needlepoint Alice had exquisitely worked from designs by Picasso? She named a once talented friend who after being treated by a psychiatrist no longer cared to paint. And surely that was the worst, said Alice in her honey voice, relighting a cigarette—not to use one's talents, to have beauty and intelligence at one's fingertips and not *let it out* into the world? I nodded, shamefaced, thinking how gladly I would have traded the creative life for that of the senses. It didn't escape me that Alice focused her concern upon the two realms my parents were least able to explore—my writing and my loving—and I marveled at her sound instinct. As I left she asked me to bring my mother and Bill to tea later in the week. I thought of warning her that Bill wasn't notably, how to put it, in the cultural swim. But Alice had eyes and ears; she'd find out without prompting.

A message awaited me from "la Princesse Canada," a name not even the concierge of the Ritz was able to gloss. When I called the accompanying number, however, a familiar voice answered: "Ah, there you are!" It was Tony. Yes, yes, my recent postcard had been forwarded to him in Paris. Nina— who by the way called herself the Princess Conan Doyle, a title far zanier (I thought) than its form garbled by the hotel switchboard—hoped very much I and the Plummers were free to dine that evening or the next. As it happened, Bill had been stewing over how to see some dull Americans in Neuilly without pointlessly involving us; my mother and I needed but the exchange of a glance to save him from Tony and the Princess.

The Bentley picked us up. Tony leapt out, kissing my mother's hand before settling her in the back seat next to a large dim perfumed cordiality, and off we were swept to the Tour d'Argent. "It is a vulgar restaurant," said Tony, squeezed between me and the chauffeur, "but Paris, too, has a vulgar streak, and one might as well *en profiter*." Our table overlooked the floodlit buttresses of Notre Dame. Along the black, excited river stretched a planetary system of radiant orbs. Tony wore a dinner jacket, and Princess Nina—at whom we were now getting our first good look—a loosely cut gown of tangerine silk. She was a theatrical, fleshy woman, much powdered, with red plush lips and iron-gray bangs. Over her balcony flowed a *rivière* of dime-sized diamonds, whose lights rivaled those of the Seine. "What an amazing necklace," I said without meaning to. Nina made a gesture of largess: "For you, darlings, for you!" Tony meanwhile saw to our pleasure with an easy assiduity I might have envied but didn't; to be that conversant with sauces and labels, with headwaiters and wine stewards, was surely a life's work, and I hoped I had better things to do.

Well, he was still the most insufferable boy at school, but with one immense difference: Nina. They were leaving early in the new year to join Denis in Ceylon. "Now tell me, who is Denis?" asked my mother. "Denis is my husband," said Nina. "And," Tony added, "considered by Those Who Know to be a very remarkable person." ("He would have to be," said my mother later, "to put up with *that* situation.") From Ceylon the three planned a slow move north, maharajah by maharajah, to the foothills of the Himalayas. The pure air would do Denis good, as would a certain saint in Kashmir, whose latest letter Tony just happened to be carrying. He passed it to me. The stationery was imprinted with the holy man's name and address on such-and-such a road, "above the tailor shop." I read that my friend was always to carry upon his person a small piece of iron and a sapphire wrapped together in silk and that he must feed bread every Thursday to a black dog. "Not so easy in Geneva or Paris," said Tony archly, "where the dogs are used to filet mignon." But he took out his magician's silk handkerchief and showed us its contents.

By comparison, Princess Nina came across as an earthy

realist who understood the stock market, loved her position in the world, and wanted my honest opinion of Tony's poetry. Was he too sensitive, did I think? Was it not a pity that so rare a spirit—he'd taken to reading an act of Racine aloud to her every night before they retired—had to publish his work himself and be known only by his friends? Couldn't I give him an introduction to my New York publisher? Of course I could, but it wasn't the kind of poetry readily accepted nowadays. Nina nodded; that was Tony's line—editors were slaves to fads and trends, unable to tell the real thing from the trash they marketed. "But that is his pride talking," Nina continued. "*You* are published in New York, yet you are a true poet. I know because I am Russian, so I feel the temperament, the soul, feel it *here*." A plump crimson-tipped hand came to rest upon her diamonds. "Also my sister-in-law is a poet." "Who is your sister-in-law?" I asked, wondering if I had seen her name in the quarterlies. "No, no"—Nina shook her head—"Barbara is like Tony; she will not risk a rejection slip. But her work is pure and beautiful, like his." Here Tony, interrupting whatever he was telling my mother, identified the unhappy heiress among whose six or seven husbands had been one of the "marrying Mdivanis." "Why, I remember Barbara Hutton from Palm Beach!" my mother exclaimed. "Was she writing poetry then?"—as if asking whether she'd had bobbed hair in 1931. Tony rolled his eyes my way. Was this the kind of talk our work would inspire twenty years hence?

As we left the restaurant he took charge: "Dearest, Jimmy and I thought we might walk a half hour by the river—if you don't mind dropping Hellen at the Ritz?" Whereupon he again kissed my mother's hand, then Nina's, which stayed extended in my direction. Though I did no better than to shake it, "You have a friend in me," she said with gracious emphasis. Then the Bentley purred off into the night. Sighing, relaxing, our topcoat collars upturned, Tony and I walked in silence through the mild moist glistening leaf-plastered dark. The evening's wines had made me giddy, and when an old Eddie Cantor song—from a record Tony'd had at school—floated into mind, I began to sing under my breath:

"Give me a limousine
And diamonds like the Queen,
Give me most anything else you have to spare—"

breaking off in embarrassment at this unthinking allusion to Nina's car and necklace. But with his old devil-may-care smile Tony took up the lyrics himself:

"And if my marriage should prove a phony
Give me plenty of alimony—
[Both] This is the Twentieth Century Maiden's Prayer!"

Another spell of silence. Then in a new faraway voice: "I have seen a panorama that I wish to portray. Given five unbroken years of work, I am convinced that I could make the first revolution in prose fiction since Proust."

"Is something preventing you?" I asked innocently.

"What do you think? I don't complain." He shrugged. "What has one to give, in the long run, but oneself?" These were familiar words. I'd heard them week after week in New York, during that season when Bill Cannastra had glanced at the gift and waved it aside. His voice more and more like a sleepwalker's, Tony now began to relate an incident from his first weeks with Nina in Geneva. They had gone together into an elegant shop, of luggage and leather goods. "Nina's *maladie d'achat* is really a case for the specialists," he sighed. "Here in Paris I've been unable to write even a line of Poyetry. Do you like to shop? Come along! We go every morning. The car takes us to Fauchon, or the Galeries Lafayette, or the Samaritaine."

"What do you buy there?" I really wanted to know.

"Ah, you have put your finger on it." He gave up the ghost of a laugh: "Something that must be returned in the afternoon . . ." But back then in Geneva, the pattern, insofar as it involved Tony, was just beginning to take shape. They stood in the leather shop, pursuing, as people will in an unlikely place, the kind of idle, hushed, dreamlike conversation that changes the rest of their lives. As they talked, Nina kept playing with a limber riding crop she'd picked up from a display table, bending it this way and that until—"until it snapped . . . like the spine of Vronsky's horse," whispered Tony, stopping on our Parisian pavement, overcome. Nina had handed the broken crop to the startled Swiss clerk and in her grandest manner told him to put it on her bill and have it delivered to the hotel. With which she took Tony's arm and left the shop. "I knew then," he said, starting to walk again, "that I could never live without her."

It was from Tony that I first learned how effective a cliché can be at the right moment.

"You'd been looking for her a long time," I said to break the silence.

There was a sense of Tony smiling in the dark. "My *sage-femme* . . ."

"What about her husband?"

"Nina and I are twin souls. We have loved each other in many, many lives. It would be a great wickedness if we were to be kept apart in this one. In fact," Tony finished, his voice still that of a dreamer, "if you can keep a secret, we expect to marry next year. We are going to Ceylon to ask Denis for a divorce."

"What if he . . . ?"

"It is out of the question. A bond such as Nina's and mine is understood by Those Who Know."

I did not keep the secret. "He made it sound like a kind of celestial shotgun wedding," I told my mother the next morning.

"It's the end of him," she said somberly. "With a woman like that, Tony doesn't stand a chance."

"He said he's had no time for his work. His writing."

164

"It's her *age*, son; it's the unsuitability. She's older than his *mother*. It would be ludicrous if it weren't tragic. Just when he could have been enjoying his youth." This reversed my mother's standard line, which I had heard only a few days earlier following our lunch with Barney Crop. What was he *doing* here in Paris—painting a picture or two, having fun the rest of the time? That wasn't a life! His poor parents must be worried sick. As we pursued the subject of Nina, my mother's words called up, at a merciful remove, her first, spontaneous objection to Kimon: not, curiously, the nature of our love but the difference in our ages. The "unsuitability" of such unions was no mere formula. It had taken a diplomatic embassy from my paternal grandmother to win over my mother's parents to the dangerous notion of her marrying a divorced man fifteen years her senior. Such conventional wisdom was the *Code Napoléon* of a society, the unadorned, bedrock prose Stendhal aspired to; once *it* was set down clearly and forcefully, flightier forms would come to seem beside the point. I never fancied that "prose" of this rigor was anything but much, much harder to bring off than Barney's bachelor doggerel or the stately alexandrine couplets of Tony's liaison. Where Tony was concerned, however, I saw eye-to-eye with my mother, a state of affairs so refreshing that, instead of contradicting her out of long habit, I kissed her and went out—for, like Nina, I myself relished a morning in the shops—to buy spats for Robert, of heavy dark-gray felt with bone buttons.

The day of our tea with Alice, we had lunch by ourselves near the hotel. "There are some things Jimmy and I have to talk over," she told Bill, as my heart sank. Must I be lectured yet again about my "life"? I needn't have worried. That subject had become Dr Detre's affair and was off limits for the duration, perhaps forever. The closest she came was a single question, over our beet-and-celery salads in the bistro: "Have you anything to tell me?"—which I took to mean anything "reassuring," anything she could repeat to her friends without embarrassment. Excited by my imminent return to Rome, I did my best. The hours with Dr Detre, I said, absorbed me totally. Whatever listlessness I'd felt with the motherly therapist in New York had melted away. Just as a careful reader might help me to write a better poem next time, analysis would enrich the text of the years ahead. Something Dr Detre had emphasized at the outset came back as I spoke. I mustn't expect to be "happy ever after" when he finished with me. The problems that had sent me to him weren't going to evaporate. But when they recurred I'd know, for once, how to face them. Who wanted the bland diet of happiness anyway? Bring on the sizzling mixed grill, the chilled and sparkling flute! *"Surtout pas le bonheur!"* as Oscar Wilde had said, though I knew better than to quote him to my mother. "The point," I did say, since we were at lunch in not only Wilde's but Lambert Strether's favorite city, "isn't that a given life be 'happy' or 'sad' but that you have the appetite to live it. It's such a waste, such a loss, if you don't." The phrases came easily; I'd written them not long ago to my father, congratulating him on his now-final divorce from Kinta. "That's why your marrying Bill is so splendid. You've left your sickroom, you've taken hold of your life. You've become a new person!"

"No, I haven't," said my mother, placing her hand over mine. "Please understand one thing. Bill Plummer is a fine man. He has more gentleness and consideration in his little finger than Charlie Merrill ever showed after the first years of our marriage. That was your father's nature; don't think I'm blaming him. Bill's life hasn't been easy, but I love him and I promise you I'll make him a good wife. But, son, we're not talking about what I felt for your father. It's not only that I'm past the age. There are things I couldn't put myself through again, things I can count on Bill to spare me."

"The pain, the humiliation . . ." I echoed words often on her lips after my father left.

166

"*And* the whatever you want to call it. Rapture? I couldn't face that again either. So don't dismiss happiness too quickly, Jimmy. It looks pretty good from where I sit."

I was sorry that rapture played no part in my mother's new marriage. The romantic in me would have liked to see her not just watched over but swept away. In any event, Bill got high marks in an unexpected quarter. When I telephoned Alice to thank her for having us all to tea, she said how pleased she was to have met my mother and how truly delighted she had been by General Plummer. "He's bound to be a blessing in your life, Jamie. So decent and sensible. Just the kind of man Gertrude Stein liked best."

In my father's divorce from Kinta, my mother (I learned recently) played a small but gratifying role. Soon after she and Bill were married, my father gave them lunch at a Palm Beach club. Over coffee he asked Bill, with a comradely frankness used through the years on many a husband, to grant him and the new Mrs Plummer an hour alone. Life with Kinta, he admitted once Bill had strolled out onto Worth Avenue, was now intolerable. My father didn't know how much longer he had to live, but he'd be damned if he wanted to die while still married to that bloodsucker. He had always trusted my mother's judgment; what did she think? They discussed in some detail his provisions for children and former wives, the present state of his finances, and so forth. At last came the bittersweet, long-to-be-savored moment. He and my mother exchanged (or so I imagine it) a look brimming with something far rarer than love—with unspoken if, on her side, not wholly disinterested intelligence. "What on earth are you waiting for?" she asked in her mildest voice. The question sealed Kinta's fate. Two weeks later his divorce was under way.

Nor was my pep talk over our lunch in Paris wholly disinterested. I wanted my mother's marriage, and the freedom it promised me, to last. It did. Bill would "watch over" my mother devotedly for fifteen years, until emphysema sapped him; then her turn came. Since his death she has stayed on in Atlanta. Betty and her husband drive over from Anniston every two or three weeks, and countless local friends—younger and younger as time passes—make much of her.

A tinted oval photograph shows her at eighteen with soulful eyes and Cupid's-bow lips, her forehead ringleted, the whole wrapped in a fichu of pink tulle against a studio backdrop of plantation oaks. It bears a clear likeness to my mother even now, while giving no clue to her uncanny, lifelong vitality. (One clue, no doubt, is the daily quarter grain of thyroid extract she has taken since my birth. This emerged when she broke a hip at eighty. Hospitalized without her medication, she lapsed before our eyes, like the beautiful girl at the close of Lost Horizon, into an old, old woman. Then she mended, and a tiny white pill again reversed the process.) Late in life, still glancing longingly at the dance floor, all animation from her first drink, her dark hair barely frosted by the years, she has not lost the ability, or the desire, to draw her companion into that old complicity of vigorous nods and knowing smiles, her slender hand coming to rest on his arm for emphasis. At ninety my mother has the smooth legs of a girl. Her breasts, glimpsed through a loose peignoir, are large and unwrinkled. The only physical sign of age is in the shoulders—giving out, as if they'd borne too much—and in the slow erosion of her once military spine to a fragile question mark.

Last year in Atlanta I was helping to pack her latest boxful of clippings about me (reviews, interviews, magazine appearances, and the like) for mailing to the university library that collects my papers. Presently she sat back and turned my way her delicate unlined face—unlifted, too, by any surgery more drastic than her oiled fingertips as she listens to the morning news. "The articles about you always tell who your father was," she said without petulance, "but there's never any mention of me. It's as if you'd never had a mother." I reminded her of many exceptions to this new pronouncement, including how she figured in my own writing, but it didn't convince her. Peering into that open grave of paper and newsprint between us, I thought of the letters she had destroyed so long ago—my letters from Kimon and Claude, from Freddy and Tony, destroyed not to punish me but lest their evidence harm me in the eyes of the world—and for a sad, startled minute saw these already yellowing heaps of "favorable publicity" saved over the years since her rash act as a kind of penance, like a conscientious little girl's smudged apology for a blunder that had better be tenderly forgiven, once and for all: any day now it will be too late.

On the last morning of my visit my mother kept an appointment at Atlanta's most genteel funeral parlor. Made comfortable in a room full of antiques, each piece labeled with donor and date, we were duly joined by one of the firm's junior partners. I watched this bloodless youth turn human, rosy in the glow of my mother's warmth as she answered his questions and told him her requirements. Since I'd showed no eagerness to be buried in the family plot in Jacksonville—where, with Bill Plummer already settled, there was, she offered hesitantly, just enough room for her and me and, if I wished, David Jackson— she had decided to "bring" Bill to Atlanta and lie beside him in the Cathedral garden. I felt her pain, as a Christian believer, at knowing that our dust would not be mingled, and then and there considered granting her that posthumous satisfaction. After all, what earthly difference could it make? But no; I wanted a return to the elements, wanted my ashes to be scattered upon dancing waters by hands I loved, and I kept silent. We rose to take our leave. Something I'd said recently about ecology and the need for biodegradable packaging must have been in her mind, along with all the rest, for on the sunny threshold she turned to her funereal friend, resting a hand on his arm:

"One last thing. Did I make it clear that I want to be buried in a biographical container?"

XIV *Arrivederci, Robert.*
Translating Montale.

IN THE PIAZZA NAVONA, its ring of Christmas booths an enchantment after dark, Robert and I bought tree decorations out of Mozart and Ariosto: eighteenth-century ladies with powdered hair, knights in quicksilver armor. Other, humbler booths evoked the *trattorie* of Elfland. Impossible to resist their little painted dishes of vegetables, spaghetti with tomato sauce, a whole roast chicken or grilled fish on a platter three centimeters long, baskets of glistening bread, bowls of tiny apples and pears. Remembering these miniature pop sculptures from childhood Christmases, I felt I'd come home. My half-brother and his family arrived from Austria. Our nephew Merrill, who had replaced Robin at the famous Swiss school, joined their party. Day after day was filled with shopping, sightseeing, restaurants. My father had commissioned me to buy presents for everybody; so had my mother. A production of *The Emperor Jones* showed us—the text in Italian, the singers in blackface—the charms and pitfalls of cultural exchange. On Christmas Day nine grownups and six children met in Via Quattro Novembre. Dr and Mrs Simeons brought their sons. Robert found a recipe for eggnog; there must have been a fruitcake or a *panettone*. Claude appeared, all smiles and packages. Marilyn's red-nailed hands fluttered over the keyboard, and out came, in her hilariously high small voice,

"She's gotta be cool in summer, warm in fall,
Hot in the winter and tha-at ain't all,
In the springtime she'll be fine as wine—
She's a four-season mama and she's mine, all mine!"

while Umberto listened in suspended disbelief. A week later we drank a bottle of champagne, and it was 1952.

But no sooner had we begun to trust the steadying joys of a life shared than the blow fell. Checking back at his landlady's one morning, Robert found an urgent message. His grandfather was dead, his mother needed him at home, he had no choice but to pack up and go. The misfortune shook us both. Neither was ready to take the other for granted. Each day began and ended with naked, electric arousals and the license to satisfy them at shameless length. Over meals we talked inventively, self-delightingly—no tense misunderstandings, no restful silences. Couples more set in their ways, used to communicating in platitudes, pricked up their ears at nearby tables. One morning when our *permessi di soggiorno* needed renewing, we armed ourselves against boredom by taking along *The Way of the World* to read aloud in the waiting room of the Questura. The other petitioners, a slow-to-dwindle crowd, lowered their newspapers as our performance gathered momentum. Mirabell and Millamant's wry declarations brought tears to our eyes. Robert got to play Lady Wishfort's scene in the last act. "Begone! begone! begone!—go! go!—That I took from washing of old gauze and weaving of dead hair, with a bleak blue nose over a chafing-dish of starved embers . . ." Unable to contain myself, I cut him off in mid-tirade: did he realize that was Hopkins? I quoted from the famous sonnet, ". . . and *blue-bleak embers*, ah my dear! / Fall, gall themselves, and gash gold-vermilion." Really, it was too uncanny. —Oh? Why should Hopkins not have read Congreve? asked Robert pettishly, still in character; Jesuits were famous for liking naughty books. Yes, but to take the actual words (I said) and use them in a poem dedicated to—! Robert interrupted me to cite the reverse example of Chabrier, who, borrowing precisely those themes from *Tristan* praised by the critics for their intrinsic loftiness, had used them in a suite of music-hall galops for two pianos. I saw his point at once: hadn't I gone through a phase of marking passages in *Walden* that proved it beyond all doubt a clever forgery by Proust? The reclusive temperament given to worldly images, the set pieces wherein nature is seen revolving through seasonal prisms. "Concord" itself, the fictive town nearest to the narrator's retreat, had been transparently named after a famous square in Paris. . . . We agreed then and there to collaborate on a scholarly article—"Lady Wishfort and the Windhover"—and were discussing its strategies when a scowling official called our names. No doubt our giddiness was ill-considered. But being young, we wanted to display it in public, and neither was musician enough to modulate into a more natural key.

Before Robert left we gave ourselves a weekend in Naples. The city fed our taste for the exaggerated, the bizarre, the frivolous. (For human beauty too; every other man looked like Gino the goalie.) We lingered among Pompeian frescos of dainty gods and heroes. "Profoundly superficial," I jotted on an envelope. We saw the *Cristo Velato,* so realistic that its marble shroud was said to sweat; and, at the aquarium, a jellyfish of live, fringed crystal big as a skull, hovering over a much littler one. "Madonna and Child," Robert murmured. We heard *L'Assedio di Corinto,* our first tragic opera by Rossini. But no matter how grave a juncture had been reached in the libretto, his music was unable to keep a straight face. Like our hours together, it bubbled, winking and flushed, from some deep well of delicious amusement. Back in our room we lay exhausted, stroking each other's cheeks, exchanging reassurances. Rays from the bedside lamp barely transgressed its flounces of pink glass. I would miss all this terribly. Since I was tied to Italy by my analysis, Robert promised to return and spend the summer with me.

"It may be just as well for you to be alone for a while," said Dr Detre. "You have been creating a duplicate self out of Robert."

"Is that bad?"

"Put yourself in his place. How would you feel?"

"If someone did that to me? Oh dear. Misunderstood, ignored . . . But if he is 'me,' then by loving him I could be learning to love myself. At least that's to the good?"

"No doubt. But there is only so much to gain from paying court to the mirror."

"None of it gained by the mirror . . ."

"Regrettably so. It is a one-sided transaction."

Robert left. In the light of Dr Detre's comments I felt almost relieved by his departure, as though, had he stayed in Rome, I would inevitably have caused him pain. It was going to be hard, after the delights of companionship, to resume a solitary life. But I trusted my analysis would progress by leaps and bounds now that it had no rival for my attention. There was always, to be sure, the opera. Like some midwinter cold snap, a transalpine company descended upon Rome with *Siegfried* and *Elektra*—an opera my mother had forbidden me, at thirteen, to attend. Did she fear my learning what sons under stress were capable of? Now at last I was free to look and listen, tingling with expectations no performance could have lived up to. Wagner brought out a formidably serious audience who shushed for quiet throughout the first act, only to sleep, heads rolling like a seal colony, in the brilliant stagelight of the last scene. Other works unknown to me kept being mounted—*Der Freischütz, Adriana Lecouvreur, Sakuntala.* The score of this last, by the Alfano who completed *Turandot,* had been de-

174

stroyed when a bomb fell on a library in Bologna. Unfortunately the composer was still alive and had nothing better to do than to re-create it from memory. He must have overlooked a few instrumental parts, for one came away giggling like an idiot from an overdose of harp, woodblock, and triangle—not to mention the old man's curtain calls after each act, hands clasped triumphantly above his head, while five or six students cheered in the half-empty house.

At last I began work on the two Montale poems Ben Johnson had given me months ago. The first, "La Casa dei Doganieri," turned out to be relatively easy, but the second, "Nuove Stanze," even after I'd looked up every other word in my new dictionary, kept resisting the intelligence, to my theoretical approval and practical dismay. Its elements were a cigarette-smoking woman, a chessboard with a game in progress, a room above the towers and bridges of a town, and various unspecified dire events looming on the horizon—which the woman's glowing gaze, her "eyes of steel," appear to challenge and oppose. Montale was clearly taking pains not to say all he knew, and to say what he did say with such mysterious force that any reader except for that ideal *tu*—the woman pondering the chessboard—would have an awed sense of eavesdropping upon a prayer. A wraith of tightly knit logic—a syntax to be followed at your own risk, for the thread might snap at any turning—marked even the least of Montale's poems, any one of which called for as much constructive guesswork as did an ode by Horace. Rhyme and assonance surfaced at tantalizing random—hazards of the medium rather than part of the blueprint. For me it was the ladles and love-letters, the furniture and pets, those blessedly ordinary nouns embedded like votive plaques in its walls, that drew a reader ever deeper into the labyrinth. Their translator had to go a step further and pretend to know what dwelt at its heart.

Our short-lived collaboration behind us, Ben and I were

pleased that its fruits found approval in Umberto's eyes. He, it emerged, was on good enough terms with Montale to suggest my calling upon him should I ever go to Milan. "I'm sure he would welcome you also as a friend of Miss Brandeis," Umberto added, lowering his eyelids and weaving his fingers together. I assumed a look of interest but, having recently seen in a bookshop a sullen, unprepossessing photograph of the poet, made up my mind to leave well enough alone.

"What was it you disliked about his appearance?" asked Dr Detre.

I saw what he was getting at—Dr Simeons had already tried the Szondi test on me, with its disturbing or lunatic faces—so there was no harm in going along with the game. "Montale? Oh, he looked, I don't know, like a hedgehog. Mean and unloving. As if he would take everything and give nothing. That's absurd, I know, because in his poems he's already given more to the world than most people ever do. I simply didn't want anything to do with him myself. Besides, what language would we speak? His English is bound to be awful."

"When did you see this photograph?"

"Just after Robert left. Perhaps a month ago? Just as I was getting down to those translations."

"Strange that you persisted in so antipathetic a project."

I half rose from the couch to look round. "It's no reflection on the *work*. The work is marvelous! I guess I'm just a Platonist," I said, falling back and thinking that if Dr Detre knew anything about poetry, now would be the time to quote that stanza where Spenser asserts that the more heavenly light there is in the soul, the more physical beauty will show in the person. Not that this could possibly be the case. On the contrary, beauty was terrifying, and only a very foolish moth expected any good to come from his affair with the flame. But Dr Detre and I had covered this ground many times. Montale's repulsiveness was the topic at hand. "So," I went on with a touch of sarcasm, "I suppose you want me to say who I've really been describing under the aspect of Montale. A rival for the Muse's favor? Closer to home, an older male presence with some sort of prior claim on an important woman in my life? Bill Plummer? How many father figures can one *have*?"

"Excuse me. Mean? Unloving? That doesn't sound like General Plummer. Taking everything and giving nothing? Are you comfortable with this description of your father?"

"Montale . . . I don't know the whole story, but I somehow picture him treating Irma shabbily. Like my father when—"

"Who is it in your *present* life who does not love you, who takes everything and gives nothing in return, who has encouraged a temporary separation from your sexual partner, and whose peculiarly accented words you are condemned to translate every day as best you can?"

A dreadful silence spread through the room. "You," I managed to breathe.

Those early Montale translations failed in part because the poet's ambiguous textures called for the kind of judgment Ben and I might never acquire. (The pianola in a phrase from the "Motetti" could be rendered by Irma as belonging to "the people downstairs" or by Dana Gioia as part of the furniture of Hell—in either case justifiably. How to know?) Yet our essential failure lay in not yet having a full command of our own language. This is the rock on which nine out of ten translators founder and accounts for the baby talk of poets who, writing under the spell of Rilke or Neruda, have read them only in user-friendly versions geared to "accessibility."

Today "Nuove Stanze" is less opaque than it once was. Familiarity with other poems by Montale—more often than not, picked out by Irma as worth attempting in English—has no

doubt helped. So have the notes in the 1980 Opera in Versi
(Einaudi), which, on my way through Italy that year, I bought
for Irma. But it seemed that she'd already received those two
volumes from another source; my gift was sent back to me.
Here, opening it for perhaps the second time in ten years, I see
that "Nuove Stanze" dates from the spring of 1939 and deals
with "la guerra che matura. Ultimi giorni fiorentini di Clizia"—
a name that would have meant nothing had I come across it in
1950. One poem, however, which I later undertook at Irma's
behest ("L'Ombra della Magnolia"), is addressed to this enigmatic Clizia. Who was she? When I asked Umberto for help,
he said he imagined she was the nymph in Ovid who was
changed into a sunflower. Through my head darted the radiant
last line of the poem Irma had read aloud to Claude and me before presenting us with the book dedicated to I. B.: "The golden
trumpets of solarity." Yet I held back from putting a face to the
sun-worshiping nymph.

Move by move over the decades, slow as a chess game, it grew
clear that she was Irma herself. One day I heard of a picnic she'd
gone to with Montale. Two years later she showed me a fat
biographical dictionary of European literary figures. Montale's
entry was illustrated not by the usual glum portrait but the
snapshot of a cat striding across a book-littered table on which
rested—seen from the back, yet that tangled hair looked familiar—a woman's head. Irma's. More years passed. No single
revelation marked the point at which I "knew." Somehow, one
afternoon, I felt entitled to wonder why they'd parted. Ah well,
Irma said without emotion, war was about to break out; as a
Jew, she couldn't possibly have stayed in Italy. Montale,
though—mightn't he have come to the States? Irma shook
her head. She'd done everything in her power, got him the papers, secured him the university position. By then, however, the
other woman—for yes, there had been, finally, another woman—had staked her claim. Montale remained in Italy. Irma re-

turned many times. After the flood of 1966 she worked in Florence as a volunteer, salvaging the precious documents. But she and Montale never met again.

Or did they? There were always third parties to whom they could, if they wished, apply for news of each other. But only after Montale's Nobel Prize—after, too, the death of "Mosca," whom he had married—did the question of a meeting arise. Irma broached it to me one evening in New York. Suppose she wrote—the merest line, you understand, expressing pride in his fame. Then what? Gestures like that had consequences. After all this time, was there anything to be gained, any point, any pleasure, on either side, in the notion of coming face-to-face? What did I think? What did I think! My eyes were shining with the romance of it. Write him, I urged her. Who knew where it would lead! She turned upon me, if not the "eyes of steel" of the woman in "Nuove Stanze," then surely that "hard crystal glance" of the anguished but divinely prescient muse in "L'Orto." Would I never, said that look, act my age? Again, months went by. One day at Casaminima, Irma's cottage near the Bard campus, she reopened the topic. "I heard from Montale, did I tell you? Oh, sometime last winter. Here, let me show you." I looked over her shoulder as she unfolded a page of heavy white paper. At its center was a square, not much larger than a postage stamp, of cramped, elderly script. "Irma," it began, "you were ever my godess [sic]"—switching to Italian to ask where and when they should meet. It was signed, with no suspicion of a flourish, "Montale."

"You see," she said, managing to laugh, "this won't do. Either his mind is gone or . . . I never called him 'Montale.' If he doesn't remember that . . . !"

"I'm always forgetting which people call me what," I said lamely.

Another mineral look. Then: "I'm flying to Milan at the end of the month. I had thought in spite of everything to see him.

But now I hear from G."—indicating a second letter at her side—"that there's talk of his marrying his housekeeper. Under those circumstances a meeting is out of the question."

Which is all I know of Irma's final trip to Italy. Meanwhile, in the wake of Montale's worldwide fame, "Clizia" had been identified as Irma in a learned journal. Another year, and this scoop reemerged on the front page of The New York Times Book Review. A flurry of interest peaked and died down. The woman who long ago foresaw the doomed pawns blinded by war madness, who beneath her high room's "frightened ivory mouldings" stubbed out another cigarette, eyes blazing with scorn and despair, turned back into words. In the notes to "Nuove Stanze" Montale is quoted telling a friend that its latest draft has made the poem "more Florentine, more like intarsio-work, a harder surface"—phrases that turn his chessboard to inlaid marble. Above Irma's bookcase hangs (or did until her recent death) a portrait of herself done in the 1930s. Modigliani would have liked that face—proud, pale as fire, but amused too, and without a shred of pathos. Everything fits. Montale's poem, like the forces behind it—the approaching cataclysm, the convulsed loyalties, the bell (la Martinella) rung only to signal a disgrace— grows daily more alive and clear, at the usual cost of whatever human presences brought it into being.

(David and I naturally called up Irma on the Ouija Board. We like to make sure that friends who've died aren't left cooling their heels by some minor bureaucrat but get in with the right set from the start. We needn't have worried; Irma sounded altogether at home. As death's pain and confusion ebbed away, she told us, she came to herself ECSTATICALLY SKIPPING ROPE. ENDS OF THE ROPE HELD BY MONTALE & DUSE.)

About to return those two volumes of L'Opera in Versi to the shelf, I'm stopped in my tracks. Heavens! Did Irma mail the wrong books back to me ten years ago? Or was it more like her to have trusted this final discovery to undo me at its own sweet pace? For these I am holding came to her from the poet himself. On the flyleaf of the first volume, in that cramped elderly hand I seem to have glimpsed once before, appears the inscription "a Clizia." And beneath it is . . . a name? The name Irma called Montale by when they were both young? One would need to have known it in order to make it out today.*

---

* A false conclusion: the books were inscribed and sent (according to Luciano Rebay, the distinguished montalista) not by their author but by their editor. Yet having basked long months in the sunset glow of fable, I'll just sit here awhile in the gloom before switching on for good the poor lamp of fact.

XV   *Broken vows.*
Nils.
Franco.
The unlit garden.
Goodbye to Luigi.

D<small>R DETRE SEEMED PLEASED</small> by my having at last expressed, however indirectly, some feelings about him. Popular psychology had led me, at the start, to anticipate falling in love with my analyst. It turned out, however, that "transference" covered a wide spectrum of emotion and that the veiled resentment brought to light by my fantasy about Montale's photograph was a not unacceptable form for this phase of the pilgrim's progress. Although we were never to dwell long upon the moment of truth, I knew from my praise of Montale's work that—whatever coldheartedness I might project upon a Dr Detre of flesh and blood—my faith in his professional skill had come through intact. Not long after my little breakthrough he volunteered that we were "on schedule." I felt I'd been given a prize at school.

Another early misconception had to do with dreams. Before entering analysis I fancied them to be the very meat on which patient and doctor breakfasted insatiably together. Each night therefore I set off in catlike pursuit of a new one, and next day proudly laid the dead mouse at Dr Detre's feet. But far from praising my cunning, he let it be felt that all this dreamwork was an elaborate ruse to keep the real issues at arm's length.

182

These—the real issues—were coming more and more to seem of my own devising. It was as if my life until now had been governed by certain vows I'd made—the vow, for instance, to keep my heart open, as my father did, to anyone I'd ever loved; or the vow always to be truthful and do my "level best," in my mother's phrase; above all, never to break faith with the pure, gemlike feelings of adolescence lest I turn, like Dorian Gray, into a hideous and corrupt thirty-year-old who lived for sensual delights and treated his lovers as means to a shameful end. The crayon colors of these projects, and their iconography of stick figures, boxlike house, and all-seeing sun, ought to have ensured their removal, long before this, from a grown person's refrigerator door. My mother, after all, that day at Hadrian's Villa, had confessed her old duplicity as to an equal. In Claude's arms after hearing that Hans was dead I knew the pain my father must have caused his latest love by never quite relinquishing the bygone ones. The feelings my poems drew upon were no longer a schoolboy's, but how was a reader to tell? What if my efforts to resist that reader's intelligence were masking not just the gender of my loves but the insidious onset of manhood? Heaven forbid! Sleeping Beauty hadn't been meant to age even a day during her long coma.

The task ahead was to release that wise but ignorant young person from those vows he had made to himself. This would have to be brought off—like all dealings with unhappy teenagers—patiently, amicably, diplomatically. "Look," I might say to him, "there's someone at this party who keeps glancing your way. Why not risk talking to him? You're not committing yourself to anything." Or: "We've never walked through that unlit garden on our way home. Yet other people seem to be making the detour. Why not try it tonight?" The party in question was given by a film director I'd met through Wayne, and the person looking my way was a young Swedish scene designer named Nils. The unlit garden, no distance at all from my apartment, turned out to be a hotbed of fickle silhouettes, a world that could be craved, possessed, and forsworn, all in twenty minutes.

Nils's beauty blinded me to his dull wits and melancholy nature. Indeed, this last may well have been caused by his beauty, or by the advantage so many people had taken of it in his short life. Blond, with dark brows, blue eyes, and meltingly chiseled lips, he had already learned—perhaps from the films of his compatriot Greta Garbo—a minimal, enigmatic play of feature. Was his deepest wish, like hers, to be left alone? On just the break with his middle-class parents Nils seemed to have squandered a whole lifetime's allowance of imagination; now it was up to the rest of the world to look out for him. But what could he hope for from his new milieu? His stage designs, when he brought them to lunch, were pitifully inept and obvious. In bed, a few nights later, he might have been a sack of potatoes. The rest of the world, that season, boiled down to me. One day he showed up in great fright and pain. I took him to Dr Simeons, who diagnosed a duodenal ulcer, psychosomatically induced to be sure, and prescribed six weeks in hospital, where Nils could be overseen, body and soul. He had no money; I offered to take care of it. But lest he imagine that these expenses—like the settlements made by my father upon his ex-wives—in any way replaced ongoing love and interest, I ran errands for him downtown and took a bus to the hospital every afternoon. Unable to amuse him, I stayed out my hour and left, promising to come the next day.

Time passed and he was cured. One wet night soon after his leaving the hospital for a friend's apartment, he invited me to the ballet. Featured that evening was the premiere of a new work choreographed by Anton Dolin, a famous dancer then past his prime. I offered Nils a bite to eat first. He arrived carrying a single rose of an unusually vibrant red, which I put in my buttonhole. We were both rather dressy; I wore a pearl-gray waistcoat with my dark suit. After supper, when we were on the point of leaving for the theater, Nils flung his arms round me dramatically, harshly too, as if to say, *Here, this is what you expected, let's get it over with!*—waking no response in me and mangling my rose. I salvaged one brilliant petal, tucked it in my waistcoat pocket, and out we went. Why we were sitting through this inane performance became clear only at its end. Dolin himself, whom Nils had to thank for our tickets, expected us backstage. Small, trim, hair blackened and cheeks rouged, the former *premier danseur* extended both hands in welcome. I was about to mention that I'd seen him dance in New York, before the war. But Dolin now drew back, shooting me an abrupt head-to-toe look of dreadful gravity. "What is that peeking out of your pocket?" he inquired.

"Where? Oh. It's just . . . a rose petal."

Dolin's eyes kindled. So that was what the boy had done with his morning's gift of roses—given them to this young American! Moments later I was on the street, alone, having had the uncharacteristic good sense to excuse myself. I'd been shown too many things at once—Nils's weakness and banality, the famous old dancer's airs, his unloving drive to dominate, and my own contribution to the whole hothouse farce. Worse yet, how plausibly I myself could slip, over the years, into Dolin's role. Did I see Nils again after that? If so, it was with the sense of a narrow escape. Better far the photograph I'd taken of his beautiful head gazing mysteriously up from the hospital pillows.

Yet something told me that my impulse towards Nils was more than a matter of looks. On Dr Detre's couch I recalled the afternoon at Amherst when Hans played the "Spring" Sonata on my phonograph; I was catching cold but gallantly fought off his offer to bring me soup and make me comfortable. Why? Perhaps it was less urgent for me to receive care than to dispense it. If my need was to be needed, Nils's very instability may have drawn me to him.

"Need is an infantile form of love," said Dr Detre. "Going

to bed with someone just because he or she 'needs' you might be compared to taking sexual advantage of a small child."

I thought of the years I'd languished unmolested.

"Be glad that you were not too much needed as a child," he went on. "Your father and mother had admirably full lives without you. Nurses kept the little boy clean and amused until the summons came from downstairs."

I remarked that after my parents' separation my mother seemed to need me very much. But by then it was as if—did Dr Detre recall that caption to my picture in the newspaper, "Pawn in Parents' Fight"?—the most expendable piece on the chessboard was within a move or two of becoming a queen.

Undeterred by my wit, Dr Detre proceeded. "The proofs of concern you received from your parents in adolescence came too late. You were already inventing your superior way of responding to an appeal—not only with money but with time and love. To this day anybody who needs you, or appears to, even for a half-hour, can have you."

There were no obvious psychological pitfalls in that unlit garden near my building, where I might far more readily have consummated my desire for Nils—and *with* Nils, it belatedly occurred to me—than by troubling to invite him to lunch. Here were shrubs and benches, and one of those turn-of-the-century urinals I'd seen all over town, which looked like something fathered upon an Iron Maiden by the Beast with Two Backs. You could pretend to be relieving yourself while waiting in double obscurity, with pounding heart, for the next stranger's hand to reach round the partition that divided you from him. Sometimes, before entering his side, he would light a cigarette, allowing you to judge whether to stay put or to yield your place to another. Sporadically the striking and extinguishing of matches transformed the whole garden into a mating ground for fireflies. At first I preferred the security of my hunter's blind. But gradually realizing that everyone else was nearly as frightened and furtive as I was, I ventured out into the shrubbery. Nowhere—as far as I could tell—was there any question of all-out copulation. (One went, according to Wayne, to the Colosseum for that.) Distractable as dogs, we sniffed from partner to partner, making do with the sort of exploratory thrill a boy of fourteen is meant to have outgrown. If a climax occurred it seemed like an inadvertent disgrace, and the culprit promptly banished himself from our midst. On my fourth—and final—visit, thinking I'd found someone I liked, I urged a man to come home with me. He did, but reluctantly; once behind closed doors, he would not undress, or lie down, or meet my eyes. As Dr Detre pointed out, I might as well have stayed in the garden.

One bright midday in late February, as I was passing the Albergo da Raimondo on my way home, a voice in my ear began singing a popular love-song. I looked round into the eyes of the rather dashing man, perhaps eight years my senior, who was picking me up. But just like that, on the street, in broad daylight! Out of simple discretion I hurried him past the *portiere* and up to my apartment. In a half-hour we were again dressed, and talking. His name was Franco, he worked—well, let's say that his work kept him out of Rome a lot of the time. There was really no address or telephone where I could reach him. He had a confident, bohemian air and gazed at me ardently throughout this explanation, so I saw nothing wrong with it. He told me of his good heart and sincerity as well. One indispensable phrase rose many times to his lips: *io invece*—I on the other hand—words that favorably distinguished the speaker from those thousands who were using the very same formula, wherever Italian was heard, at that exact moment. Somehow it added to Franco's credibility; had he been play-acting, he'd have had a better script. I gave him my telephone number, and when he called two weeks later asked him over right away. Separation had inflamed us both. We fell into bed.

"*Ti voglio bene, Dzim, ti voglio bene,*" Franco kept breathing as he sought to turn me facedown beneath him. But this position alarmed me, for all its exciting novelty, and besides—*ti voglio bene?* That wasn't saying very much. If Franco merely "wished me well," as Luigi had his ugly fiancée, he had better go by himself to the tavern where his friends gathered and where he'd suggested on the telephone that I accompany him this evening. Obviously this Lothario had all along been trifling with an innocent boy's emotions: why should I let myself in for a lifetime at the beck and call of such a heartless person? His clothes furthermore were shabbier than I'd remembered, and he had a blackhead on his neck.

I expected Dr Detre to applaud my mature decision. Instead he allowed himself a youthful laugh. "You have proven to my satisfaction that the only way to learn a foreign language is in bed. Do you honestly not know what *ti voglio bene* means? It is how an Italian says 'I love you.'"

I protested. *Amo* was the verb, just as in Latin. Lovers were *amanti.* "*L'amo,*" confesses Violetta in Act III—I love him. "*M'ama*"—she loves me—sings Nemorino in *L'Elisir d'Amore.*

"I do not question your experience of nineteenth-century opera," said Dr Detre, "only of the Italian language as it is spoken today."

I bit my lip. Franco loved me! But how would I ever find him again?

"Nevertheless," Dr Detre pursued, "from your account of this admirer and the circumstances under which you met, I have to agree with your appraisal of his character."

Well, there was always Luigi. Over the Christmas holidays he had joined an excursion to the zoo with my brother and his family. Many of the cages were empty. Others contained domestic animals—dogs from Africa, North American poultry. Luigi himself was voted the most popular exhibit. I saw the kind of father he would make and identified wistfully with four-year-old Bruce, perched high on his shoulder. From Austria the two older girls sent him valentines in my care—wasn't Valentini his family name?—which I gave him when he came to lunch. Quinta liked him, too, and fed him well those days. If I expected him to regret our evenings by the fire, just the two of us with our leftovers, our wine, our dreams, and shake his head over What Might Have Been, I had misjudged my man. Luigi was now the friend of the family. I knew his people, he knew mine. His place at table was assured, his second helpings were forthcoming. When an idea crossed his mind he expressed it; otherwise—companionable silence, the cheerful munch, the meeting of eyes as when old friends share food. A day came when I could bear no more.

"Luigi, I must talk to you," I said in Italian. "These last months have been difficult for me. I want only to go back to my country, yet I cannot. I must stay in Rome until the therapy I am pursuing for a nervous condition comes to an end. Among Italians—even with you, my good and sincere friend—I feel an estrangement, *un disamore*, which does them, and you, a great injustice. But my one consolation is to be with my fellow Americans. Do you understand?"

"*È naturale*," said Luigi, nodding slowly, as though my speech, which to my own ears sounded so perfidious, summed up what he had long ago come to realize. "You are a poet; your nerves are not like mine. Shall I not see you again?"

"If the mood lifts," I promised. We finished our *dolce*, drank our coffee, and parted with unfeigned affection. It was that simple.

It was a truth universally acknowledged in those innocent decades from 1950 to 1980 that a stable homosexual couple would safely welcome the occasional extramarital fling.

David and I, still in our early thirties, found that a good deal of anxiety could be finessed by setting out together when we felt the itch, rather than carrying on behind each other's backs. We kept on the lookout for a threesome or a "double date" with some other couple on our wavelength. Like high-school buddies we compared notes afterwards, laughed and commiserated, took care to smooth the plumage of any third party who felt he'd been badly treated. By and large, though, we gravitated towards the kind of exploit offered by that unlit garden in Rome, or a New York bathhouse. For me those hours were the adolescence I'd been too shy or repressed to put into action at the time. Their polymorphous abundance spilling over into our lives kept us primed and sexually alert towards each other.

The pattern takes on new colors and dimensions when we begin our annual trips to Greece. There are of course many non-libidinous reasons for going—our delight in Tonáki and Maria, the diamond-clear air (of those first years) that dries out David's sinuses, the charm of the new culture and the new language. The fun also of being Foreigners. Thus labeled, we feel a great burden of personality—individual history—lifted from our shoulders, and set about playing our parts in the ancient Athenian comedy.

And the Greek youths we take up with? Don't they have personalities themselves, and histories? No doubt; yet it seems to us that they primarily have humors, choleric or melancholy, sanguine or phlegmatic, as in pre-Renaissance psychology. Also our friends strike us as creations of their Mediterranean society far more than we are of ours; one of the surefire words in the jukebox songs is yitoniá—the neighborhood—shaper of these young men and ongoing arbiter of their behavior. Emerging all aglisten from the gene pool, too proud to notice us just yet, the newcomer puts his coin in the slot. What will "his" song be—the exquisitely good-humored "Myrtia"? the noble lament of "Kaimos"? Something at any rate from that golden age before Theodorakis turns political, discovers Byzantine chant, and begins writing plainsong cycles too bleak and pretentious to hum or to dance to. By the mid-seventies only busboys are shameless enough to perform a floor-show hasápiko. But in those early days . . .

One evening Barney Crop, who'd given up Paris for Athens, took us to a tavern near some barracks at the edge of town. Here soldiers got up to dance and a handful of civilians or foreigners sat ready to applaud, send wine, try out the phrasebook phonetics for The Rendezvous, or deftly slip a telephone number into a khaki pocket. One of the camp-followers kept glancing at our table. With a show of pique, Barney addressed the ceiling: "Very fetching, but no, thanks. Not my type at all. The idea of going to bed with a 'sister' couldn't interest me less."

David protested. The young man didn't look—

"Then he's probably trade. Or still doesn't know what he wants. Don't mind me, I like my men straight."

Such pedantic taxonomy made my heart sink. Yet Barney's words shed a light that had eluded me under the Roman trees and in the New York steam, though I might well have seen it in the pages of Margaret Mead. The soldier on the dance floor, like nine out of ten from his class and culture, would count himself lucky to catch a permissive male lover—one who wouldn't appear in the yitoniá making a scene. No reflection on the dancer's masculinity. Girls weren't easy to come by in 1959, outside of marriage or the brothel; and who on a military wage of thirty shoeshines a month could afford either one? Your own fiancée, supposing she escaped her mother's eye, wouldn't go "all the way." A hussy might now and then grant access to what Barney in his racy French called the entrée des artistes— but, he grinned, "we" could do this as well as any girl and with far less fuss. The affair might last a night, a season, years. Deep affection might blossom on both sides. As Barney talked, a vague longing I'd felt in Luigi's presence took detailed and plausible form. That the dancing soldier hoped one day to marry and raise a family struck me as the best news yet. More than the barriers of language and background, it seemed to ensure our never going overboard in Greece. David and I could follow with no harm to him the faun incarnate in this or that young man, and without losing ourselves or each other. We were very optimistic to think so.

—Why, why does all this have to be spelled out? my mother sighs in the long conversation we never have. You're not hurting me; you're diminishing yourself. Don't imagine, son, that these are things people need to know.

—But they are things I need to tell. If they were boy-and-girl adventures no one would bat an eyelash.

—There you're wrong, said my mother. A young couple, married or living together, as you and David were, doesn't behave in the manner you describe. That's what shocks me.

—I'm sorry. The young people you have in mind have no taboos to exorcise. Society protects them when love fails to. (If you've missed seeing your values embodied, ask Betty to bring her grandchildren over.) David and I had to patch our lives together out of ethical snippets woven originally as protection in a climate we chose to live as far away from as possible. Too much to keep under wraps! No wonder that in my case, over the years, the forbidden fruit of self-disclosure grew ever more tempting. The spirit of the times ripened it like a kind of sunlight. The very language was changing. An article saying that I "lived with my lover in Athens" sickened you—what would the world think?—until I was able to point out that by 1970 "lover" denoted, as it hadn't in your girlhood, either a man or a woman. . . . Came the day when even the behavior you find so shocking, which by then lay decently buried in my past, or in my poems, was clear to anyone who still cared. As in the classic account of Sarah Bernhardt descending a spiral staircase—she stood still and it revolved about her—my good fortune was to stay in one place while the closet simply disintegrated.

192

XVI *Easter in Graz.*
By myself in Ravenna.

$\mathbf{M}$Y BROTHER'S LIFELONG passion for Central
Europe was somewhat gratified by his year as an exchange
teacher in Austria. Naturally he would rather have left his
school in St Louis for Poland or Hungary or Yugoslavia, where
the history was more colorful and the intellectual life more
intense, but would those hardship zones have been fair to his
wife and children? Graz, where they had settled after the first
months in Vienna, was an interesting compromise, a small,
abashedly Germanophile city staggering back to peacetime,
with its own university and an unbombed opera house. By the
time I arrived to spend Easter with the family, Charles had already given several extracurricular lectures and been unnerved
to see how many citizens in the intimate hall were studying
him through opera glasses. I suggested that the glasses, unknown to him, might have been reversed for the sake of aesthetic distance. "Giving," he said, delighted by the joke while
adapting it to his own ends, "the impression of a larger room,
hence a more *hörenswürdig* lecture." Humor was our common
ground. Six years apart in age, we hadn't greatly troubled to
know each other until I was in college. Even then, his taste for
history and politics left me cold, and I hereby erase from the
record a remark he made, at twenty-four, about "The Rape of
the Lock." But Charles had an appealing flamboyant side. He
loved opera long before I did. At Harvard he wore an ankle-
length Polish military cape and played the flute like Frederick

the Great. And he took, over our father's initial, knee-jerk objections ("How can he say he loves her? She's the first girl he ever dated! The damn fool—can't he see she's just after his money?"), a wife whose wit and equanimity charmed me from the start. His marriage, like our sister's, was extremely stable. Longer than I these children *du premier lit* had seen the havoc caused by our father's restless libido. Forewarned was forearmed.

Charles and I had quite different ways of coping with the paternal menace. He'd actually taken a course in Military Strategy at college. Thus, while I sought to postpone or altogether avoid confrontation, my brother's breathtaking repertoire of shock tactics, diversionary movements, positions secured by verbal barbed wire, and so forth, kept the old man on the defensive and the rest of the family on the edge of our chairs. By 1950 the war had been won. Neither Charles nor I was expected to join the Firm. Hands had been washed of us; thanks to our trust funds, and to being American, we could do as we liked, live far from home in poorly furnished apartments, wear suits of burnt-orange Turkish wool tailored in Prague or cheap puce velvet too tight to sit down in, entertain left-wing ideas or moot young men—it hardly mattered which. All these parodies of luxury were made possible by our baffled, hardworking, womanizing parent in his English cambrics and cashmeres; one could hardly blame him for the hour when he saw red.

Doris meanwhile worked to restore the balance, helping the career of a smart and successful husband, naming one of their sons after the Firm, planning family holidays in attractive resorts, redecorating their three houses at frequent intervals, not to mention the enormous "beach cottage" at Southampton, which our father, once more a bachelor, now decided to move into—all this at the cost of those crippling headaches she couldn't spare time for Dr Simeons to treat. The old man, I'm

194

afraid, often took for granted her desire to be the perfect daughter, while yearning in the best tradition of patriarchs after his prodigal sons.

This season we were all, for once, in his good graces. With Kinta out of the picture, he wanted to draw up a new will and saw no reason to include the children whose future he'd already so handsomely assured. An old-fashioned Florida lawyer, retained more for piquancy than pertinence, spoke up: "Charlie, you can't just cut your children off. They've got every right to contest this after your death." Original to the end, my father proposed that we simply sign away any future claims upon his estate. The lawyer mopped his brow, but we naturally agreed; whereupon each received a bonus of one hundred dollars as full quittance. Charles now brought out an Easter letter from our sister. Visiting Daddy in Palm Beach (Doris wrote), she'd appeared one morning in a beautiful dressing gown, and when he teased her for being extravagant, silenced him by saying she'd used up her inheritance to buy it.

Dr Detre gave me the whole week off for Easter—nine days counting both weekends. Charles and Mary had wanted to meet me in Yugoslavia, but one of the girls was recovering from chickenpox, so we sat tight. On Easter Eve we attended *Parsifal* at the Graz Opera. The production was old and shabby, the tenor wore brown street shoes along with his tunic of moth-eaten skins, one Flower Maiden used pince-nez in order to see the conductor, and Kundry woke at Klingsor's bidding with a shriek that sounded suspiciously like a sneeze. Yet the reverential audience willed into fitful being a performance they could leave exalted by. We ourselves slipped out after the second act. Next day, church bells, the apartment-wide egg hunt, the feast. Every so often the children—Cathy and Amy in their dirndls, little Bruce in his lederhosen—abandoned their play to overrun me like vines and come to rest heavier than a lapful of watermelons. Would they have happy lives? Would I be a father myself one day?

The best we could manage in lieu of Yugoslavia was a night in the little border town of Radkersburg. Our hotel hung over the narrow, fast-flowing river; we could see the ruins of the bridge, or keep warm in bed gazing wistfully at the Croatian landscape. Charles brought along a novel he'd just finished writing—he filled notebooks in longhand, like Sir Walter Scott—and I began reading it as dusk fell in the warm *Stube* where we would presently order a bottle of wine and, later, dinner. Radkersburg couldn't have seemed farther away from Rome, or Charles and Mary (he knitting his brows over a political biography, she placidly sewing) from the people I'd been seeing there. No less remote was the heroine of Charles's tale, a young Austrian who'd survived the war. Worthy of the noble ideas she embodied, she shared her author's gift for discourse but fell short of his irony and prodigious floor-pacing sulks.

"How's Marilyn?" asked Mary the next time I looked up. To my surprise I felt able to follow every stitch of her thought. She'd begun wondering how the children were getting along, entrusted to a favorite baby-sitter, but still . . . She'd savored anew, as I'd been doing for the past hour, the glow of family feeling. Sensing how much Charles's and my slow evolution from wary siblings to respectful and affectionate grownups owed to her, hadn't she then—an only child—gone on to dream by the fire of an ally, a lively younger sister-in-law with whom she could marvel at their two impossible husbands who kept refusing to grow up, who would always . . . ? Marilyn had been a hit over Christmas; from St Louis herself, she knew the school my brother and a friend had opened there, knew people he and Mary knew. . . . Then, too, surely the problems I was being treated for, my touchy sparks and green splinters, would begin to settle, like the blaze in the *Stube*'s porcelain stove, for an overall companionable warmth, if only . . .

"Marilyn's fine," I said. "She sent love."

*   *   *

They saw me off on the night train. I am not, however, going straight to Rome but to Ravenna. This daring plan, wholly without precedent, leapt from my head full-grown as I was booking my tickets at American Express. I would for once do something by and for myself, unaccompanied, unsupervised. It is cool sunless midday by the time I check into a hotel and consume, standing up at a dented metal counter, my ham sandwich and Campari-soda while poring over a map of the town. Had Dr Simeons' injections not kept me in Rome the previous June, I would no doubt have gone to Ravenna with Claude, ticked it off my list of places to see, and never found myself there now. I leave the bar and head for San Vitale. It comes over me, as never before, how dull and full of self-pity I made those two or three days in Rome. At the time, I thought I was spending them wisely, writing an anniversary poem, for it was already a year since my reunion with Claude in Cassis. But the poem—which imagined us together among the mosaics I knew merely from postcards—came out willed and sour, re-sentful between its lines of the carefree time he was having without me. His dry peck on the cheek was more thanks than I deserved.

As I approach San Vitale, a small brick building, squat and clumsy beside its tall domed neighbor, like an X in some ar-chitectural tick-tack-toe, catches my eye. This will be the Tomb of Galla Placidia, where the oldest mosaics are to be found. One may as well begin at the beginning; I go in. Noth-ing has prepared me for what I see: a midnight-blue dome, an old skull thick with gold stars; in the vaults, more stars, precise as snowflakes and big as streetlights enlarged by mist. The space, effortlessly anthropomorphic, has been created, it seems, to dramatize the inner life of a seer or a sibyl, the mira-cles hidden beneath weathered, baked-brick features, upraised in thought. The means to this lavish end are simple, durable,

197

anonymous—nothing of the "personal" brushwork that marks a square inch of canvas as the work of such-and-such a master. Yet instinct and initiative are everywhere at play. Thousands upon thousands of glass-paste dice—each by itself dull and worthless as a drawn tooth—have been shrewdly cast to embed a texture now matte, now coruscant, with colors fifteen hundred years have failed to dim. Through narrow alabaster panels, their art-deco patterns lymph-washed and bloodless, like human tissue on a slide, comes a glow I try to resist, if I am going to make out . . . Look! There's the *buon pastore* seated among his lambs. But this young shepherd hasn't yet evolved into a Christian savior. Cross held upright like a primitive bass viol about to be played, he is still Orpheus, or Apollo; and I recall from my dictionary that "mosaic" derives from a Greek word meaning the work of the Muses.

I step outside, gasping, as if having run up three flights of stairs. Tomorrow at leisure I can take it all in more sensibly; now is the time for rapid impressions. I enter San Vitale. Here is greater splendor yet, placed higher up. No night sky overhead. The old astronomer's heavenly vision gives way to quadrants of a cupola where green foliage on gold alternates with gold foliage on green, like sun filtering into a rain forest. I stand as though in the mind of some young, wide-eyed god, extravagantly in love with detail, and grieved by nothing under the sun, not even the bigotries he has already begun to foster or the self-determined faces in those two imperial retinues above my head. Here gender confronts gender, and gaze, gaze. Real people are being caught in this act; the emperor needs a shave, one of Theodora's ladies twiddles her ring. But reality throws no lasting wrench into works of such sumptuous invention. Round each panel runs a border, no, a series of borders, each a decorative *idée fixe* of the utmost plainness, which notwithstanding, when put together, become steps in an argument so daring yet so crucial to the rest of my life that I know I must get it by heart—not now, though. I have glimpsed peacocks. I've noticed that the motif of counterpoised sheaves or horns of plenty in an archway is being echoed, on pilasters elsewhere, by one of paired dolphins. The dolphins have black-and-white eyeshadow, red mouths and crests and tails. Their tails are linked and their heads thrown back, as on the last chord of some ecstatic universal tango.

I walk out into sunlight. Sarcophagi lie about the churchyard, carelessly, their contents turned to tall grass; and it is true—death doesn't matter. An old coachman, recognizing my symptoms, proposes a ride to Sant'Apollinare in Classe. Here I see a mosaic meadow full of sheep; in Sant'Apollinare Nuovo, the sages whom Yeats called "the singing masters of my soul." By evening next to nothing remains unseen. I have taken not a single photograph. I sit by myself in the hotel dining room, brimming with insights, free associations that sparkle my way from remote crevices of the past: a forest scene composed of butterfly wings from Brazil; sun rising over fish-scale wavelets; a richly iced gingerbread cottage; my grandmother's beaded evening purse, turned inside out. "Childhood is health," said Herbert, and here is mine, along with Christianity's. Merely to know that these early, glistening states are still attainable . . . ! Had Ravenna been a psychiatrist, today's hours alone would have cured me.

The next day I fill in gaps and go back to the places that struck me most. Morning light in the starry vaults of Galla Placidia show up textures piteously withered; it is like gazing upon the mummy of Ptolemy. In San Vitale, by contrast, Jesus stands waist-deep in ripples. His genitals are visible through the lucid warp. I open my notebook and begin to sketch a section of the decorative borders that, like an idealized circulatory system, here tracing a groin, there confining some pious vision to a lintel's brow, link quite a number of structural elements. Its central nerve, one golden tessera in width, bisects this blood-red passe-partout, branching at fixed intervals to create a run of alternating ovals and oblongs. These enclose perhaps a dozen tesserae apiece, just enough for the nice gradation of greens in the oblongs, blues in the ovals, to convey depth—so many gold-framed, kohl-rimmed swimming pools reduced to snuffbox size. Punctuating the spaces between pool and pool, big pearl-white colons invite the eye to pause, then move on. A second border, which parallels or diverges from this one at whim, resembles an awning of white flounces, each blazoned with a squat black cross. A third—but no matter. The profusion of motifs, their vigor by now a reflex long past thought, gives out a sense of peace and plenty in the lee of history's howling gale. It isn't the creeds or the crusades they tell of, but the relative eternity of villas, interior decoration, artisans, the centuries of intelligence in fingers not twenty years old. While empires fell offstage, these happy solutions to the timeless problems of scale and coherence stretched, like flowers to the light, wherever a patron beckoned. Palmyra lies in one direction, Addison Mizner's Palm Beach (for better or worse) in the other. Or Tiffany glass. There is no limit to the life encoded by my anthology of mosaic borders. For this morning hour in San Vitale I feel like the aborigine who can describe all the people and animals who have traveled a road, just from whatever grows along its edge.

Back in Rome, I telephoned Claude. "I'm so proud of myself," I said. "I did it!"—no sooner realizing that he might be hurt by what I was about to imply than not caring if he was. He of course, I went on, had been living that way most of his life. And while even I had been known to go to the opera by myself—did that explain why I loved it so?—I'd never believed, never trusted, never been told what rapture solitude could be in a place like Ravenna. The sheer hours on end of *seeing*, of never having to exchange remarks or keep looking around in case one's companion was bored—why, it made all the difference in the world. "Like a note struck once," I finished, "that turns suddenly into a trill. To be *alive* and *alone* . . . !"

"I know," said Claude gently. "It's so sad."

Scripture and fiction are full of nicely opposed brothers; why shouldn't life be? At Ravenna the decorative elements moved me to tears, whereas Charles would have exclaimed "Tiens!" on reading in the guide that Charlemagne had built a replica of San Vitale in Aachen, and agreed with those visitors who valued the basilican purity and thrust of Sant'Apollinare in Classe above the pastoral charm of its mosaics. He would have been more interested yet in what it was like to grow up in such a town, in schools and labor unions, employment rates and the chances of survival for a chamber music society. He would have gone out of his way to meet the priest or the podestà over a lunch I'd have sat squirming through. Perhaps his being a family man, with five clever children, caused him to focus, wherever he went, upon community issues rather than the natural or artistic splendors of the place. In my view these concerns held one back; it was important to travel light. But where, if it came to that, were we all going, and what was the big hurry?

William James once described Henry as his "younger and shallower and vainer brother," and that is how I tend to see myself next to Charles. A devout pragmatist, he founded a school (Commonwealth, in Boston) where the lessons of history were paramount. Here students met their opposite numbers from Poland or Ghana, sang the "Lord Nelson" Mass, and learned to draw their own conclusions about Job, Mao, capitalism, and the right to die. Years later they would speak of him with reverence. He has gone on missions of mercy to far corners of the earth and worked for understanding between blacks and whites.

Among countless low-profile good deeds, he helped with the renovation of the Graz state theater. (His reward? A festive luncheon at the motorcycle factory.) My brother writes voluminously still, always in longhand, the burden involved but graspable, his whole message behind every word. I have done none of these things. Low on public spirit, without "ideas" in his sense of the word, or should I say ever leerier of their frontal presentation, in writing I have resorted, after the first scrawled phrases, to keyboards of increasing complexity, moving from Olivetti to Selectric III, from Ouija to this season's electronic wizard. Now each morning, risen like Kundry in Parsifal with a shriek and a shudder to do my Klingsor's bidding, I make for the arcane, underworld glow of a little screen. Presently minimal bits of information, variable within strict limits, like the tesserae of a mosaic, flicker and reassemble before my eyes. As best I can—here slubbing an image, there inverting a hypothesis—I set about clothing the blindingly nude mind of my latest master. Line after line wavers in and out of sense, transpositive, loose-ended, flimsy as gossamer, until a length of text is at last woven tightly enough to resist unmaking. Then only do I see what I had to say.

Soon after my return from Rome I settled down. With David Jackson it was easy to renounce New York and its pitfalls for the stabler routines of life in Stonington. My New York friends— like Robert or Hubbell—complained that I'd let myself be "taken out of circulation." How could I give up the music, the exhibits, the midnight suppers? In truth I asked nothing better. I'd seen so many paintings, heard so many operas—fuir, là-bas, fuir! It was time to get to work.

We were both writing novels, David on a table in the kitchen, I on a sideboard under the tin dome of the dining room we'd painted flame red, perhaps to placate the powers that one day, such was our delight in the old wooden building, might set it ablaze. (Sages standing in God's holy fire? Each time we left we shut our manuscripts in the refrigerator.) We had a record-player, a rowboat, a brass bed, but few invitations and no telephone. Just then, when life had never been more fulfilling, the genetic angel, as in a parody of the Annunciation, struck. What was this—nearly thirty and not yet a father! If through childlessness I'd been spitefully putting my parents in their place, parenthood would put me in theirs; how else to make peace between the generations? But I had better act quickly lest I be too old to enjoy my children. (David's marriage, unrewarding to both parties, though his wife was now our best friend, had cured him of any such nonsense.)

In real distress I relived that Easter in Graz, with Charles and Mary, the restless play of growing limbs and minds, the heart-stopping repose of moonlit sleepers glimpsed through open doors. And now Freddy wrote that he'd fallen in love; soon he would be on his way. With no mother lined up for my child, I began to look, willy-nilly, at the local females. Was that tomboy divorcée still fertile? What about the teenage daughter of new friends, whom David was teaching how to drive? Anxiety swept me. Dr Detre, by then conveniently in New York, felt that "settling down" was itself the issue; young men like us didn't belong in resorts for the idle or retired. He made a few suggestions (go back to teaching, don't spend so much time by yourselves), and the crisis passed. Another summer, and the house had filled up—not quite what Dr Detre had in mind—with Ephraim and Company, who were prepared, like children, to take up as much of our time as we cared to give, but whose conversation outsparkled Ravenna, and who never had to be washed or fed or driven to their school basketball games.

XVII
Claude plans to leave Rome.
Visiting Umberto.
The Piero Resurrection.

CLAUDE HAD ME to lunch. It was a lovely spring day. His French windows, open onto tiny balconies, overlooked the Piazza di Spagna six flights below. Quinta presided in a cheerfully visible kitchen—how unlike mine—and the round table had been set for three. Above it hung a mobile of wire and wooden balls, vaguely planetary, a new addition. I'd seen his apartment just once before but felt greeted by things I recognized, above all by the serenity they achieved under his roof, which my own unruly belongings could never aspire to. The books stood in thoughtful order, a little Murano vase I'd given him held a fresh flower, the Olivetti slept like a parrot beneath its patterned kerchief next to the densely typed pages of Claude's vast, ongoing journal. Over a glass of wine we talked of Ravenna. Out came a book on the mosaics I might like to borrow. Alice had written; she was well and said I owed her a letter. They were doing *I Puritani* next month at the opera—had I ever heard it? I understood: he was treating me as a guest. I glanced again at the third table setting and waited for the doorbell to ring. Or did the new person already have his own key?

"It's gone on ten months," Claude was saying in his diffident murmur, but with a merry twinkle. "We've agreed that the end's in sight."

What had I missed? It was unlike him to talk so openly of a failed romance, but I supposed he had Dr Detre to thank for this new, rather callous frankness. Ten months? So the affair had begun while we were still together, soon after our move to Rome. Feeling wronged in retrospect, I asked—since I had to say something—if "he" was Italian.

Claude stared. "I don't understand."

"Your friend of these last ten months . . . ?"

"I was talking about my analysis, about Tom," said Claude, still puzzled. (He called Dr Detre Tom, just as he used *tu*, like a true Italian, when speaking to Quinta—with whom I had locked myself into the formal *Lei*.) "The year he'd originally estimated is nearly up. I forgot an appointment the other day. It's a classic sign that the patient is ready to move on. But you thought—" As the nature and implications of my mistake dawned on him, Claude broke into uneasy laughter. The doorbell rang.

Quinta admitted a frail, black-haired young man, who greeted her familiarly. Claude introduced him as Jorge, an artist from Peru. His was the assemblage of hoops and spheres that hung above us as we sat down to lunch. At once I liked it less. I found Jorge plain, his deferential manners at odds with my latest notion of table-talk on a sunny day. Of course he and Claude were lovers; the lunch had been arranged to make this clear. Was he the "best Claude could do" in Rome? It pleased my vanity to think so, and to remind itself that Robert would soon be returning; the part of me that wished Claude well was depressed.

Not that I was entitled to show any of this. Love had once allowed us to read each other in the dark. Now the psychic lens opening had contracted; we must let what could be made out by friendship's plain daylight guide us, without reference to that secret nocturnal terrain we no longer stumbled through. Here a more exciting thought broke in. If Dr Detre was planning to send Claude home—cured!—in six or eight more weeks, wouldn't my own term end shortly thereafter? I decided not to ask the doctor this question; it would have been like glancing at one's watch during the salad course. Nor did I intend to bring up my impressions of Jorge lest, like Montale, he dissolve on closer inspection into Dr Detre himself. Whose precise, amused voice I could hear already: ". . . this yellow-faced foreigner Claude has been seeing secretively, who has replaced you at the center of his life." I didn't need to be told by my shrink that I'd been chafing under his schedule. After Ravenna, I wanted to visit new places by myself and taste the drug of solitude in each of them. And for the first time in months, at the risk of sapping the creative energy I was expected to bring to our analytical work, I found myself fiddling with a poem. It began with some negatives of photographs I'd taken of Robert and ended by returning him—or "her," as convention dictated—to the status of a perfect stranger:

> Here where no image sinks to truth
> And the black sun kindles planets in noon air
>
> The lover leads a form eclipsed, opaque,
> Past a smoked-glass parterre
> Towards the first ghostliness he guessed in her . . .

Quinta's *risotto primavera* was delicious. I mentioned my forthcoming weekend in Cortona. ("It is now officially spring," Umberto had said in his deep drone, "and the rooms are no longer freezing.") "You will be near Arezzo," said Jorge, "where the great Piero della Francesca frescos are. Have you ever seen them? For me he is the supreme Italian painter." I had not; I knew Piero's works chiefly from photographs. Marilyn had visited the famous *Flagellation*— "In Urbino," said Jorge reverently, and began to enumerate the other Pieros, peasant madonnas and farmboy saints, rendered with a dispassion itself amounting to saintliness, which studded central Italy like solitary gems, while Claude gazed fondly at him, pleased that our talk was giving his friend a chance to shine. Although these things were worth hearing, Jorge's account of them struck me as wooden and impersonal. What, I wondered not without slyness, was the best book on Piero? The dim young man named it eagerly; it was the source of his passion; no more than I had he stood before the paintings themselves. Claude's eyes now met mine in a brief, intensely neutral look. "You and I may feel," the look said, "that it is pitiful to boast of secondhand knowledge; nevertheless Innocence is as precious as Experience, and I will thank you not to snub my friend." I felt the justice of a reprimand that must have been made more than once on my behalf, when Claude was my lover and I rattled mindlessly or tipsily on. So the luncheon party left a sour aftertaste.

Umberto met me at the Cortona station. A sunburnt man of forty, introduced as Mario, drove us uphill in the tiniest conceivable Fiat. Each summer of his childhood, Umberto explained, ox-drawn wagons would move the entire household—people and bedding and so forth—from the winter house in town to the purer air of the "country" place five kilometers away. Mario turned down a long tree-shaded drive and stopped on gravel in front of a façade three stories high. The house looked suitably old, of mottled gray-gold stucco, with green shutters and a quaint escutcheon: the head, in relief, of a blackamoor—for *Morra*—above a date in the 1760s. The front door, framed with green and red stained-glass panes, opened into a cool, frescoed parlor I was given no time to study. While Mario took my suitcase, Umberto led me—past (good heavens) a sedan chair and a stuffed bear rearing seven feet tall in the stairwell—to the kitchen, where a couple of children fled our approach and Mario's . . . sister? wife? mother? bowed us onward. "There is someone here who expects to meet my guests as soon as they arrive," said Umberto.

In a sunny chair outside the kitchen door sat an old party of considerable presence. His features, above a knitted cardigan, wore the noble, sclerotic bloodlessness of a bust. One big inert hand lay tucked along his thigh. The other took mine in a marble grip. Words of welcome surged from the living half of his face. "This is Tonino," said Umberto, leaving me prey, as we returned indoors, to wild conjectures. Had they been lovers long ago, when Umberto was a student and Tonino a . . . gamekeeper? E. M. Forster would have known what to make of the situation. I did not.

I'd noticed, in the kitchen garden where Tonino sat, an outbuilding on whose plaster wall trompe-l'oeil fruit trees had been painted. Back in the house similar touches came to light. A small barrel-vaulted library had been made into a tent of pale red-and-white hangings. A ceiling upstairs dissolved into the heaven of a sun-beamed attic storeroom. The dining room walls were painted with broad stripes of lime and silver, to simulate wallpaper; while those of the little parlor through which guests came and departed, and where Umberto and I sat over aperitif or camomile, had been enthusiastically decorated with a ruined pyramid, a stone sphinx, a pair of lovers on a pedestal, all in a landscape of hills and lakes and blue willow trees. The chairs we sat on were covered in pretty (patriotic?) stripes of red and green and ivory cut velvet, but so old that the threadbare, tattered fabric had now to be stitched back into place after every washing. Under a hanging lamp the round table at the center of the room was piled with books and international periodicals; I had never in my life seen such absorbing clutter—that is, until I entered the formal drawing room upstairs. Here, along with draperies, vast mirrors, sofas and chandelier, a larger round table, piled higher yet with culture, stood a seven-pedaled ottocento piano. A forest of photographs on its lid could hardly be seen for the family trees they faintly but imperiously summoned up: Savoy, Romanov, Hohenzollern. Not for me to recognize the crests on the frames, or ask—we Americans having evolved beyond all this twaddle of rank and royalty—who that tiaraed beauty was, or that fat-faced child wearing a toque of pearls.

One small room downstairs—between the parlor and the dining room—was hideous beyond description. Heavy, turn-of-the-century furniture that looked machine-made, dried grasses, glassed cabinets jammed with medals and bibelots, surrounded a full-length life-size portrait of a man in uniform. A tapestried stool in front of it invited the guest to kneel. Curiosity at last banishing my republican feelings, I asked Umberto if this was his father. "That is the King," he replied. "Or *was* the King."

"Your family knew him?"

"My father was a general, in charge of, well, regiments, campaigns. Later, an ambassador. I believe they were on rather close terms."

"Do you remember him?"

"The King? No. I was a baby when he died."

"Was this . . . Victor Emmanuel?"

"The son of Victor Emmanuel. Umberto."

"Oh? Then you were named for him!"

Umberto gave his helpless drone of amused constraint. "Well, that is one way of putting it. In fact mine will have been, to all intents and purposes, a family name. . . ."

Mario put on a white jacket to serve our dinner: broth, an omelet with vegetables, stewed fruit, and a carafe of stunningly bad wine, which Umberto knew to pass up but for the single tablespoon stirred into his broth. We saw each other so regularly in Rome that I was no longer shy in his company, yet I still couldn't be sure what interested him or how much he wanted to know about me. At least he himself enjoyed talking, and without his in any sense holding forth, I heard a good deal about Berenson, Edith Wharton, Salvemini, and others. Here in Cortona he had quite a circle of friends, many foreign; a few were coming to dinner the following evening. We might go into town next morning to see the Signorellis; not painting of supreme interest, still . . . His hands sketched a gesture of modest pride: in so rural a backwater, what could one offer but these cultural equivalents of fresh eggs and milk straight from the cow? I asked if anything by Piero della Francesca lay within a reasonable radius. "Ah," he smiled, "you give me an idea."

Back in the parlor, over our camomile, I mentioned that Robert Isaacson would be returning in a couple of weeks to stay through the summer in Via Quattro Novembre. Umberto blushed—with pleasure *for* me, I somehow felt—and said I must be sure to bring him along on my next visit. As we parted for the night he took my hand in both of his and wished me *buon riposo*. I fell asleep wondering if I could find my way to his bedroom and how my barefoot presence there would be received.

The next morning it was all arranged. Mario was driving us to Sansepolcro, where Umberto had a brief but long-deferred errand and we could see the Piero *Resurrection* before lunch. Arezzo would have been a shorter excursion, but then we'd have needed more time to study the frescos, so it worked out. The masterpiece awaiting us at our drive's end had yet to be properly installed after spending the war in a bomb shelter; its own provisional resurrection, Umberto remarked before leaving me alone with it, was quite as moving in its way as that of the central figure. Banner in hand, one foot on the rim of his sarcophagus, Christ was climbing back into the world. I tried my best to see through Freddy's light-filled eyes, while summoning to my own lips Freddy's faint inward smile, this haggard, glaring adult. It didn't work. After the green-and-gold childhood of faith, glimpsed at Ravenna, so stark an embodiment of its maturity left me cold. Deep down I feared that Jesus and I, both, had reached our zenith as children and that I would be hard put to avoid a terminal phase shot through, like his, by showmanship and self-promotion.

Weren't those, however, among the traits I saw Jesus as sharing with the artists I most admired? Like Baudelaire he had a weakness for loose women. Like Mallarmé he enthralled and mystified his disciples; like Oscar Wilde, courted ruin at the height of his fame. Like Proust he had dipped, with miraculous consequences, a cookie into a restorative cup. These figures—themselves moved in rare, subliminal ways by his example—moved me immoderately; why not Our Savior? Well, it is one thing for an artist to behave like a god. How many charming and eloquent young men have we not seen idealized, exploited, "crucified" at last by their power to attract a large audience? (In my youthful poems I was already taking measures to keep this from happening to me.) But when a god behaves like an artist—! I might gladly have accepted Christ as a kind of living ideogram for the imagination, a spark of godhood breathed upon in each of us. In the Sistine Chapel's *Last Judgment*, the central dancing figure, like the great marble arm detached from the same artist's unfinished *Pietà*, was pure Apollonian radiance. What chilled me was the (so to speak) movie version of that supreme fiction. Pulpits the world over urged it upon the whole family. Stills from it hung in a thousand museums, luridly fleshing out the leading man's looks and attitudes and—always the thorn in my side—history. How to disown one's mother, fulfill prophecies, hypnotize crowds, and serve oneself up to the cannibalistic instincts of the tribe weren't, I hoped, the things I lay on Dr Detre's couch in order to learn. What then: to love my neighbor as myself? Well and good; but that meant figuring out how to love myself without, for once, a lover—human or divine—to make the difference. While these ideas hovered just out of reach, I went on studying Piero's *Resurrection* avidly, storing up the precious painterly touches that compensated, if anything did, for so grim and "significant" a subject.

Yet it was a subject that seemed to elude an American couple who had joined me in front of the Piero when Umberto returned from his errand. "Excuse me," said the husband, making signs of recognition. "Count Morra? We met last year in Basel at the XYZ conference. This picture—what does it mean? Is it a story we should know?" Umberto rose to the occasion; indeed, he said, Piero's "unidealistic" view of Christ might easily puzzle the pilgrim, and so on—assuming, as a man of the world and against all evidence, that his American acquaintances properly valued the myth at the heart of the Western world. Intelligence dawned at length upon husband and wife; yes, yes, it was all coming back: Sunday school, loaves and fishes, "on the third day," yes, thank you, they remembered now—drifting cordially away, the weight of centuries light as a feather upon them.

"That might be described as a surreal moment," Umberto said with a smile, over lunch. "Or is it a trait of the American mind to have declared its independence from Christian things? Of course Piero is a case apart; his images are not *bondieuseries*. And I am not a 'believer,' " he went on, with a headshake of self-deprecation for standing perversely outside the fold. "Even so, religion like poetry being an almost irresistible form of hearsay, it is hard to envision a world in no way nourished by these grand rumors."

I didn't mean to waste my weekend with a father-figure of rare sweetness like Umberto, complaining about somebody else's son. Yet if there *was* a God, I ventured, it seemed to me that I would have to be His child no less than Jesus was, and the idea of needing an older sibling or "mediator" in order to approach my parent struck me as offensive if not absurd. Did that count as an American trait? Umberto's laugh showed his brown teeth. "Rilke," he said, blushing now for unavoidably dropping another name, "once compared it to trying to reach the Almighty by telephone, only to keep getting the operator. *Allora*." He made a sign to the waiter, and the subject was closed; neither of us cared to agree further upon matters about which it was seemlier not to have spoken at all.

The party that evening included a young French diplomat who had a house nearby, a Swiss musicologist, and a professor of history who had come down from Turin to spend a few days with Umberto. Close to him in years, the Professore looked ageless as an elf; his blue eyes sparkled in a face like a fresh rose. I joined him the next morning after breakfast for a walk up and down the long alley of trees and heard—after months of vain conjecture—a great deal about our mutual friend. For instance, he had spent his earliest years in St Petersburg, where his father was *en poste*; the Czar was his godfather. (Would he and Mina have met at a party for diplomatic children?) Umberto had gone on to do brilliant scholarly work in his youth; had translated Voltaire and Trevelyan; been a protégé of Berenson's; was presently writing an extremely valuable memoir of the young socialist Piero Gobbetti, dead at twenty-five. Umberto's infirmity resulted *not* (my companion emphasized) from throwing himself in front of a carriage in order to avoid military service, as rumored in certain quarters, but rather from a tubercular hip in childhood. His stamina was nonetheless remarkable. In 1943, on the eve of Italy's surrender, he had gone *on foot* from Rome to Naples in order to make the vital liaison between the Italian antifascists and the Allied forces. He had stood on a balcony with General Mark Clark and megaphoned the terms of peace to the crowd below. Absorbing and admirable as these facts were, I'd hoped for something juicier, less journalistic.

"I can't get over this house," I said. "Has anything been done to it in the past fifty years?" "No," the Professore laughed. "A twinge of electricity—nothing more. And closer to one hundred years than fifty. Umberto's mother, you see, died young. This was his family's place. In the normal course of things the bride would have done it over from top to bottom.

But all she got round to was that little chamber of horrors dedicated to the King. The rest is a time capsule from the preceding generation, when *I Promessi Sposi* was the best-seller and 'Eri Tu' led the Hit Parade." The Professore began humming the famous aria from *Un Ballo in Maschera*. His words set in motion a train of thought that lurched from a king's friend and his faithless wife to the old invalid, so much nobler in aspect than Umberto, sunning himself outside the kitchen door.

"And Tonino? Does he go back to the beginning too?"

"Ah, Tonino," said the Professore. "I presume he is a kind of relative. Have I been indiscreet? Hadn't we better turn back?"

Until his death eight years ago, Umberto's was the house I returned to most regularly in Europe, either alone or with an array of companions as dear and diverse as David Kalstone, Grace Stone, and Strato. It never occurred to me that any part of my life needed to be hidden from this kind friend. Not long after my return to America, Umberto and my father both found themselves in New York, and I asked them to dinner together. I dreamed up, for the occasion, an appetizer of shrimp with orange-garlic sauce, in whose polite rejection, if in nothing else, they were unanimous. (Alice put it in one of her cookbooks, though; to my recipe she suggested adding, before serving, a tablespoon of warmed curaçao.) On his next visit my mother gave a party for Umberto in Atlanta. Whatever his view of these meetings, they gratified me no end. My parents could hardly fail to be impressed by the priceless human antique I'd acquired abroad for next to nothing.

David Jackson and I stayed with Umberto when he ran the Italian Institute in London. He visited us in Athens. He was cordial to our lovers and courtly to the Alexandrians who'd taken us up. I can see him now at a party, bending an ear to little eye-fluttering Mika, a fifth highball clutched in her bird claw. Sudden panic crosses her face: does this Italian man of letters expect her to broach a topic? "Ah," she giggles instead, "you're so sexy—yum-yum-yum!" In an article about his trip Umberto evoked these ladies as having emerged "stanche e sfatte"—tired and unmade—from the pages of Lawrence Durrell.

His tolerance for people unlike himself—indeed, his attraction to them—underlay his friendship with Grace Stone. Grace was the most cosmopolitan of our Stonington neighbors. Formed like me by exposure to opera at a dangerously young age—open on her piano still lay a tattered score of Manon with one-word appraisals of each aria ("ravissante" . . . "exquise" . . . "parfaite") in her schoolgirl hand—she had gone on, as a navy wife, to break hearts from Paris to Shanghai. Umberto was an easy, platonic conquest, dating from those last Roman winters, when her sight was failing. His letters to her, which one summer afternoon I was asked to read aloud as respite from Don Juan or the Odyssey, were virtual declarations of love for her charm and courage, qualities he wrongly feared were lacking in himself. The affection was mutual, though tinged by snobbery on Grace's side. From her I learned that Umberto, according to Roman gossip, was not only the old King's namesake but his son by the wife of his trusted friend, the general and ambassador-to-be. People still spoke of our friend's uncanny resemblance to the King.

"Umberto must know—or does he?" I wondered, thinking of the portrait in that hideous parlor. Ah, Grace breathed, exhaling smoke and taking on the aspect of the famous novelist she had once been, who knew what Umberto knew?

As for Tonino, gossip had it that he was the general's son by a peasant girl.

"Umberto's half-brother . . . ?"

"Well, no," said Grace. "That's just the point. No relation at all. It's the world of Beaumarchais—false identities and the droit de seigneur. In our world Tonino would have been half black and Umberto a corpse at Gettysburg. They arrange these things better abroad."

If Umberto knew himself to be the subject of such unblushing speculation, he gave no sign. "Wax to receive and marble to retain," his friendship, once bestowed, was never withdrawn. On his last, brief trip to Washington and New York, a man in his seventies who by then navigated with extreme discomfort, he had gone hours out of his way to spend an afternoon alone with Ben Johnson in the Veterans Hospital outside Boston, where Ben was dying of lung cancer. When Umberto was dying, Mario and his family overflowed the corridors of the clinic. Umberto left the wonderful house to them.

Visiting Umberto one chilly April when he was still in his low-ceilinged "winter quarters" downstairs, I was given the master bedroom, a dim white cavern, all pillars and mirrors and hangings. A tidy brazier in a wooden frame—the "priest," as it was known—had been slipped between my sheets to warm them. Alone in the huge lumpy bed of a man I loved, I remembered the night in Southampton when I'd insisted, at seven, on being allowed to sleep with my father. (He and my mother had lately moved into separate bedrooms.) Neither of us shut an eye; I lay awake till dawn—when Emma, peeking in, beckoned me back to my room—marveling at my situation and waiting in vain for the pajamaed form tossing and groaning at my side to place a soothing hand upon me. In Umberto's bed, finally, I slept like a child.

My bedroom wallpaper in Southampton was a hypnotic tangle of vines on which sat elves dressed in olive or puce. Above the bed hung two pictures: one, a manger scene all radiance and oxen and wise men; its companion, a Jesus no older than I, in a white nightie, alone and barefoot on a woodland path. His smile promised safe-conduct through that forest not yet Dantesque, and after my prayers I fell asleep watched over by the adorable little boy overhead.

To run Christ down in later life, as I'd done that day with Umberto, gave me no satisfaction. What prompted such talk? An intricate campaign of disenchantment, set off by the changing of my wallpaper. A romantic couple—"boy in gray" and crinolined belle—beside a cannon, the Stars and Bars unfurled above, one summer replaced the elves. Jesus ascended to the attic. No more make-believe, the message read; history would be my fate from then on. The red-blooded boys of Southampton were expected to serve unreturnably fast balls in tennis, not Our Lord. Certain white-haired English teachers in tears over the Victorian poets confirmed the impression of a creed outworn. By the time my mother (with no justification in the Gospels that I ever found) called on Christ's teachings to straighten me out sexually, or Freddy's novels made their pitch for his gentling presence in our lives, the damage had been done. I'd thrown the baby out with the churchly bathwater. But "there is no purification without myth"—Jan Kott. Of late Peter cannot stop talking about his month in a Trappist monastery ("High time I gave myself the silent treatment"), nor Jerl about the rehabilitation center for victims of early sexual abuse, where he recently visited his lover. There the therapeutic sessions concentrated upon the Inner Child, a self-image of helpless innocence in each of us, that never deserved its rough treatment at the world's grown-up hands. Listening to Jerl, I've tried to picture my own Inner Child—and who but the smiling towheaded Jesus on the threshold of the forest springs to mind? I'm sixty-six; second childhood plucks at my sleeve. Time to make peace not only with that little boy who may, for all I know, have seen me through the glooms and forking paths of the middle years but with the man he became on its far side. Some nights I even say a prayer to him.

217

XVIII *Reunion with Robert.*
Regression with Rolf.
Auden unmet.

Woken from a heavy sleep, I seem to have grown a new set of arms and legs. A voice—my own?—is murmuring my name. These novel proliferations have time to both worry and comfort me before I decode them: Robert returned yesterday, and I will never be lonely again. Rome's cup, as well, has begun to overflow. Summer's here. Hubbell is taking us to Ostia for a noon picnic. And Robert expects Rolf— his onetime lover—to pass through a month hence, on his way to photograph bright-eyed urchins in the Blue Grotto. "Such a German idea of a holiday," Robert snorted, draining his glass at the restaurant, earlier. He was groggy from the long flight but looked wonderful—tanned, flushed, eyes sparkling into mine. Now in the narrow bed I shift gingerly, inhale his skin and hair, give thanks for the weight of his head on my arm. Together we sink back into sleep.

The separation has been hard on him. His grandfather's death, the lawyers, his mother's state of mind—Robert is the only child. But he withstood every inducement to stay at home; the thought of Rome, of joining me and prolonging—as we all were doing—the magic glow of a life not fully answerable to the grownups' world, kept him sane. As during our first weeks, I've given in to the charm of loving "myself" in the person of another. The likeness is no longer chiefly physical, although a cluster of similar impulses and reactions, shrugs and smiles, sleights of mind and turns of phrase, once made it seem so. Hubbell as well—despite airs distinctly more mannered than ours—partakes of the family resemblance. The way fledgling artists write a manifesto and start a "movement," or like the generic movie star of the twenties—blonde, enigmatic, with a suspicion of baby fat, before fate transforms her into Garbo or Dietrich, Elisabeth Bergner or Carole Lombard—each in his fashion lends himself to an image of the elegant young gay man of the period. This composite figure has a stylish assurance none of us will attain as individuals for some time. Not that twenty or thirty years later the style in question still seems worth trying for; but we bear its scars, like an old face-lift.

The style may have derived originally from the manners of our divorced mothers at the bridge table or at dinners where it behooved them to sparkle; also from the assumption, in America at least, that a boy can do better than to grow up like his old man. Yet it's the paternal note I miss—if I miss anything—with Robert and Hubbell at Ostia, on sand so exactly the shade and texture of our mixed pepper-and-salt in its wax-paper nest that we dip our rubbery eggs more than once into the wrong condiment. Our topics are those usually classed as feminine—personalities, culture, "dirt"; our mode is telegraphic and face-tious. Lacking is the restraint of sons who have looked to their fathers for emblems of conduct. Yet our flapping sallies and diamond veerings need some such centerboard to keep them on course, to remind us that the world is periodically real and life now and then a serious business. Well, I can always get back in touch with Luigi—*he* would eat that last sandwich! But no, what I dream of is what I never had from Luigi: a steadying male presence who, finding in me elements of both mate and child, would bind himself to me sexually, for a while.

"Sex between men is by its character frustrating," Dr Detre said. "The anus is full of shit; the mouth is a well of flattery and untruth. The honest penis is left with no reliable place to go."

Embarrassed, I studied the ceiling.

"It might be worth considering," he went on, "that this masculine self you crave is available within you, only you have not accepted the power to harm that goes with it."

"Must one do harm in order to be a man?"

"You seem to have received that impression."

"From . . . ?"

"A woman who, hurt and rejected, turned to you."

A woman whom I, on the beach with Robert and Hubbell, kept echoing in spite of myself. "Are you saying it's time I went out and hurt someone?"

"Not necessarily. Is there someone you wish to hurt?"

"No, but . . ." I couldn't shake the idea. "Supposing there were, though, and that I did. Would I inflict the man's kind of harm or the woman's?"

It seemed to be the ultimate question until Dr Detre took it a step further: "Or the child's?"

Robert bought a little car, which gave us new mobility. Collecting me on the bright noon pavement outside Dr Detre's building, he could whisk us out of town—to the beach, to Tarquinia or Cerveteri for the afternoon, to this or that celebrated villa or garden. One weekend we drove Umberto from his house to Lake Trasimeno, where he sat in the shade and watched us in scanty swimsuits disporting ourselves, consciously athletic, to give him something to remember. That evening our host cleared dozens of princely photographs from the seven-pedaled piano so that Robert could unlid and soothsay from its entrails, mute for generations. Equally silent was our subsequent lovemaking—just a twang from the old outraged bed, and stifled giggles as we imagined Umberto's eye glued to a secret peephole.

* * *

Like figures on a clock, our former lovers retreated and advanced. Claude was sailing home, Rolf was due any day. Claude and I dined by ourselves on the eve of his departure. Inquiring for his Peruvian friend, Jorge, I learned that he'd left Rome. "He had become totally dependent upon me," said Claude. "It was a sad, unhealthy situation." The soft reluctance in his tone called to mind how dependent I'd once been on him myself. Claude wasn't beyond bringing that out in people, through his many disciplines and convictions. The point, no doubt, would have been to develop a few of one's own. I felt a pang for poor banished Jorge, and another for Claude. Who wanted these neurotic alliances!

About his year with Dr Detre he was sad, euphoric, silly, and wise. "Absurd as it sounds," he said, "I feel equipped for a long and complex adventure." I was close enough to gaining my own freedom to know what he meant. If his plan (to join Vira in Houston, where she'd moved after the Saudi Arabian fiasco, and help run a restaurant she had, with winning resilience, opened there) didn't quite answer to the splendor of the challenge, Claude could be trusted to make the most of it.

"The future looks possible, for a change," I suggested. "Not the sheer cliff it was last summer. We've found footholds, a way to get up there."

"The process seemed so gradual," said Claude dreamily. "Almost automatic. I hardly noticed the changes until they'd taken place. Remember Psyche's tasks in Apuleius?—having to unscramble all those different grains and seeds, the lentils and millet and poppy, into separate piles. The ants do it for her. It must be the earliest allegory of psychoanalysis. I never felt Tom 'doing' anything. What happened in our sessions, from week to week, was more like the work of time than of any human agent. Dali's pocket-watch swarming with ants. I never asked him about that. Maybe you will. . . ."

We smiled and raised our glasses. Each of us had seen the other through, from start to finish—at a distance, to be sure, like mowers in neighboring fields—and those nearly parallel labors and their harvest filled us with pride. Not long ago, before Robert's return, this mutation from love to friendship had seemed to me a step down in the world. But now, "I'll really miss you," I told Claude as we wandered into the cobbled, saffron-and-indigo night. "You'll come to visit," he said. "Alone or with anyone you like." I tried to picture that house in Vermont, not as I'd seen it before, icy and stern beyond the glow of its blazing hearth, but open to all the fragrant winds of summer. We had reached my door. It was the turning-point. I wouldn't have come to Europe without him; now I was here independently—alone or with anyone I liked. "I could spend the whole night wandering through Rome," Claude was saying. "I've loved it so! Goodbye, dear Jamie." We embraced. He waved from the corner and was gone.

On Rolf's first evening Robert and I picked him up at his hotel and drove to an outdoor restaurant in Trastevere. Rolf turned out to be in his late thirties: tall, pale, soft-fleshed. He had left Germany as an adolescent, before the war, and spoke with only the hint of an accent. He wasn't a "verbal type" like Robert or me. His observations, dogged and humorless, discouraged response, as did the superior airs he gave himself. "I am a serious, somber person," Rolf's manner asserted, "not above shouldering my cameras and my backpack and striding off right now into the hills in search of the nourishment I derive neither from this *saltimbocca alla romana* nor from your bright, piss-elegant behavior." What *did* nourish Rolf? I asked Robert at the evening's end.

"Oh, you know, the elements. Sunlight, the sea, boys . . . platitudes of the *Zitronenland*—"

"Boys? Were you too old—that's why he left you?"

"Whoever said he left me? After the first months I thought I'd go mad. I was twenty, he was thirty-five. He was getting older, *I* was getting *younger.* Who wanted a father, let alone a Hamburger!"

Our other guests had left. Across the room, at the piano, Hubbell sang on in a husky undertone: "There were two little babes in the wood . . ." Marilyn sat beside him, already matronly in her happiness. She'd arrived bubbling with news: date fixed for her return, plans to marry before the year was out. Her fiancé, an art historian named Irving Lavin, had thus far figured so sketchily in her talk that I half disbelieved in him. He could, however, be inferred from her conduct. The unattached American girls we knew that year were in the throes of disastrous love affairs with Italian men. Cute little Ruth from Iowa had been caught up in a ring of young doctors who drank ether and staged orgies in the x-ray room of a respectable private clinic; close-ups of skeletal hoopla were held to the morning light in coffee bars. How sensible of Marilyn to prefer the amusement, the absolute safety of *our* company. We watched our language in front of her, treated her with brotherly fondness and respect. (Robert came and went, collecting glasses, emptying ashtrays. "Two little hearts," Hubbell sang on, "two little heads . . .") Yet it was odd to think that, all during these months, Marilyn's inner compass had been pointing towards another person—faceless to us, a mere silhouette, not unlike the self awaiting me even now at the end of the reverberating Roman tunnel.

I'd had too many cocktails. I sank down on the sofa next to Rolf.

"You've been flirting with me all afternoon," he observed quietly.

I shot him a naughty smile. "Why would I do a thing like that?"

"I don't know," he said with a look that wiped the smile from my face.

Another three days, and I thought of no one but Rolf. He spent an afternoon photographing Robert and me at the piano, then at the little skylit kitchen table, whispering behind a big palmetto fan: images of each other in our interchangeable Roman suits. His camera wooed us. Robert had learned the hard way to resist that mechanical courtship; I was powerless against it. Rolf's eye—perceiving, whichever way I turned, more new Jimmys and Jamies than a tailor's mirror—stole my soul. Qualities I'd found tiresome on our first evening I now saw as gravity, mature independence, freedom from Claude's or Kimon's bookish airs. Then, too, Rolf counted as a foreigner—better yet, my first German. "Know Your Enemy," urged posters during the war. Had I been older, had Rolf not emigrated, we might have met, soiled and battle-weary, in no-man's-land and surrendered to each other in a barbed-wire bower. The great, original attraction, I realized to my dismay, was his having been Robert's lover.

Rolf, keeping to his plan, left for Naples two nights later. At his request—and virtuously telling Robert where I was going—I dined with him before seeing him off on the night train. We went into his sleeping compartment, where Rolf put strong solemn arms round me and kissed me. "Let us meet in ten days. Give me time to get my old winter body in shape. Come with Bobby. It will be all right. You'll see." Whatever that meant.

The train pulled out, disclosing further platforms, studded with family groups. Fathers kissed their children, women wept; this, after all, was Italy. I stood by the bare tracks, unwilling to break the spell of Rolf's last look, uncertain, too, of what awaited me at home. Robert drunk and sarcastic? Robert senseless in a pool of his own blood? No; for as a train in the middle distance began pulling out, a voice I knew cried "Archie!" and a figure in nimble pursuit proffered a forgotten briefcase to a frantic golden-haired man leaning halfway from his compartment window to receive it. Mission accomplished, the sprinter turned back flushed and panting. It was Robert.

He saw me. Like mirror images, abreast but with the tracks between us, we approached a limbo where parallels dissolved, and fell into a taxi. "That was Archie Colquhoun," Robert said. He'd dropped the name in the past, but the fat old party it conjured up bore no resemblance to the Apollo on the train. "He phoned just after you went out. I had no idea he was in Rome. He was catching the sleeper to Milan, so we had dinner. Pure opera buffa there at the station: his briefcase left behind— you saw? Five years' work on Manzoni. Well. I think he saved my life tonight. . . . How about you? Rolf got off?" "Yes." "Did he kiss you?" I nodded. "Was that all?" I promised that it was. "You were lucky"—Robert laughed, facing away from on-rushing lights—"because if he'd made love to you you'd have been disgusted. Disgusted! Do you understand?" I did not; it sounded like something a writer ought to know about.

Still, it was all at a puzzling remove, like faraway things re-flected in nearby glass. Dr Detre agreed; dynamics of two or three rather different situations had come into play. In one, Robert stood for my mother. Assured of love from this quarter, I nonetheless needed a father and saw one in Rolf; had for that matter seen one in Archie, as though any man my lover ran after couldn't fail to set fantasies in motion. Or else I was my father's own son, never more loyal to an old flame than when a new one beckoned. Finally, at some level wasn't I my mother as well, and Robert the child neglected in favor of a demanding, all-too-familiar intruder? It took me two hours on the couch to figure that much out.

"Do not forget," added Dr Detre, "that Robert has thus far been primarily an image of yourself, an innocent, vulner-able self, whom you are this week subjecting to an ingenious punishment."

"Punishing myself—him? What for . . . ?"

Time, which for the moment had run out, would tell.

* * *

Robert and I joined Rolf in Naples. He'd said it would be all right? He was wrong. We sailed for Ischia, sitting on deck in bursts of spray; the waves were gunfire-bright. Ten days of beach life had left Rolf looking handsomer than he'd been in Rome. Back and forth we talked, saying whatever came to mind, seeking each other's eyes. Robert sat between us, taking swigs from a bottle of whiskey. At one point he deliberately stubbed out a cigarette onto his bare calf. "Oh, don't!" I cried, appalled, but he looked past me and shrugged. So did Rolf, who then rose to stroll down the deck. He seemed used to Robert's self-destructive behavior; in his day he must have provoked enough of it himself. As I gazed after him desire scorched, leaving a stench of fear and distaste. The stew it had taken me all that time to prepare was suddenly inedible. I touched Robert's arm. Why didn't he and I stay on board, return to Naples, leave Rolf behind forever? But things had gone too far for easy amends. Robert stared as though a stranger had spoken. "What can you be thinking of?" he inquired in clipped, withering tones. "Are you trying to spoil our holiday?"

So we did our time on Ischia. In those years, W. H. Auden was that island's Prospero—invisible to us, though a compatriot of Rolf's, joining us for dinner on the terrace of the *pensione*, repeated this season's gossip about the increasingly eccentric genius. Many bottles of wine had glazed over the miseries of the day. "But I mean!" I cried, adopting Robert's huffiest voice under the tipsy impression that any note of solidarity would please him. "Auden really goes too far. In New York he wears his carpet slippers to the opera, with a dinner jacket. Being a great poet doesn't excuse that sort of affectation. Of course I've barely met him, so it's not for me to say . . ." (trailing off into pettish inaudibility).

Rolf was looking at me with delight. "You're a great mimic," he laughed. "You've got Bobby down to a T."

I turned to my friend in dismay. I hadn't meant—! (Or had

I?) But Robert's gaze was fixed elsewhere. "I wish I could see Wystan," he said.

"You know Auden?" asked the German.

"Would I call him Wystan if I didn't? But it's not because he is famous or in order to make fun of his slovenliness behind his back that I want to see him but because he is a kind man who can put me in touch with a priest. I mean to receive communion tomorrow morning."

"Oh, no," Rolf groaned. "You're not still going through that old religious crisis? Spare us, please!"

Although I'd seen Robert's odd behavior in churches we visited for their art, I tended to dismiss his bobbings and crossings as reflexes more worldly than virtuous—when in Rome, and so forth—and secretly wished for the style to get away with them myself. But any port in a storm. Why not find Robert a priest? I'd found a psychiatrist. It was, however, too late to seek out Mr Auden this evening; he was famous for retiring, said Rolf's friend, on the stroke of nine.

"Can't you just show up at a confessional before the service?" I asked.

"Of course he can. Anyone can." Rolf chuckled. "The Church would go bankrupt otherwise." He winked at me good-naturedly, as if his presence were sunshine.

"It all depends," said Robert, answering my question, "on the gravity of the sin you're confessing."

"Is yours so very grave?"

"No, I suppose not. A bagatelle, now that you ask." He looked into my eyes for the first time in hours. "I've wished I were dead."

"Oh, what are you saying?" I moaned.

"I'm saying that if we treated our bodies the way we treat our souls, none of us would live past twenty."

There was a circle in the Inferno for the violent against themselves. Must I confirm Robert in his misery by assenting to his theology? Sin be damned. To feel for my friend it was enough to recall my own jealousy when Hans and Seldon showed up together at Maggie Teyte's Amherst concert—only neither Hans nor Seldon had ever returned my love. That both Rolf and I had returned Robert's made his corner of the triangle— to say the least—pinch more acutely. One soprano led to another: I thought of the deranged heroine of last month's *Puritani*, so ravishingly sung by an ungainly newcomer named Callas that I went to all three performances. "*Ah, rendetemi la speme o lasciatemi morire!*"—give me back my hope or let me die! Over and over the piteous refrain rose and fell, while two baritones with swords and lace collars wished they had acted better. A needle on my dial registered in decibels the pain I'd caused. But on a nearby wavelength someone quite different was jazzily bewailing his lost opportunity to find out what made Rolf so "disgusting" as a lover, and blaming Robert for making a fuss.

Dr Detre saw my behavior as "regressive"—that of the child I feared I would no longer be after therapy. "This trick," he said, "of stealing from your lovers someone to whom they are or once were attracted, you and Robert have already played on Claude. Try not to get into a rut."

In short, I wasn't as far along as he'd thought at Easter. Did he mean I wouldn't be through by August? Well, he replied, perhaps October; certainly November. Hearing this, I felt like a child indeed—kept after school—and said so.

"All the more reason to get on with the assignment," said Dr Detre.

A stubborn silence. Then, with many pauses between one unit of insight and the next: "You said I was punishing Robert; that sounds right. . . . But why? . . . Strange how soon I lost interest—had I cared for Rolf at all? Robert was the one I . . . Perhaps I cultivated our mirror likeness because, left to myself, I'd never have attracted anyone . . . like the orchid in Proust, masquerading as a bee. . . . When Rolf lit on me, I was able to punish Robert for . . . loving me? For being like me himself?"

"Put it simply: to punish both yourself and him for being homosexual," said Dr Detre with his flair for the last word.

The house I return to most regularly in America is Claude's. Its rooms remain of a gleaming, exemplary bareness, the books high-minded and intently read. The sad truth is that I shall never live up to him—he who has no more than one lover at a time; who seldom travels farther than thirty miles from home, and then only to meet his students at Bennington; who, exchanging his recorder for a shakuhachi, came back from Kyoto a Buddhist. By now he looks like one, rotund and roseate, eyes alert under heavy lids, a loose, much-mended kimono sashed round him: Zenmaster Time's favorite pupil. Visiting him is restorative. For chronic complaints like my weakness for a new face and the resulting guilty sense of

> Love, too frequently betrayed
> For some plausible desire
> Or the world's enchanted fire

my old friend dispenses, if not exactly comfort, a twinkling tonic all his own. "A little pain never hurt anyone," it isn't beyond him to remark, or "The fire begs to be played with"— quoting a sutra? I wouldn't know. (The lines quoted above, by the way, are Auden's, from The Rake's Progress.) I climb the stairs to bed with a lighter heart. Waking at Claude's—alone or with David, or with Peter—I blink up at a ceiling blanker than any mirror, and slowly, peacefully calculate how old I am this year.

It should go without saying that my early dismissal of Auden had to do with his being so openly homosexual—an impression based not so much on any active naughtiness, or the relative chastity of his voice in print, as upon the reported promiscuity of his talk. Invoking "Miss God" or referring to himself as "your mother," he must, I see now, have chosen his listeners with care. Nowadays, of course, in my young friend Jerl's eyes, letting one's hair down is a political act, a step towards reality, self-esteem, and enlightened legislation. But thirty years ago gay idiom (unless one was abroad, where it was risky fun to assume that the natives didn't understand or one's fellow tourists eavesdrop) served as a deshabille to be slipped into behind closed doors. In this it resembled shoptalk. The Wystan who held forth at blissful length about poetry and opera in a seminar would have sat mum with distaste in those literary cafés where public impersonation of the stereotype is taken for the real thing. To the artist a closet is quite as useful as it once was to the homosexual: what John Hollander calls, in the lingo of spy thrillers, a cover life, allowing us to get on with our true work as secret agents for the mother tongue—a phrase itself grown ineffably off-color, thanks to Wystan.

Athens, 1965. Auden arrives late, rumpled and wrinkled. Nelly's rooms are full of people eager to meet him. Catching sight of me, he smiles. Although we aren't yet the intimates we shall become after his death, he approves of my work and fancies that I exemplify moderation to Chester.

"What I'd really like, my dear," he says, "is to sit down somewhere and enjoy another drink."

"Follow me." I lead him to the sofa from which Maria Mitsotaki, a reclusive star, warily observes the crush. "Look sharp, Maman," I say. "Here's the guest of honor."

"Enfant, this time you've gone too far," she murmurs, even as he lowers himself beside her. Dressed in her eternal black, wreathed in the smoke of her eternal Gitane, Maria is the closest I'll ever get to having a Muse. There is no one saner or more sympathetic, more in love with overtones, quicker to register anything said or left unsaid. Her genius for listening comes across like a drop of scent dabbed behind each ear. So it hardly surprises me, returning with Wystan's full glass, to find them— ten years hence, the leading lights of Sandover—already deep in talk, eye-to-eye like accomplices.

"It's the great, great pity with Mediterranean men," Wystan is stating with his usual frankness. "They like sex, but love stumps them. Love is giving, and they simply don't know how to accept it." Intelligence flickers behind Maria's dark glasses. She has no trouble fleshing out this dictum with succulent particulars: Chester and his evzones, David and George Lazaretos, Strato and me. Wystan continues:

"They can't be bothered to learn our language, they've no conception of culture, ours or theirs. I mentioned guilt in a talk I once gave in Rome, and it was translated over the earphones as gold leaf. South of the Alps, guilt has only its legal or criminal sense. The rest is all bella figura. When you love a Mediterranean man there's nothing whatever you can give him. Except children."

"Or money," whispers childless Maria, smiling.

"Exactly."

Meanwhile my mother and I pursue our imaginary argument:

—From the age of nineteen I've been made to feel (first and foremost by you, dearest) my difference from the rest of the world, a difference laudable and literary at noon, shocking and sexual at midnight—though surely from the beginning my nights were part of the same vital process as my days. Age, however, has brought one blessing: the sense of how much like everyone else I'm becoming. Young people trust me; they never used to. Elderly taxi drivers see my gray hairs and talk to me like a brother. You wanted me to conform? I have!

—Since when? inquires my mother, intent upon her Bullshot. (I was hoping to make her smile.) And to what?

—To that composite gay young man I thought up on the beach at Ostia. To the sexagenarian poet kept young, like Wystan, by past and present indiscretions. To my type, if you like, in the human comedy.

—Anyone who lives long enough gets to be a "type." I could name plenty we both know, but I'd die before I called them that to their faces. It's no compliment and no blessing that I can see.

—You're looking in the wrong direction. In nature the type is everything, and you and I are tolerated only to the degree that we're true to it. If in the process we refine it, better yet. The first and hardest step is getting into Nature's good books. One reason my behavior was "unnatural" a hundred years ago was that Nature found on her shelves so few texts proving otherwise. But in our day she's had to build a whole new bookcase! Wonderful, isn't it, how she keeps working to improve her mind? Just like you.

My mother makes a helpless gesture. Compliments to our intelligence are seldom refused.

XIX *A glimpse of Istanbul.*
Second visit to Poros.

Perhaps sixty feet underground, we had the wooden platform to ourselves. A stone forest fanned outward into gloom, inscrutably plotted; the two or three spotlights lit only those columns nearest us. They rose from shallow water, supporting a groined monotony of brick. The air was stale and cool. We breathed it guardedly, as if buried alive and having to conserve oxygen. At length an unseen hand put out the lights; our time was up. Back at street level, Robert checked off the great cistern in our *Guide Bleu.*

It had been folly to dream of seeing Istanbul in two days, yet a brief impression was better than none; better as well, I'd begun to think after Ravenna, than a prolonged, studious one. It was mid-August. Dr Detre had released me for another nine days. (He himself was going to the seaside. He, too, had a "normal life"; a human heart beat beneath that white shirt-front and funereal necktie.) Thanks to Robert's little Fiat, merely en route to the Brindisi ferry we had seen: the octagonal gem of Castel del Monte, the old bare church on the harbor at Trani, the fourth-century bronze giant in the square at Barletta, the euphoric ocher baroque of Lecce. We took care never to look at anything long enough to reduce it to a known quantity. Going through the Corinth canal we craned from our porthole at clifflike walls close enough to touch, then fell back for another hour's sleep. Our flight to Istanbul took us over Samos, Lesbos, the tiny islands in the Sea of Marmora,

233

on one of which Kimon was born. We checked into the Pera Palas just after sunset.

This was our first non-Christian city, and we meant to drink in as much *orientalisme* as we could. A muezzin woke us at daybreak. Opening the wardrobe onto our Roman summer suits, hanging alike as two peas, I was mystified.

"Why is your suit covered with snails and not mine?"

The snails were tiny and conical. Robert's suit looked like an aerial reconnaissance photograph of the stalagmite chapels in Cappadocia.

"It's too tiresome. I never wear my decorations on holiday, but try getting that into their heads. Give it here."

He brushed them off. They knew better than to cling.

Downhill, past moribund blocks of flats, a flash of waters, distant minarets. Seen close, Istanbul illustrated all the evils of the industrial revolution. Forges roared. The air tasted of coal. Cars long extinct in other countries served as taxis. Thanks to Ataturk's reforms, the street signs were laughably intelligible. POLIS, TUVALET, KREDİ (a bank). Should the tourist go astray, Greek shopkeepers fluent in six languages peered from doorways, ready to direct him past the actual reek and noise of the streets to the true city they dreamed of reconquering; to seawalls and Hippodrome; to the handful of miraculous structures on which, a thousand years later, the upstart mosques would be modeled. Byzantium glimmered at every turn. Who could say but that the Bazaar might yield a bird "of hammered gold and gold enameling"?

In 1952 the available postcards of the interior of Hagia Sophia were sorry affairs, retouched so that only the big gold-on-green calligraphic lunettes and hanging lamps like instruments of torture stood out against a dim oatmeal of pillars and bays. Not knowing what more to expect, we weren't at first thrilled on entering. Where were the mosaics promised by Yeats, by Gibbon for that matter, who described the dome as a "glitter-

234

ing spectacle"? Lacking these, we turned to the celebrated marble facings, Rorschach blots in porphyry or verd antique that had once mirrored the torches and gems of Theodora's retinue. But they'd grown stagnant, unresponsive, barely giving back our shadows as we approached. Starved for ornament, we were reduced to dull immensity, and here our preference for the fleet impression helped not at all. Spaciousness implied leisure, time to expand the psyche to the height of certain prodigiously intersecting arcs, vaults within vaults, sheer walls that themselves appeared to lean back and gasp as the dome's peeling cabochon slowly floated to rest within its setting of pronged sunlight. But now we were outdoors again.

We went to Topkapi and saw the arm of John the Baptist, ostrich-plume fans and turbans Hubbell would have wanted for Christmas, jeweled dirks, a small fish-tank half filled with emeralds. "Exactly like sucked candies," said Robert. "Have another, Roxane? I can't possibly finish the box by myself." A gleaming collection of celadon vases and platters, gifts from a seventeenth-century Chinese emperor, filled a further room. Their preservation, we read, was due to the sultan's pique on opening the first crate; no gold encrustations, no embedded garnets and pearls. And no reflection on him—hadn't I hoped for mosaics in Hagia Sophia?

"I met a woman," said Robert, "whose husband did business with the sultan of somewhere-or-other. Over the years she made friends with the Swiss lady in charge of the sultan's household. One day they were strolling through this endless storehouse of china and glass, you know, Limoges and Baccarat, and my friend said, 'What became of your lovely dessert service, two hundred pieces of pale-green opaline?' 'Oh well, you see,' the Swiss lady said, 'it is wicked to value things for themselves. By strict Moslem law, any household possession that hasn't been used in a given year must be destroyed. We called in the men and had it smashed to bits.' Like a wife past childbearing, I suppose. . . ." Robert's voice trailed off.

Beyond the Hippodrome a steep path led down to the "little Hagia Sophia," as the Turks called the old church of Sts Sergius and Bacchus. It was closed. A child with shaved head saw us, cried out, and ran off—in dread? No—to fetch the custodian. Leaving our shoes on the porch, we entered a space perfectly scaled to the play of human attention. Again, no mosaics. Calligraphy in bolts of ultramarine lightning lit the shabby whitewash overhead. The dome's marble rim was solid with Greek. Were we allowed upstairs? Our host gestured like a pasha. A wide gallery paved with rosy stone led round to an overview of threadbare blues and crimsons that carpeted the church—the mosque, rather; for from this vantage we could also see the apse reoriented, by an oblique dais, towards Mecca. Next to it a flight of narrow marble steps led nowhere. Members of the congregation had left slippers and prayer beads roundabout. An artisan's cotton smock hung, limp with wear, one pocket torn, from a row of five wooden pegs painted orange.

While Robert sniffs at so much adulteration of past splendors, I find myself drinking in those humble objects the tide of daily use has filled brimful. Such visions were denied me as a child. I was told to look away from the broken bedstead on a curb or the eyeless doll in an old woman's lap. At home we had "nice things." There I could learn the difference between good and bad, with respect at least to silver and china and furniture. But the lesson of our Meissen plates and Sheraton chairs intimidated me. They kept their own counsel; our postures and hungers affected them hardly at all. The chair shrugged us off, each careful washing rinsed the dish of us, and the objects resumed, like heroines in Henry James, a gleaming, inviolable fineness their uncouth admirers could only fall short of. By contrast the smock on its peg, the beads and slippers I gaze down upon in this hushed corner of Byzantium or Islam, move me in mysterious ways. They belong. They shine with a proud, illiterate life given over to their users. True, they've seen better days. I picture my mother throwing these things out to make room for new ones, or ridding herself of them without quite seeming to, the way she sends me Aunt Mil's latest letter marked "Destroy—have answered." But I am weak. I side with Mademoiselle, with Luigi's grandmother, whose instinct is piously to mend the smock, polish the slippers, add the letter to a cache of others. It comes to me for a rare, unselfish moment that Lambert Strether's may not be the last word, that what one wants in this world isn't so much to "live" as to . . . *be* lived, to be used by life for its own purposes. What has one to give but oneself?—as Tony himself asked from within his gilded cage. The willingness of the beads to be held and numbered, of the slippers to be worn and scuffed—or, put more sensibly, the continuing honor in which they are held and worn—leaves these objects proud and mindful in subjugation, old dogs on a warm hearth.

We glimpse their masters as we pass the Blue Mosque on our way back to the hotel. Prayers have ended. A huge congregation is disbanding—all men. This in itself is worth remarking after a year in Italy and a lifetime in America, where the churchgoing male more often than not wears the look of having been dragged there by his wife. Surely, with less than fifty years to the next millennium, such militant belief is old-fashioned, out of step with the times. Yet the eyes of these Turks blaze with doctrine. In dark trousers, cheap striped shirts, a collar-button in lieu of a tie, here and there a uniform jacket from the Great War, they could be an army streaming past us. I try to imagine myself part of a society fueled by such monotheistic carbons. As a scribe, the very way I form my letters— regardless of the word they spell—would express some aspect of my faith; the same phrase can be rendered as a dish of sweetmeats or a nest of scorpions. After seeing the intricate gold-and-black squid-shaped tugras and firmans on display in the calligraphy rooms at Topkapi, I can't approve Ataturk's decision to romanize the written language. Inflammatory as

Beethoven, hieratic as Mallarmé, the Arabic script gives a thrilling, godlike primacy to the most banal slogan. Well, the milk is spilt; now, less than three decades after the reform, only scholars are able to read the archives and the sacred texts in their original glory. A few more generations brought up on roman minuscules, and perhaps these men melting wild-eyed into the dusk will simmer down.

We crossed the bridge to Pera, the old foreign colony—hotels and embassies, restaurants and shops. Looking back across the Golden Horn, we tried to decipher, from so many domes and minarets, where we'd been that day. But the skyline, too, had grown unreadable. We dined on staid "European" food at the Rejans (Régence!), its dingy elegance overseen by a life-size oil of Ataturk in white tie and tails. Between courses Robert fished out the notes given him by the fat English diplomat he knew in Rome. The Rejans was starred on a little handmade map, with the following scholium: "Set up by Ataturk for a White Russian mistress; scene of riotous drinking parties; at one of them Kemal's wolfhounds ate the belly-dancer." That heyday was long past. For good measure our informant listed two or three louche hamams—recommendations Robert flung aside: by what right had such interests been attributed to us? Sanctimoniously I agreed although, truth to tell, I fancied that lovemaking from country to country—from class to class, if it came to that—could hardly fail to yield a treasury of ethnic and professional variations. In the spirit of disinterested research I might have enjoyed comparing the courtship dance of a Turkish blacksmith to Franco's or Wayne's. Another indelibly surcharged stamp for my album . . . But the recent drama with Rolf, and its effect on Robert, had for the time being cramped my style.

Next morning at the Bazaar—a warren of blazing bulbs, coffee smells, exhortations edged in dental gold—we found its one quiet shop and bought rings, not as love gifts but each for him-

238

self. Robert's was bronze, a circlet of verdigris flattened to a seal at the crest. Mine, of soft gold, wore a half-effaced bunch of grapes; a child's jewel, it fitted just above the second knuckle of my ring finger, making the hand look paintable by Memling. We also bought a backgammon board and played with gusto throughout the wait at the airport, the next day's long bus ride from Athens to Delphi, and on the afternoon boat to Poros the day after that—always to nods of the greatest friendliness. It was one of the approved male pastimes.

Back in Athens after Delphi, we walked barefoot over the burning bald marble of the Acropolis, until a guard (*"Kyrii! sivouplé!"*) made us put our sandals on. It gave visiting diplomats, he explained in what might be called Freek, the wrong impression. We drank a can of retsina under vine leaves and philosophized until it was time to collect our baggage. On the way we found a dry goods shop and bought meters of cheap local cotton—dark chalk blue, a turmeric orange—to have made into shirts that wouldn't last a dozen washings. One kept an eye out for the perfect souvenir. We stood at the rail, counting islands. The brilliant warm dry wind carved our faces into archaic smiles.

Poros wasn't the same without Mina. She had stayed in New York that summer. For a year now, she and Kimon had occupied my apartment. It was deeply gratifying to shelter these grownups from afar, like the porcelain parents in a doll's house. Their being under my roof implied acceptance of countless choices made by me in the past. If above my bed hung Blake's engraving of Job affrighted by visions, or if (as Kimon wrote, genuinely puzzled) I owned neither a toaster nor an ironing-board, these pluses and minuses were as much part of the package as my personal mannerisms; friends would have to take them or leave them. But just before I left Rome a letter had come from my New York landlord. He and his wife wanted my floor of the old brownstone for their newlywed son, and to that end, with many apologies, weren't renewing the lease. Kimon and Mina would therefore have to move out earlier than expected, and everything go into storage—on the virtual eve of my return. "It must be symbolic, don't you agree?" I laughed crossly. "I mean, now that I've been made over by analysis, my former life washes its hands of me. Does this throw a terrible wrench in your plans?"

Kimon was smiling and shaking his head. "On the contrary. I, too, have some news. Mina and I are to be married."

My face snatched one of my mother's smiles to cover its nakedness.

"Next month, as soon as I get back," Kimon went on. "My classes start right after Labor Day. Mina's already looking at apartments. She's become a real New Yorker; she rides the subway! Can't you arrange to be home by then, Jimmy? I want you to be my best man!"

Quick as Kimon was to explain his marriage as one of convenience, enabling Mina to stay in America or to come and go as she pleased, a dozen gratifications not wholly beside the point fluttered round him like putti as he spoke. The homosexual's desire for a conventional life. The slum child's dream of marrying "above" him. The exile's newfound world embodied in a lover. Elements, too, no doubt, of real tenderness, devotion, gratitude. My heart sank nonetheless. If Kimon of all people was taking a wife, what hopes had I of resisting the undertow of generations? I noticed Robert listening attentively, his large eyes lowered. When they met mine he blushed.

That afternoon I opened a door into Mina's room—tidy, austere, more a space to wake and get dressed in than a shrine to her personality. Yet a shelf under the windowseat held certain children's books I recognized, books from which Mademoiselle had taught me nineteenth-century French and nineteenth-century virtues. Their dark-pink bindings brought a lump to my throat. Where was my copy of *Le Pauvre Blaise* or *Les Mal-*

heurs de Sophie? Had I outlived their precepts, could my lips still form their birdlike vowels? I missed childhood, I missed Mina. Gone were the wildflowers; the hills looked parched, the sea dusty. Our silver-haired Persephone was doing time in the New York subway system. Mitso had gained weight, and this year's baby cried a lot. Too late I remembered how little there was locally to admire—no freestanding column, no pretty Hellenistic theater, just the sun and moon and Kimon's discourse. I'd been wondering, after Ravenna, if I didn't prefer places to people; a scene can mirror more expressively than a friend the confusions we bring to it. Poros, though, was a place that recalled what it would have been kindness, in a friend, to forget. Here was the tree I'd dozed beneath, the table where Mina brought me tea. At every turn I met my listless, enfeebled self of two years before.

Leaving his cottage, with the Medusa above the door, to Robert and me, Kimon had moved into the main house. "That way you'll have privacy," he said. But we were together for meals, walks, talks, swims in the cove. Like the setting, without Mina's transforming presence Kimon showed at a disadvantage, by turns gushy and sententious. "He's as bad as Rolf," Robert sighed at our second evening's end. "What a taste you have for the serious-type queen." Robert had undressed and was pensively draping his tanned body, this way and that, with meters of blue. I shook out the long folds of orange and followed suit. We found straw hats and wore them at smart angles, like Tanagra figurines. Woken by Kimon for the early boat to Athens, we were still entangled in the vivid lengths we'd gone to.

While Dr Detre listened I expressed Oedipal petulance. Kimon was joining a frieze of vital figures moving into the sunset with their Minas and Ninas. Months of silence from Tony—still in Ceylon?—told as much, in their way, as my mother's irrepres-

241

sible bulletins from Atlanta. Two perfectly unheard-of women had entered my father's life. Could people never stay put? Much as my grown-up self understood, the neglected child in me was pouting.

"I thought we outgrew our useless old feelings," I complained.

"Why? The horseshoe crab is an ancient creature—ugly, obsolete by human standards. Yet it continues to thrive and multiply."

I silently congratulated Dr Detre on having returned from his seaside holiday with a metaphor.

Robert also, within two years of his return to New York, marries a delightful woman older than himself. He opens a gallery and buys his first Gérôme. As with Kimon, I feel obscurely to blame. Did my shortcomings drive him into the arms of women?

"Angel," says Hubbell, "you can't have been the easiest act to follow. Après toi they take the pledge, if not the veil. Try to be flattered."

That first winter Mina enrolled at Columbia to study Chinese. Even married life might seem easy by comparison. They found an apartment uptown. Instructed by Kimon, the doorman called her Baroness. Kimon taught his classes; Mina gave lessons in English and Italian to the young daughters of a diplomat. Money remained a problem. Later came the phase, freely dramatized in my second novel, when the two began to think with real bitterness of each other; yet there was no reason to divorce. The bitterness passed and, with it, the intimacy. All at once Mina was very old, back on Poros for good. "They no longer say 'Live to be a hundred' on my name-day," she said, laughing, when I saw her for the last time, "since that's just a few years off." She stayed alone in the big house; her cats filled Kimon's cottage; Mitso, a grandfather, had moved to his daughter's in Patras. "People look in every so often," said Mina vaguely, "but they bore me." She had decided to publish her translation of Lao-tzu into modern Greek, but whom to trust with the project? It had absorbed her for nearly three decades, ensuring a sophistication and purity of spirit that might otherwise have rubbed away. To illustrate the danger, her grandson, once a little boy crowned with water-lilies, now an architect in his thirties, entered the room announcing that he and his girlfriend would after all not stay for supper but try to beat the traffic back to Athens. As she took in his words, love changed Mina before my eyes into a crooning, head-waggling peasant granny: "Eat something first, my child! Take a warm sweater with you!"—not until he was out of sight reverting to the woman I knew.

Mina was born in Istanbul, but no Greek has ever stopped calling it Constantinople, or just the City. In the popular imagination it is simply a matter of time before the City is theirs again. The years following my first visit saw the dispersal of the Greek community; before long nobody on the street spoke anything but Turkish, or a little Gastarbeiter German, and the social give-and-take suffered accordingly. But the dream persists. Shortly after the young King Constantine was crowned, Strato assured me—for once not laughing, his green eyes lit with conviction—that here at last was the long-awaited hero.

"The prophecy tells of a Constantine with twelve fingers who will reconquer the City," he declared.

As it happened, a recent photograph had shown the King in action: a karate leap with five-fingered hand extended. Strato had seen it too.

"My golden one, don't you know that they touch up all those

pictures?" He used the word eikónes. "But I who have seen the king on horseback, with my own eyes, know differently."

Why argue? Thanks to the Turks, there had been no Renaissance in Strato's history. Never, I smiled to think, could such an assertion have crossed the lips of an Italian youth, with Machiavelli in his veins. These much-handled properties of Strato's mind—like the slippers and beads seen at Sts Sergius and Bacchus—filled me with delight. Our days were numbered; his faith in long shots had already handed him over to an underworld of cardsharps that would be his ruin. His smile owed some of its brilliance to my not knowing this. We promised to go to Constantinople together for the fireworks when it became once more part of Greece.

Meanwhile I returned to Istanbul without him, with others, time after time. One winter dusk David and I tried out the louche hamam. One June, after wishing my mother goodnight at our hotel, I was roughly treated in a park. By and large it was the beaten path I kept to, from Hagia Sophia to Topkapi, to the Suleymaniye, to St Savior in Chora, to the Bazaar, retracing my tracks again and again as if I'd learned nothing, or had lost something precious. (One year, at an all-night party in New York, it seemed poetic to let my gold ring fall, like Mélisande's, into a French girl's highball; I never saw it again.) On perhaps my sixth visit a street vendor's trinket caught my eye—a kind of pendant or pennant, chevron-shaped and fringed, entirely made of tiny glass beads: blue-green, white, orange, lemon yellow, pink. At the center, on a perch of beads, a beaded bird swayed; above it, beads spelled out MAŞALLAH (Glory be! Praise the Lord!) No two were alike; they cost nothing; I bought several. In Stonington I hung one in the doorway between our domed red dining room and the shoe-box parlor with its huge gilt mirror and its bat-and-cloud wallpaper designed by Hubbell. The longer I lived with the bird, the more it charmed me. Istanbul was a city of birds; a vortex of birds, Wyndham Lewis might have called it: sparrows and swifts, fishwife gulls, storks

244

on chimneys. Storks, too, made of limber Arabic letters in the Calligraphy Museum—already migrating, in what I feared was a one-way passage, from Nature's realm to that of the Mind. Chickens huddling for warmth where their tavern roost revolved above blue flames. The empire's two-headed eagle. The peacock whose cousin, Mirabell, had for one long summer at the Ouija Board sung to us "of what is past, or passing, or to come." My beaded talisman could have issued from no other place in the world. I wanted all my friends to have one, which meant a seventh trip to Istanbul.

This time, tourist buses jam the streets. Trucks at midnight unload mountains of carpets for sale the next morning. Son et lumière fill the great cistern, and duckwalks lead to two columns at the very back, resting on heads of monumental marble half submerged in dreamlike transparence. Pretty wooden hotels have sprung up near the antiquities, with tables outside, and fountains. I wonder if the Rejans still exists. All this has happened in Greece too. No sooner does the real thing vanish than it returns, with a conniving wink, as folklore. Near our hotel we find a vendor of beaded birds. This year's model, however, comes in uniform blue and yellow, with two birds to a perch. (Two twittering pangs, the finches Ralph and Ivy, flit through me for a split second.) They look machine-made, matrimonial, not at all what I . . . Days pass; the end of our stay is in sight. I've frankly given up the search, when Peter spots a glinting mound in the Bazaar, like Iris on her rubbish-heap at the opera's end. We buy the lot. No need ever to travel again; it's the perfect souvenir: a translation into the demotic of Yeats's golden bird on its eternal bough. Swaying from the rearview mirror of Claude's Volkswagen or basking in the glow of my mother's bridge lamp, the talisman (readily unstrung, but who isn't) keeps up appearances, reminding us how notions such as Joy or the Imagination—the Holy Ghost Itself, if it comes to that—out of some recurrent urge to be embodied, make for a Halloween trunk full of feathers and wings.

XX A game of Murder. Leave-takings and creative stirrings.

ⅠTS SUMMER-LONG SIESTA at an end, Rome began languidly making up for a new season. Out came the black pencils, the golden powders, the rouge of earlier sunsets. One evening we were invited to a party in the penthouse of a medieval brick tower near the Forum. The hosts were a blond Italian decorator, fortyish, and his handsome, serious-looking young American lover. We didn't know them and never caught their names. Our invitation came by way of Hubbell, who was himself unable to attend, having been hired to play the piano, evenings from seven till midnight, in the twinkling blue-and-gold bar at the Orso. At the party Robert and I were two of twenty-odd guests, all men, mostly young and American. It seemed there were more circles in Rome than we'd realized. Except for nice silver-templed Fritz Prokosch, we'd never laid eyes on any of them before. Or had we? One elegantly turned-out young man echoed my name in amazement when we were introduced. He was the son of our Southampton doctor; we'd last seen each other at age eight.

A game of Murder was to be the evening's entertainment, and its rules were now explained. Each player draws a slip of paper from a bowl and examines it secretly. All the slips are blank but for two—one marked with a black dot for the Murderer, the other with an X for the Cross-Examiner. In darkness

246

the players wander from room to room. The Murderer is free to claim his victim—a gently stylized blow to the heart will do—at any juncture, hoping to be unobserved when the body cries out and drops to the floor, and at least a room away by the time it is discovered. Lights then go up, the players gather, the questions begin. In replying, the Murderer is entitled to whatever lies he can get away with; only if directly accused must he tell the truth. The person who has been falsely challenged becomes the next Cross-Examiner. We gathered round, drew our slips of paper, unfolded them privily. My heart skipped a beat—there was the big black dot! Robert looked at me, his face a question. Mine showed nothing.

Off went the lights. We fanned out into the apartment. Its several rooms linked by a long hallway were soon filled by silently milling men. The silence and near-invisibility punctuated here and there by a glowing cigarette reminded me—and many of the others, I fancied—of the unlit garden I'd explored during Robert's absence. It seemed, during the first few minutes, not impossible that our game would develop into a kind of somnambulistic orgy. I recalled a ballet conceived, but never choreographed, by Maya Deren to three playings of the overture to *The Magic Flute*. Twelve dancers would repeat the basic action, each time at a progressively higher (or deeper) level: from cocktail party to *partouze* to sacred ritual. Suppose our game . . . ? But rules were rules; I fingered the slip of paper in my pocket and kept moving, feeling like the killer my father had wanted to hire to eliminate Kimon. In the dark corridor I spotted Robert; he went by with shining eyes—a willing victim?—yet gave no sign of knowing me, as if such compromising circumstances called for tact. Here came the Southampton doctor's son; he winked without slowing his pace. Here came our host, peering into every face with that needle-threading glance of the Violent Against Nature, in Dante. Poor fussy old queen, whom I prayed I would never grow to resemble, having to give a party for people like me, Americans he didn't even know. . . . He deserved some attention. I looked swiftly in both directions and struck him dead.

When the cry went up and the lights came on we all trooped blinking into the *salone*. Out came wine and cookies, and the interrogation began. Everyone was asked where he'd been at the fatal moment. I stuck to a simple alibi: in such-and-such a room, near the bookcase. In this highly polished crowd I must have cut a figure so dim that it was hardly worth anyone's while to doubt me. After weighing his evidence, the sleuth hazarded a wrong guess, stepped down, and the whole process was repeated by his successor. And *his*. . . . It was a chapter out of Kafka. Time trudged by, the wine was running out, Robert and I rolled eyes at each other. Half the party had been exculpated by the time Fritz, as Cross-Examiner, lit on me and I confessed. Everyone groaned with relief, rose, stretched, circulated. A few guests glanced at me with new interest. The victim, who'd been making lengthy telephone calls in the bedroom, returned to pinch my cheek and joke about his resurrection. "My dear," said Robert, "we must do this more often." Another half-hour, and the party broke up. At the door, however—

The good-looking young American lover of the man I'd killed was seeing people out. We hadn't spoken beyond my thanking him when he filled my glass. Now, about to shake hands, he looked most meaningfully into my eyes; at the same moment a slip of paper—instructions for a new game?—was being pressed into my palm. Surprised, I took a step back. "It's nothing," he muttered, stooping to pick up the note and pocket it. Our eyes met again; he looked put out. No one else seemed to have noticed. "Wait for me!" I called to Robert on the stairs. (If only I'd gone to the party alone!) What had the handsome stranger been proposing: a tryst with his lover's murderer? a life together in Montana? I would never know. Far too shy to dream of learning his name and telephoning, I found several pretexts, in the week that followed, to walk past the scene of the crime. But he never came running out after me.

The golden days grew shorter. Marilyn put aside her studies—no less engrossing now that her future was settled—and flew to Milan with us for *Falstaff* at La Scala and a day of churches and museums. "What will it be like to meet in New York?" she wondered brightly. "What will New York have to say to us, or we to say to one another? Now, I mean, that we've all become—"

"Italicized," said Robert, and we laughed in full accord, for weren't we more elegantly slanted now, more emphatically set upon the world's page, than the blunt types of a year or two earlier, into whose midst—or "chase," as Claude had taught me to call the printer's tray—we must again face being distributed? But to what end? Marilyn at least looked forward to a life in academic circles. She'd be returning to Italy for summers and sabbaticals. Culture wasn't, in her case, the blind alley I sometimes feared it was in mine.

Well, Robert and I could always bring our trained eyes to bear on St Patrick's or the Thomas Coles at the Historical Society. Yet Marilyn's question—what would we have to say to one another?—touched a sensitive nerve. It brought to mind my old longing to escape from New York and the people I saw there, whose friendships gave me no leeway to change and make new friends. Hadn't that been the chief reason for going abroad? And had I now reached the same point all over again, in Europe? Depressing thought. "You are once more putting the cart before the horse," said Dr Detre. "There is no one to prevent you from changing, if you wish to."

Robert on the telephone to a customs broker: "You mean, with tourist plates I can't. . . . It's cheaper than to. . . . Are

249

you serious? How much does having a car destroyed cost? . . . I see. . . . May I watch?" And so forth. Hanging up, he turned to me. "For three hundred dollars La Cenerentola will have her coach viciously dismembered at a government garage. The next of kin are not invited. Italy! Shall we go out?"

In those weeks of fine weather we took long walks every afternoon. There was so much of Rome we'd missed or wanted to revisit. Robert developed an insatiable appetite for Borromini, whose works weren't always easy to see. We bribed our way into the tiny church of San Carlo alle Quattro Fontane—its dimensions exactly those of one of the four pilasters that upheld the dome of St Peter's—with its pearl-gray cloister no bigger than a brooch. We were obliged to attend a Sunday mass at Sant' Ivo in order to admire the bee-shaped interior's gold-and-white cupola, where concave and convex stagger forth from the corkscrew skylight as though a New England meeting house had drunk too much rum. (Here Robert abstained from communion.) In the façade of St Agnes in Agony we sought qualities answering to the gestures of dread and distaste that Bernini's river gods, grouped round their obelisk, directed at his rival's work. Sure enough, along with his preciousness of scale and taste for perishable materials, Borromini could be seen as cunningly parading his hollows and undulations, like structural limp wrists and swaying hips, in order to provoke a limestone outcrop of homophobia from the robuster artist. (What? Borromini wasn't gay? The river gods weren't by Bernini? No matter. Fact could hold no candle to instinctive truth.)

These promenades were our farewell to the city and, whether or not we knew it, to each other. Robert was returning to New York in late October. He had come over for the summer, thinking I'd be free to leave with him at its end. Now pressure from his mother, and the need to find an apartment in New York—if he wasn't going to spend the rest of his life in St Louis with her—decided him to go first. "Where will you live?" he asked diffidently, knowing I had nowhere to stay. "I could look for a place big enough for us both. Would that . . . ?" I urged him to do so. It seemed the ideal solution, didn't he agree? Somehow, though, we failed to pursue the topic. After the intimate summer trance of throbbing engines and glittering wake, my head was filling with new horizons, faces, tones of voice. I tried to disown them. Robert deserved better from me than this guilty foreknowledge of a shipboard romance coming to its end.

A shipboard romance . . .

I'd heard a story, where and from whom I was never able to recall—perhaps from some sunburnt grandchild of the tiaraed muse seated next to Henry James at dinner parties. A couple of friends charter a boat to go fishing in the Gulf Stream off the Florida coast. An argument leads to a bet. Can one of them, harnessed for once not to his chair against the pull of marlin or tarpon but to the end of the other's line, hold out for ten minutes, a fish in water himself, to be "played" with rod and reel by his sportsman friend? The idea filled me with horror. At fifteen or sixteen I wasn't past working myself into a panic over the imaginary shark in my father's swimming pool. Think of *being* the bait in an ocean teeming with ravenous monsters! All at once it was a subject I couldn't shake. Perhaps a one-act play, set in the fishing boat . . . ? Or set both "now" and "then," the scary incident coming to life as one of the characters remembers it from a safer vantage in time and space (Ravenna?). What if this character were a woman?—since words came more easily to me in a woman's voice than in a man's. What if she were the sister of one of the friends and—yes!—beloved by the other? What if she were cold and flippant, causing pain to her lover, as I had to Claude by taking up with Robert, as I had to Robert by flirting with Rolf? The climax would come when, stung by her taunts, the lover goes overboard, underwater, fighting against the friend (for these long moments his enemy) who

251

struggles to reel him back to air and safety. He has gone deep, deep into himself, where the others can't dream of following. Back with them in the boat, he and they no longer share a language. The risk-taker is left with his solitary sense of having done all he can.

Whatever my little plot "meant" didn't detain me. I was eager to explore the form I'd chosen. Since first learning to read, I'd responded to the dreamlike immediacy of a play in print: no descriptive or analytical set pieces; rather, gesture and tone stripped to bracketed italics, allowing the reader's sedentary imagination to get into the act. Daringly the stage could encompass both the fishing boat and an Italian piazza. Best of all, thanks to there being more speakers than the single all-creating *I* of a poem, anyone who went on at too great length could be interrupted by new information in a new voice. What most excited me was this very prospect of dividing the labor of consciousness, or whatever light the murky action engendered, among reflectors at greater or lesser odds with one another. From behind a mask we tell the truth, said Oscar Wilde; and in each of my characters I saw a side of myself combined with elements of someone who mattered to me. Claude with his seriousness and intellectual courage stood behind the figure of Charles (who takes the plunge and finds himself); yet the very name Charles, my father's and my brother's, implied relative maturity and spoke for the part of me that lay, now fighting for life, now spluttering in self-pity, on Dr Detre's couch. By the same token I associated Gilbert (who wields the fishing rod) somewhat with Dr Detre, but also with that fussy, expendable person I felt in recurrent danger of aging into, like the host at the other night's party, whom I'd so neatly killed. Hating waste, I gave Julie (my heroine) phrases from my old unsatisfactory poem to Claude about Ravenna, plus a versified account of the mosaics, lifted from a letter to Freddy. Before grinding to a halt I'd filled quite a few pages of my long-abandoned notebook.

Revulsion followed. I was rusty, unused to holding a pencil. At first I hadn't thought the project worth mentioning to Dr Detre—he had shown, for one thing, so little interest in my writing—but now I did. The writer's block I'd originally gone to him to get rid of was still there, I said grimly, big as life.

Dr Detre asked what my play was about.

"It will have occurred to you," he said when I finished, "that your hero's adventure is made possible by a line attached to himself. The word 'line' suggests something besides fishing, no?"

I had to think for a moment. "You mean, like a line of poetry?" Never before had Dr Detre acknowledged my—could I say?—calling. For him to so do after all these months thrilled and silenced me.

"If I am not mistaken," he presently went on, "in one of our first meetings you related a dream in which you were a fish trying to become human. That has now come to pass. In your scenario it is a healthy and goodhearted man who is hauled from the sea by those he loves."

My heart leapt, my eyes stung. "But they don't love *him* any longer," I pointed out.

"Perhaps," said Dr Detre, "they loved a different person."

"The person he no longer is . . ."

"Exactly. The person who, by the way, is now free to decide whether he still loves *them*."

The Bait *was part of a program of one-act plays—* John Ashbery *and* Barbara Guest *wrote the other two—di- rected by* Herbert Machiz *and produced by* John Myers. *John, an ageless, hulking Irishman with the self-image of a pixie, had come to New York from Buffalo in the thirties, worked on* View magazine by day and as a puppeteer and comedian in an off-beat nightclub. I'd met him through Kimon, but only now, six years later, felt proof against his flamboyant crusade for the avant-garde. During my years abroad John had become a force to reckon with; parties every other night—merry little dinners, midnight traffic jams—took place at his and Herbert's one-room apartment. A bomb falling on one of these gatherings would have set the arts in America back six weeks. Here I met my contemporaries, the founders of the (had it already been named?) New York School. John and Herbert wanted to produce Plays by P*O*E*T*S, with Sets by P*A*I*N*T*E*R*S—not that mere asterisks can render the starry-eyed emphasis John brought to the plan. "Sweetie," he cried, darting forward on tiptoe, "you must write something wonderfully, perfectly, divinely beautiful for our Artists Theater. Hush! Don't say a word, just let it happen!" John touched my brow with his imaginary wand. A couple of months later, back from visiting my father in his latest retreat—a handsome old house on Barbados, surrounded by canefields—I showed them the finished playlet.

It was a kind of closet opera. Without singing or music, there were nonetheless arias, duets, trios, and the odd prose recitative. In truth I still hadn't learned very much about writing speakable verse. Nor did the production help. The set—a café table in Venice juxtaposed with the stern of a fishing boat in the Gulf Stream—looked messy and abstract expressionist rather than spare and ambivalent. The leading lady had a German accent. At the first performance the noble (and nearly nude) hero had begun his climactic sestina in a green, "underwater" spotlight:

> I am not one to think much about pain.
> I would not choose to dwell upon myself
> In public, sipping at a tumbler of stale water.
> It has never been my thought to preach to the fish.

254

Nevertheless if I am ever in my life
To think profitably, to see with clear eyes,

Let it be now—

when a sudden commotion shook the tiny packed theater. Arthur Miller and Dylan Thomas, whom Kimon had brought to see the play, stumbled out, making remarks I'd have preferred not to hear and dragging after them the audience's attention, along with poor Kimon himself. ("What could I do?" he said next day on the phone. "Dylan wanted a drink." Years later I learned what Mr Miller, with uncanny insight, had whispered in Dylan's ear shortly after the curtain rose: "You know, this guy's got a secret, and he's gonna keep it.") I went outside during the intermission and let a few friends comfort me. One of them introduced his companion—a slender blond man with a voice that didn't sound at all like New York, a perfectly convincing wedding ring on his finger, and the friendliest smile; if only I'd caught his name. Then back we all went to our seats for John Ashbery's play, the hit of the evening. A week or two later I'd stopped, for the first time in over three years, at my old haunt, the San Remo on MacDougal Street, when the man with the smile and the wedding ring walked in, alone. This time I got his name: David Jackson.

The Bait was done again thirty-five years after its premiere. The writer who lives long enough finds his youthful idiom yet more stilted than it was to start with, his view of society positively quaint. I used the occasion to liven it up a bit: Julie grows older, and her dim boyfriend, as if having passed under a Brazilian rainbow, changes sex. Peter Hooten played her brother, Gilbert, the trickster who initiates the action that enmeshes him along with the others. It was wrenching to see Peter, with his resonant voice, his profile of Apollo, impersonate a teasing, superficial character. Gilbert and Julie, as I've said, embodied aspects of myself I shrank from facing directly, like my cruelty and flightiness during Rolf's weeks in Italy. Peter brought to the role a volatile anguish which he would draw more deeply upon for the wrathful, suffering angel Gabriel in the performing version of Sandover. Watching him play Gilbert, I felt, in ways I couldn't easily explain to him, that these youthful sins of mine, like so many games of Murder, were being lifted into the light and forgiven. It was a catharsis overlooked in antiquity: that of the poet by the actor's uncanny grasp of his role. So The Bait with all its flaws and affectations, and despite the miserable situation that inspired it, remains close to my heart. Its rainbow has spanned my life, early to late, leaving a pot of gold at either end.

XXI
End of therapy in sight.
Hubbell's repertoire.
My favorite words.
The pillow book concluded.

I WANTED A Roman gift for Robert. Here at last was reason to enter the old engraver's shop near the Trevi Fountain. Among his round red or violet cardinal-hat seals I'd noted a few secular ones and wondered if he could make the bookplate I had in mind: a unicorn's head, the motto CANDOR & RARITY, and the initials R. I. The old man's eyes slowly lit up—busy as he was, a real commission. Six weeks later he greeted me with satisfaction. This very day, *proprio oggi,* he'd made a start—indicating his workspace, dwarfed by an antique marble fragment, the quarter-life-size head of a horse. It came, he smiled, from his personal collection; how else to model the rarely seen *liocorno?* The bookplates—white on tobacco brown, small as silver dollars—were ready before Robert left. He spoke his pleasure, yet I had the oddest feeling that he would never use them. Rarity and candor were a dew that dried up when one called attention to it.

Dr Detre confirmed his summer prediction. I could go home, if I wished, at the end of November. The long-awaited news disoriented me. Wasn't I still the anxious, unhappy person who'd dropped his amber cigarette holder at our first interview? Now a mere month remained. How could I throw away my crutches at its end? There'd been no shattering breakthrough, no climax out of Hitchcock.

"I often think," said Dr Detre, "that the relatively uneventful cure is the most lasting. Like a good dark suit." Before I could ask his opinion of my colorful shirt and tie, he continued. "I have some news, by the way. I, too, shall be moving to New York. I have secured my visa from your State Department."

So! That's what *he'd* been doing these months in Rome: waiting for clearance. His internship at an American hospital would begin next January. Thus, though our "work" was finished, any bits that came unglued could be fixed on the spot. Dr Detre was after all a fellow mortal, with worries and aspirations of his own. The war's end, which found me eager for wicked, blackened old Europe, found him—the rest of whose family had disappeared at Auschwitz—among those millions dreaming of a passport to Freedom. Who could blame him?

I'm not used to living alone. With Robert gone, with my life aired and swept clean like so many rooms waiting to be furnished (rooms whose proportions and views change daily), my ties to the present grow ever flimsier. Hubbell persuades me to fly with him to London for a week before sailing home from England on the new *Queen Elizabeth*. I welcome the plan; eager as I am to start living, it seems wise to approach life indirectly, to catch it off guard. I am proud of my years away but fearful too. If friends no longer know me, if strangers take me for a foreigner? Perhaps on docking in New York I should hire a taxi straight from the pier to Montauk—or some such equivalent of Proust's Balbec—where, during long hours in an empty dining room above the sea, I can glean from the banter of busboys and waitresses the latest cultural passwords. Am I still American? Hearing my language on the street, I look round into tourist faces wan and apathetic from the pursuit of happiness. Out of the Grand Hotel, with its memories of my father and Robin, steps a mink-coated woman crying "Whoopee!" and brandishing the *Rome Daily American* above her head. Is she drunk? A red-white-and-blue ribbon flutters from the newspaper. It's the morning after Election Day. Eisenhower (a hero of Bill Plummer's) has won.

As my departure draws near, I contact a packer and shipper for the things I want to keep—books, a lamp, the harpsichord. See to returning the rented piano. Give lunch to Dr Simeons, to Marilyn, to Umberto. Join the Bakers for a farewell "feast of fat things" (Isaiah 25:6): fried chicken with gravy, rice, frozen succotash, biscuits, salad with syrupy tangerine segments and cream-cheese balls rolled in chives, butter-pecan ice cream and devil's food cake. But most evenings I manage to keep free, not for any final sowing of wild oats, rather for a kind of refresher course. Seated in the corner nearest to Hubbell's spotlit piano bench in the dark blue-and-gold bar of the Orso, I listen to Cole Porter and Richard Rodgers, Gershwin and Noël Coward, songs from an era whose afterglow plays upon my friend's impudent, lightly pitted clown face as he puts body and soul into his next selection.

These songs evoke a period more or less coinciding with the first fifteen years of my life: from just before the crash on Wall Street to Pearl Harbor. To their lilt my parents danced and I took my own first steps. They precede Actors Studio and rock stars, precede (for that matter) beboppers and jitterbuggers; agitation has yet to become the earmark of sincerity. The tunes are catchy, metropolitan, popular without being entirely of the people—you go to Nashville or New Orleans for that. The lyrics are literate but not highbrow; witness the phrase from "Smoke Gets in Your Eyes": "Now laughing friends deride . . . ," where the redundant adjective is chosen lest a listener not know what the verb means and feel left out. No; it isn't the language so much as the tone (as they called it at Amherst) that risks being misunderstood. When the hero of "I

Can't Get Started with You" brags about his intimacy with FDR, his pilot's license, and his "showplace," is this a dangerous megalomania talking? a light-headed soup-line daydream? Vital discriminations I feel at work within me. If Rilke's poems, so comforting in adolescence, imply a handful of readers privileged by their fluent access to pain and solitude, the songs in Hubbell's repertoire conjure up, in another wing of the house, a Byronic elite of fox-trotters classy enough to crack jokes while their hearts are breaking.

Before closing time a stunningly handsome figure entered the bar: not Gino the goalie this year but Enrico, with his elegance, his title, his sense of humor. When the last set ended he swept my friend off to a late supper. Urged to go along, I seldom did. The streets were empty, moon-misted as I walked home, singing Hubbell's songs under my breath.

Pronouns ricocheted through their lyrics, relationships being of prime importance. The heartless She, the unempathetic They (who asked how I knew my romance was through, who threatened, evening after evening, to begin the beguine); foremost, of course, the eternal You and I. . . . Would there never be a poem purged of the whole love-addicted crowd? Clichés meanwhile rolled past like Hollywood vamps in open, vintage cars. Clever polysyllabic rhymes, allusions to remote places (Spain!), to cigarettes and exotic drinks, hinted at the vocalist's sophistication, even as recurrent words like "tears" or "heart" or "Baby" confirmed the soft spot beneath a glamorous, know-it-all veneer.

What were my recurrent words? No longer, as at sixteen, "pale" or "dim," or even the irresistible names of colors— "violet" or "rose," scented respectively by turbulence and upward movement. The words I never wearied of were rather those adverbs like "still" or "even," or adverbial phrases like "by then" or "as yet" or "no longer," which, sharpening a reader's sense of time, suggested a reality forever in the process

260

of change, that had "only now" come into being or was "already" on the point of vanishing. "Still," with its triadic resonance of immobility, endurance, and intensification ("Eleanor grew still more animated"), was perhaps the hardest to resist. Deep in the pinewoods of my vocabulary, it yielded an intoxicating moonshine I would keep resorting to in small, furtive sips.

The evanescent reality mirrored in such dewdrops of syntax came as a vast refreshment after my trek through the cut-and-dried. Young people in my day—in any day?—believed that a comprehensive account of everything would presently be rendered. With the development of the hydrogen bomb, matter had begun to yield its inmost secrets. The poets we read most carefully seemed to have the last word—witness the transcendent certitudes of the *Four Quartets*, or Stevens when he wrote, "The prologues are over. It is a question, now, / Of final belief." But *final* belief, or ultimate truth, was the last thing I wanted. That it should be in a fiction, as Stevens went on to say, or that Eliot's vision kept rippling off into wordless radiance, was a paradox to whose height I had yet to grow. "Central man?" I saw a totem pole of rigid, glaring faces; while belief and believer—why, just to breathe the words set up a green rustling in my mind.

I'd been ravished to discover that (in English at least) "truth" and "tree" shared a single Indo-European root. Truth, then, could be felt as a living organism, varying from time to time and place to place. Now a seedling among thousands, now a gaunt trunk crowned with fire, it grew and withered in natural cycles. So did the various tongues in which it was couched. Wasn't my own psyche, cradled and fed by those out-of-date lullabies Hubbell gave gravelly voice to, night after night at his spotlit piano, already outgrowing them? Any creative spirit truly à la page came most to life, I hoped, by the perpetual freshening of human language—the slang of each successive decade, the gaudy breakthroughs of folk idiom, the body English explored in a new dance craze, or the latest concept in astrophysics.

These blissfully self-sufficient hours left me convinced of having changed but vague as to how deep, or how cursory, the change had been.

"Remember," said Dr Detre, "it has been a time of breaking for you." Breaking, I understood, with my mother's stifling scenario; with Tony's exhibitionistic solutions; with Freddy's calm and conventional ones. Teaching that year at Lawrenceville, Freddy was also courting a girl whose parents and his had been friends. Such fidelity to beginnings would have been the end of me. My dream, a love flowering far from Palm Beach and Southampton, mirrored Freddy's centripetal one toward early figures and scenes. But did it truly matter—both inner and outer space being curved—which direction one set out in?

"Now I've broken faith with Robert too," I observed faintly. "Is this what I'll more and more find myself doing?"

"Robert, like Claude before him, contributed to your present freedom. Through him you explored and rejected the choices he stood for."

And having served his purpose, was he now simply to be shrugged off—Sleeping Beauty's last dream before waking? I hated seeing myself in that light.

"You were warned at the outset not to make too deep an emotional commitment while undergoing treatment."

Well, it appeared I hadn't. But henceforth I'd be free to—?

"Of course," said Dr Detre in a fresh, amused voice, before I could decide what.

Sitting up on Dr Detre's couch, tingling all over, I felt I'd had a rubdown with salt and oil. Was it the moment to ask Claude's question? "Tell me," I said, with a laugh part apologetic, part euphoric, "how much of this was really necessary?" How, in other words, was a patient ever to know that time

262

mightn't have brought about the longed-for changes? Time passing normally, without all the probing and soul-searching, the cost to oneself and others.

When Dr Detre smiled he looked like a different person. "Time," he said, "approximates with surprising accuracy the work we do. But we"—his satisfied pronoun embracing a host of colleagues—"we do it faster."

One morning I've set aside an hour, before catching the bus to Dr Detre's, for errands. I pick up my new passport photo in Piazza di Spagna. I photograph Claude's building, the boat-shaped fountain, a policeman directing traffic like a ballet-master. (For two years now I've killed time with my camera, focusing the image, making the moment stand still. But all this while, if Dr Detre is right about "doing it faster," my inner life has been a speeded-up movie, one that the principal actor, however enriched by it, never gets to see.) Next I buy a couple of ties in a smart shop nearby. It's a short walk to the English bookstore. From there I make a detour to the Villa Giulia and say goodbye to the Etruscan couple reclining on their terra-cotta sarcophagus. They look past me, as always, with calm, enraptured smiles. I continue through the Villa Borghese Gardens, down Via Veneto to the American Embassy. Here I complete the necessary forms and submit them, with my old passport and new likeness, to a white-haired woman full of questions. Aimed at obstructing the prodigal's return? No such luck.

"We'll have everything ready by noon tomorrow," she gloats. "VIP treatment for all our citizens!"

I step back into Roman sunlight the more precious for these minutes on American soil. Going by way of the National Museum will see me home in good time for Quinta's lunch. In the museum's cavernous brick antechamber (originally part of some great Roman bath) hangs a black-and-white mosaic of a human skeleton. The technique, after the wonders of Ravenna, is crude and cartoonish. The figure reclines, skull propped on bony forearm; above it in big capitals float the words GNOTHI SEAUTON: Greek for "Know Thyself." Was self-knowledge, even in ancient times, a kind of death? or brooding upon one's nature a lifelong career, that carried over into the grave? Heaven forbid. Above the sober "consolations of philosophy" I'll take my constellations of peacock and seraph twinkling forth from vaults of gold. Yet the motto's starkness pleases me. Obviously for anyone undergoing psychoanalysis—oh my god!

Bells were ringing. My hour with Dr Detre was up, and I had forgotten the appointment.

At my first appointment with Dr Detre in New York I arrived on the wrong day and his jolly American wife opened the door. Confusion. Apologies. A glimpse of my confessor without necktie. What had been bothering me in the four months since my return, I said when eventually we sat face-to-face, was my calendar: black with names and numbers, lunches, cocktail parties, drinks at intermission, nightcaps after the opera. Would I, like Tony, never have time to write? True, in the odd hour between engagements I'd finished The Bait and was at work on a second play. On a visit to my father in Barbados, I'd begun planning a novel about his life there, surrounded by former mistresses, new loves, the inevitable disapproving nurse. Poems, too, like comets at whose tails I grabbed, whistled overhead. What did it mean, I asked Dr Detre, and where would it all end? He reminded me that I could answer such questions myself.

On arriving in New York I stayed at the Plaza. My mother and Bill were coming to spend Christmas with my grandmother and me. Over the days ahead I planned to find an apartment and move into it by the new year. Robert phoned from St Louis. He was eager to see me, would be returning shortly to the small flat he'd taken on Irving Place. Though I was welcome to share it as an interim measure, it seemed best at present for him to live alone.

Outside the Plaza that first evening, dusk had fallen. Before drawing the curtains of heavy hotel-green silk, I looked out into the gemlike reds and whites of traffic. Good-natured horns blew, a crystal fringe gusted and shivered beneath Karl Bitter's bathing nymph. A sleighload of gifts—I'd done my Christmas shopping in London—filled a corner of my room. As for my presents, I knew that my mother's needlepoint family crests had been framed and mounted; I would try for a suitable glow of pleasure when I unwrapped them. But here awaiting me was a package, not in Christmas paper, from Freddy. The card read: "Welcome home. You know you've always wanted one." It was a Ouija Board.

Thus, while Freddy never won me to Christ, he once again—as when at fourteen he made writing a poem seem the most natural and desirable thing in the world—put me in touch with a whole further realm of language. Within a couple of years David and I, having escaped New York and its merciless cultural calendar, begin holding candlelit séances after dinner. We change to a homemade Board—more spacious than Freddy's—with an overturned willowware cup as pointer. The messages are from the start arresting:

> . . . born in Cologne,
> Dead in his 22nd year
> Of cholera in Cairo, he had KNOWN
> NO HAPPINESS. He once met Goethe, though.
> Goethe had told him PERSEVERE.

These lines, for all their parlor-game tone, turn out to be as crucial to my poetry as Aeschylus's bringing onstage an "answerer" (the hypocritēs) was to the development of Greek drama. Two voices—my narrative one in lower case, the young German ghost's in upper—together compound the cozy lyric capsule. A promising start; yet I am slow to draw further upon our transcripts. Dr Detre calls the Board a folie à deux and wonders if we aren't "playing with lightning." Besides, who at thirty wants to spend hours each day communing with the dead? Past fifty—our age when cold, inhuman voices usurp the Board— we shiver a bit but go along for the ride. By then we'll have guessed that the very flimsiness of the Ouija apparatus somehow protects us, obliging the lightning to articulate itself by slow degrees. So that even when flashes come from highest heaven we are seldom blinded to the fruitful suspicion that they dwell all along in a manner of speaking.

Late in the summer of 1990 the dramatization I'd put together, for Peter, from The Changing Light at Sandover is videotaped. Nothing in life, short of the gradual coming into being of that long poem itself, has ever thrilled me more. Peter is both actor and producer. Airline tickets, hotel suites, caterers. Lighting and stage crews, director, settings, a cast of nine. We have taken over the Agassiz Theater in Cambridge. Countless ganglia connect a magic truck, denser with technology than a pharaoh's tomb with hieroglyphics, to our soundstage, two flights up. Finally all is ready. I play myself, and each day now begins with the magic of having wrinkles painted out, temples darkened, eyes and lips brightened by a makeup man. Time reversed, the Princesse de Guermantes's terminal reception run backwards. One by one the key figures of the poem (of my life as well, if the two can be told apart) gather round the coffee urn: Ephraim in his Greek miniskirt, Mirabell in peacock leotard; Wystan and Maria, side by side, smiling like accomplices. Here is Peter, sportshirted and sandaled, who before long will reappear in skintight archangelic silver. Too keyed up for words, we make do with a powerful hug.

Here now comes DJ—or Terry, as I'm learning to call him.

266

Once a street clown in Paris, he is hunkier than strictly necessary. But his easy American manners and infectious smile recall the David I knew when this impostor was in nursery school, so that I almost forget the real friend left behind in Stonington—who with no one to paint out his wrinkles will be spending today in bed, chain-smoking, eyes fixed on quiz shows or sitcoms.

What worries Terry this morning is having to react to the Ouija dictation without being able to lean over and read it. He's left with nothing to do. JM at least is seen to keep transcribing. I tell him how in real life David often foreknew the messages, tears welling up on the verge of some especially poignant passage. Terry brightens at once: this means business. At noon he will bring me a present, a tiny clay pot containing a smooth miniature pinkish-gray boulder cleft in twain, like Gertrude's heart in Hamlet. From the cleft a pink flower has opened. I've never seen the like; is it a kind of succulent? Pleased by the success of his gift, Terry himself turns a shade pinker. "It's called a living stone," he explains. Alice's name for David—Dr Livingstone! I'm once more on her horsehair sofa in rue Christine; a cleft thirty years deep is filling with light.

Back to 1952. There was time, that evening, to walk to my grandmother's. She lived on East Seventy-second Street, in the same building my mother and I moved to after the divorce. My grandmother, long a widow, had given up Jacksonville to cast her lot with us in New York. Having first leased this apartment, she agreed to buy it in 1941, when the building "went cooperative," for fifteen hundred dollars. So astonishing a bargain didn't keep her from fretting over "tying up that kind of money in real estate." She'd been poor for the first fifty years of her life, poor but genteel. She had painted on china as a girl and played the piano pieces of Grieg and MacDowell. A genuine Dresden doll—her muse?—in panniers and lace fichu perched on her dressing table. Settled now in four comfortable rooms, with a live-in maid and no friends of her own to entertain, though my mother's and mine fussed gratifyingly over her, my grandmother harbored all the reflexes of frugality. "I never thought I'd live to see the day," she said as we sat down to the coquilles of deviled crab which I'd asked to taste again, "when crabmeat would skyrocket to two dollars a pound."

It is rare in America that a given address figures in one's life for more than a decade. The upward or downward mobility of tenants makes for turnover. Or else the house itself vanishes— as when my first home, the brownstone on West Eleventh Street, was inadvertently blown up in 1970 by student activists. Yet this apartment of my grandmother's, in a building where I lived fifty years ago, can be seen to have gradually passed into my hands since her death. The latest clue, bought in Athens for exactly what the old lady paid for her apartment, hangs on the wall: an outspread black-paper fan painted by Tsarouchis. It shows—my answer to the Dresden doll?—two swarthy, wasp-waisted soldiers in boxer shorts, winged like cabbage whites or some companionably low order of angel. A key turns in the lock. Peter enters, rosy from the chill dusk outside. But he wears a remote, melancholy face I know better than to question.

Saying he's in a hurry to change and leave for dinner, he hands me the mail I overlooked this morning on purpose: the friends who fifty years ago wrote long, eagerly awaited letters nowadays reach for the phone. Here accordingly is the usual haul of kitchen-appliance catalogs, fund-raising for AIDS, beachwear from Saks, organizations to save the planet. The unspeakably urgent coupled with the utterly inane. A far more absorbing pile awaited me on a table in this very room, the night of my return from Europe. After our crab, our stewed fruit and peanut-butter cookies, I poured myself a drink and while my grandmother readied herself for bed—immemorial pantomime of shoe-trees and quilted hangers, ablutions, face-cream and hairnet, the aquamarine brooch and earrings wrapped in tissue, the drawers evenly closed, the faucets ritually strangled—gave this hoard a preliminary glance. Ah! here was a 1953 calendar from Irma. Next, a fat, richly stamped letter from Tony; I put it aside to read later, along with those from my mother, my sister, and Claude. This flat parcel from Holland felt like a book. . . . Opening it, I found that Mr and Mrs Lodeizen had sent me Hans's just-published second collection of poems, handsomely bound in leather, with a ("I'm late—who loves you?" Peter off so early? Faint slam) frontispiece photograph of the author.

As if I had fallen into a sudden chasm, I stumbled weeping into the next room, where my grandmother, asking no questions, held me in her arms for the moments it took to pass. Hans's immediate posthumous fame, his place today as the inventor, for Dutch poetry, of an offhand, "modern" way of seeing and putting what he saw on the page, sprang from those manners that so charmed his friends, manners at one time of a piece with his live, physical being. No longer. Between these ounces of paper and leather and print he had become—his biographical container, in my mother's phrase—and the person I'd known and loved lay all the difference in the world. It was of course myself I grieved for. I had glimpsed, through the joy of homecoming, the degree to which I was consenting to the transformation my friend had already—taking his leave with a little bow—undergone. Hungry for experience and cured of my writer's block, wouldn't I, too, turn, word by word, page by page, into books on a shelf?

On my last Roman morning I stand gazing about the denuded apartment while Quinta comes and goes. Hubbell will be picking me up downstairs in ten minutes; we fly to London at noon. I've already taken formal leave of Quinta, spoken the words of friendship and gratitude, given her a fat envelope for

Christmas. My empty bookshelves and worktable have resigned themselves to my departure; placidly they await their next user. A studious child . . . a sick old woman . . . ? The sharpest pang comes when I look out at the mild blank blue of early December sky. Never again will I see—will anyone see—today's particular morning sun, breadth and bias of its retreating path ordained by the hour, the season, the year, the millennium, as it treads the gleaming boards I can still for a moment call mine.

"*Signor Jim*," cries Quinta, holding it up from the bed she is stripping. "*Il guanciale! Non dimenticarlo!*" The pillow— my precious down pillow—so many healing and transforming dreams have been dreamed upon. Well, such pillows are no rarity where I am going. Besides, months of heavy duty have left this one battered and limp. Would Quinta like to have it? She beams with delight. A final look round, a last embrace, and downstairs in the elevator piled with luggage. On to the new life! But reaching the door of Hubbell's waiting cab, I discover from a check of my pockets that I've left something vital, wallet or passport, behind. Up again I go. What on earth . . . ? A white blizzard—feathers everywhere—fills the

(Weeks later, the explanation. No sooner have I been seen to leave, Umberto would write in reply to my fascinated query, than the elder Count Bracci—"who believes he had the pleasure of meeting you once, at the signing of your lease"—popped in to scrutinize the premises. Had the American tenant perhaps left behind a usable ashtray, a bottle of ink? Aha! That pillow appeared to be in decent condition. . . . Sharp-witted as a Goldoni hostess, Quinta said it was now hers; did the *padrone* wish to make an offer for it? Wait: how to know, the old count countered, unwilling to be duped, that it was *piume d'oca*, genuine goosedown? Because if not . . . ! Heated words and mutual interest presently led them to rip open one corner for a peek.)

270

—fills the apartment. I've walked in upon two people my parents' age struggling to contain the damage. The proscenium of the sleeping alcove frames them. Quinta's eyes flash with an embattled passion never seen before. Count Bracci, white-haired but dapper in jacket and tiepin, sputters and waves his arms like a broken toy. Before either discerns me in the storm of feathers (through which I see *them* more and more clearly), I have retrieved whatever I came for and slipped away for good.

James Merrill was born in New York City and now lives in Stonington, Connecticut. He is the author of eleven books of poems, which have won him two National Book Awards (for *Nights and Days* and *Mirabell*), the Bollingen Prize in Poetry (for *Braving the Elements*), the Pulitzer Prize (for *Divine Comedies*) and the first Bobbitt National Prize for Poetry awarded by the Library of Congress (for *The Inner Room*). *The Changing Light at Sandover* appeared in 1982 and included the long narrative poem begun with "The Book of Ephraim" (from *Divine Comedies*), plus *Mirabell: Books of Number* and *Scripts for the Pageant* in their entirety; it received the National Book Critics Circle Award in poetry for 1983. *Late Settings* appeared in 1985 and *The Inner Room* in 1988. He has written two novels, *The (Diblos) Notebook* (1965) and *The Seraglio* (1957, reissued in 1987) and two plays, *The Immortal Husband* (first produced in 1955 and published in *Playbook* the following year), and, in one act, *The Bait*, published in *Artist's Theatre* (1960). A book of essays, *Recitative*, appeared in 1986.

A NOTE ON THE TYPE

This book is set in Linotype ELECTRA, *a face designed by*
W. A. DWIGGINS (1880–1956), *who was responsible for so*
much that is good in contemporary book design. Although
much of his early work was in advertising and he was the
author of the standard volume Layout in Advertising, *Mr.*
Dwiggins later devoted his prolific talents to book typog-
raphy and type design, and worked with great distinction
in both fields. In addition to his designs for Electra, he cre-
ated the Metro, Caledonia, and Eldorado series of type
faces, as well as a number of experimental cuttings that
were never issued commercially.

Electra cannot be classified as either modern or old-style.
It is not based on any historical model, nor does it echo a
particular period or style. It avoids the extreme contrast
between thick and thin elements which marks most mod-
ern faces, and attempts to give a feeling of fluidity, power,
and speed.

Composition by Heritage Printers,
Charlotte, North Carolina
Designed by Harry Ford